Screening the Afterlife

Screening the Afterlife offers the first comprehensive examination of death and the afterlife within the growing field of religion and film. It looks critically at a range of cinematic works and considers how they encroach upon theological territory. Topics addressed include:

- the survival of personhood after death
- the language of resurrection and immortality
- Near-death experiences and mind-dependent worlds
- the portrayal of 'heaven' and 'hell'

Drawing on films from *Flatliners* and *What Dreams May Come* to *Working Girl* and *The Shawshank Redemption*, this book is a unique and fascinating exploration of the 'last things' as envisaged by modern filmmakers.

Christopher Deacy is Senior Lecturer in Applied Theology at the University of Kent, UK. His books include *Screen Christologies* (2001), *Faith in Film* (2005) and *Theology and Film* (2008).

Screening the Afterlife

Theology, Eschatology and Film

by Christopher Deacy

Routledge
Taylor & Francis Group

LONDON AND NEW YORK

First published 2012
by Routledge
2 Park Square, Milton Park, Abingdon, Oxon OX14 4RN

Simultaneously published in the USA and Canada
by Routledge
711 Third Avenue, New York, NY 10017

Routledge is an imprint of the Taylor & Francis Group, an informa business

British Library Cataloguing in Publication Data
A catalogue record for this book is available from the British Library

Library of Congress Cataloging in Publication Data
Deacy, Christopher.
   Screening the afterlife : theology, eschatology and film / by Christopher Deacy.
      p. cm.
   Includes bibliographical references (p.) and index.
   1. Death in motion pictures. 2. Resurrection in motion pictures. 3. Motion pictures–Religious aspects–Christianity. I. Title.
   PN1995.9.D37D43 2011
   791.43'6823–dc23
                    2011020155

ISBN: 978-0-415-57258-3 (hbk)
ISBN: 978-0-415-57259-0 (pbk)
ISBN: 978-0-203-35601-2 (ebk)

Typeset in Bembo
by Taylor & Francis Books

MIX
Paper from
responsible sources
FSC® C004839
www.fsc.org

Printed and bound in Great Britain by
TJ International Ltd, Padstow, Cornwall

Contents

Acknowledgements

As ever, I want to thank my wife, Caroline, my parents, Gerald and Jennifer, and my grandfather, Arthur Philip Stokes, for all their love and support. My grandfather, now 91, but with the mind and stamina of someone half his age, has been writing his memoirs over the last seven years. His ability to weave together a vivacious and compelling narrative that begins with the time he met my late grandmother, Joyce, in Newquay, Cornwall, in 1941, when they were both serving in the RAF, is a terrific inspiration to me in my own life and writing.

This book is the product of a period of study leave – my first since coming to Kent – in 2009, and I am grateful to the University of Kent for enabling me to take a semester out from teaching and other administrative duties. Despite the ostensibly 'other-worldly' character of my research (though, as we shall see, the terrestrial has a pivotal role to play in so much of the theology and cinema of the afterlife), the last year or so at work, while I have been writing this book, could not have been further removed from matters abstract. The first term of writing this book, immediately following my sabbatical, coincided with my being asked to take over as Senior Tutor for all first year students in the School of European Culture and Languages, a pastoral role which, strangely, complemented (and maybe even held in check) some of the more abstruse and metaphysical flights of fancy. At the time of finishing this book, I have moved on to the role of Director of Learning and Teaching, which is certainly no less demanding of my time. But, this is a deeply rewarding profession to be in, and I must thank my colleagues, not least Professors Robin Gill and Jeremy Carrette, who continue to be so supportive, as well as the many students I have taught over the years, especially those who have challenged me to think differently in seminar exchanges about aspects of my own research. It is to their dedication and enthusiasm that I want to say a massive Thank You. Equally, I wish to thank Lesley Riddle, Amy Grant and Katherine Ong at Routledge for their commitment to this book and for their invaluable assistance throughout.

Finding a balance in any profession is always going to be difficult, but I want to thank Caroline for her love and patience as I have attempted to juggle everything that has been going on in our lives. We first met in a university that has changed beyond recognition over the years. I look back with enormous fondness to my student days, and to the friends with whom I have, regrettably, lost contact over the years. In Chapter 4, I cite, in relation to H.H. Price's model of a mind-dependent world, Paul Badham's assertion that 'Even the best of old comrades would ultimately tire of exchanging memories of the past or weaving new theories about what might have been' (Badham 1976: 120). As I grow ever closer to the age of 40, and I am increasingly conscious of the fact that many of the students I am teaching now were not even born when I went to university in 1991, I find myself thinking (and, quite in keeping with Price's theory, dreaming), not quite as far back as my grandfather is presently doing with events of more than half a century ago, but still quite a long way back, with great fondness and affection, to all the people who, in addition to my wonderful wife, parents, sister and grandparents, have helped shape my character. I am not sure I will ever tire of 'weaving new theories about what might have been', and I hope that, some day, I will have the chance to exchange memories of the past with some of those many people who have influenced me more than they will perhaps ever know.

Introduction

The impetus behind this project is the consideration that death and the afterlife, though predominant concerns in themselves both in film and theology, have never been comprehensively brought together within the ever-growing field of theology and film. I began to be interested in this area of scholarship back in the mid-1990s when I was undertaking a taught MA programme in the area of Christian eschatology. One evening, I took some time out from preparing for a seminar on the topic of Christian perspectives on Hell in order to watch a film, *The Witches of Eastwick* (George Miller, 1987), in which Jack Nicholson plays the role of the Devil. What especially caught my attention was the way in which, on the one hand, my research entailed having to read up on all manner of erudite theological musings on Hell that I could glean from academic books and journals. On the other hand, the film seemed to synthesise a variety of film genres – comedy, romance, drama, horror and super-natural – in order to say something about an ostensibly similar subject matter but in a much more accessible and populist way.[1] It was clear that the film broached theological territory and that this was on display to a much wider constituency of people than any of the academic writings on death and immortality with which I was dealing. At the time, it had never occurred to me to even contemplate using anything other than traditional academic sources to document an academic essay. The issue had simply never come up.

Not surprisingly, perhaps, when I decided to embark on subsequent research, the impetus for this was my growing interest in film. Of course, I discovered in due course that there had already been plenty of attempts to cross disciplinary boundaries – though nothing like the volume of literature that has come out since the mid-to-late 1990s by the likes of Clive Marsh, Robert Johnston, John Lyden and Conrad Ostwalt. At the outset of my PhD (and later post-doctoral) research, my focus was on the concepts of redemption and escapism, and it was not until 2006, when I was colla-borating on a book with Gaye Ortiz, that I returned to the specific area of death and immortality when assembling a chapter which came to be titled 'Heaven, Hell, and the Sweet Hereafter: Theological Perspectives on Eschatology and Film'. More than a decade after completing my Master's, I found that some of the major theorists in the field of eschatology, among them John Hick and Paul Badham, could be brought into the contemporary theology–film exchange to provide scholarly ballast to intertextual dialogue between such theological debates as those pertaining to mind-dependent worlds, 'spiritual bodies' and the de-sacralisation of the apocalypse and the themes of a number of films such as *What Dreams May Come* (Vincent Ward, 1998) and *Vanilla Sky* (Cameron Crowe, 2001). In this book, I will take the discussion that was initiated in that chapter forward with a view to focusing in more detail on how films have depicted (as well as in crucial respects deviate from) traditional eschatological ideas concerning life and death, heaven and hell, as well as the extent to which cinematic portrayals of the afterlife have often tended to use earthly realities as the point of departure and to visualise the transcendent through the lens of this-worldly phenomena.

There have been some excellent antecedents to the study of eschatology and film over recent years. In particular, Clive Marsh's *Theology Goes to the Movies: An Introduction to Critical Christian Thinking* (Marsh 2007[a]) contains a rich and insightful chapter on 'The end', in which Marsh asks a number of key questions concerning how death is to be understood, whether physical death constitutes the end of a person, whether Christianity supports resurrection or immortality or some combination thereof, whether only believers are resurrected, whether judgement has been redefined as something which already occurs in *this* life, whether heaven and hell carry any real meaning today other than as symbols of human experiences, and what it means 'to speak of "God" in relation to death, judgment, resurrection, immortality, heaven, hell and visions of the future' (Marsh 2007 [a]: 146). Marsh takes the line that the medium of film has proven to be 'a fertile ground for the development of stories and visions about the end and "what lies beyond"' and that 'Theology cannot but be interested in such speculations' (Marsh 2007 [a]: 141). Underlying Marsh's thesis is the clear suggestion that any theology which fails to draw on agencies of popular culture simply misses the point about how and where theological reflection is already taking place, and this book will be an extension of many of the ideas that Marsh raises. Like my own collaboration with Ortiz, Marsh's book treats eschatology as one of a number of theological themes that can be brought into dialogue with Christian theology. In his case, *Theology Goes to the Movies* takes the form of a systematic theology – the ordered structuring of a number of themes or topics which are relevant to both theology and film – with particular reference to God, 'Human being', Spirit, Redemption, Sacraments and Church, as well as 'The end'. Marsh's aim is to dissect a broad range of popular films with a view to challenging and even critiquing the way in which theology is often practised, and in much the same way my co-authored book with Ortiz, *Theology and Film: Challenging the Sacred/Secular Divide* (Deacy & Ortiz 2008), set out to examine how an understanding of a variety of theological perspectives and filmic themes, ranging from violence to feminism, the environment to war, and justice to eschatology, can lead to a two-way dialogical conversation between the theologian and the film text.

This book is a continuation of such endeavours to allow both theology and film an equal voice in the exchange, in keeping with Gordon Lynch's revised correlational model, as expounded in his 2005 publication *Understanding Theology and Popular Culture*, which 'values a complex conversation between the questions and insights of both religious tradition and popular culture, and allows for the possibility that both religious tradition and popular culture can be usefully challenged and transformed through this process' (Lynch 2005: 105). According to such a model, theology and popular culture can both learn from and be challenged or changed by the other – they are not two discrete, monolithic or changeless entities. Not only is it the case that 'questions that have previously been regarded as important in religious tradition can be put to contemporary culture (e.g., the eschatological question of what end we believe the universe is moving towards)', but 'contemporary culture can generate insights that require us to challenge or revise ideas and practices that have been an established part of religious tradition' (Lynch 2005: 104).[2]

In view of such a postmodern scenario, whereby the Bible, for example, is just one of many texts struggling to be heard and read 'among the swirling, fermenting currents of contemporary culture, and none has primacy over any of the others' (Deacy & Ortiz 2008: 68), it is particularly disappointing that in film studies, while there have been some attempts over the years to examine films which depict the afterlife, there have been few attempts to engage with any insights from theology or religious studies. Rewarding though it is to come across such titles as James Robert Parish's *Ghosts and Angels in Hollywood Films* and Tom Ruffles' *Ghost Images: Cinema of the Afterlife*, what is conspicuously missing from such endeavours is a theological undergirding, especially as the films themselves are often overtly drawing upon theological material. As a result, although the content of Parish's book is about ghosts and angels, thereby ostensibly making it prime material for a theology student, or as a course reader either in a religion/theology and film or an eschatology module, the absence of any theological material somewhat diminishes the potential readership. Moreover, despite its treatment of ghosts and angels, Parish's book is also quite limited in its scope in that it avoids supernatural film subjects that are not directly related to these phenomena, such as reincarnation, Satan, Hell and near-death (NDEs) and out-of-body (OBEs) experiences. The kind of two-way, dialogical approach that I thus envisage as being important for the theology-film field has yet to be taken up within film studies, and I hope that this book will precipitate the development of such research within film studies in the future.

Ironically, perhaps, although the last century has, arguably, 'generated more eschatological discussion than any other' (Chester 2004: 255), Andrew Chester makes the instructive point that – paradoxical though it may seem to be – there has been a relative scarcity of eschatology within Christian theology. Chester's thinking, here, is that, from the Patristic period onward, eschatology was never 'as fully developed, profoundly reflected upon, or given as rigorous and imaginative intellectual probing' (Chester 2004: 255), as were such other areas of Christian theology as Christology and soteriology. The specific context of Chester's argument does not revolve around debates in the field of theology and film, but there is an important sense in which what he is arguing finds a certain resonance in film and theology circles. When he writes that 'There is still a need for a rigorous and intellectually sustainable account of Christian eschatology' (Chester 2004: 255), the case could equally be made that when filmmakers draw on traditional images and representations of eschatology in their works – and there is little doubt that themes of death and the afterlife comprise perennial themes in cinema, as evinced by the likes of *A Matter of Life and Death* (Michael Powell & Emeric Pressburger, 1945), *Heaven Can Wait* (Warren Beatty, 1978), *Made in Heaven* (Alan Rudolph, 1987), *Ghost* (Jerry Zucker, 1990), *Defending Your Life* (Albert Brooks, 1991), *What Dreams May Come* (Vincent Ward, 1998), *Wandâfuru Raifu* (Hirokazu Koreeda, 1998), *Dragonfly* (Tom Shadyac, 2002) and *The Lovely Bones* (Peter Jackson, 2009) – there is a need for serious, critical dialogue with theology.

Of course, there are many differences between how theologians and filmmakers approach the topic of the afterlife. Popular films tend to bear witness to representations of the likes of God, the Devil, angels and demons in a literalistic and supernatural manner, as shown by such films as *It's a Wonderful Life* (Frank Capra, 1946), *Wings of Desire* (Wim Wenders, 1987), *Fallen* (Gregory Hoblit, 1998) and *Bedazzled* (Harold Ramis, 2000). Conversely, many theologians are more inclined to employ allegorical language and to be, frankly, embarrassed about some of the more extravagant teachings of, say, St Augustine, according to whom hell was an everlasting site of punishment from which no-one was exempt but for the grace of God.[3] But, this does not mean to say that filmmakers have nothing to contribute to the way eschatology is understood in the world today. Even in films which are not specifically concerned with questions of resurrection, immortality or eternal life, questions of eschatology can still be found to play an intrinsic role. This should come as little surprise. After all, there is invariably going to be a link between our lives on earth and any form of future existence, to the point that Marsh is surely correct that if one holds to belief in 'some notion of continued, or resurrected, existence beyond physical death – be that immediately on death, or at some future point – then questions arise not only about the form of that existence, but also the nature of the continuity with our present lives' (Marsh 2007 [a]: 147). John Hick, one of the pioneers of looking at death and the afterlife in modern theology and philosophy of religion, has similarly indicated that we can no more refrain from speculating about death than we can refrain from speculating about life – 'the one is inseparable from the other' (Hick 1976: 21).

It is with such considerations in mind that this book has been conceived. Some of the questions that will be addressed in the ensuing pages are as follows:

- Are there any differences between how theologians and filmmakers approach the topic of the afterlife?
- How successfully have filmmakers visualised competing claims of the immortality of the soul versus the resurrection of the flesh?
- To what extent do cinematic representations of NDEs/OBEs reflect and/or differ from theological and religious accounts of the afterlife, as undertaken by, say, Raymond Moody and Kenneth Ring?

- With reference to the work of Susan Blackmore, to what extent does academic scepticism in the area of NDEs/OBEs preclude serious scholarly study of NDE-oriented films such as *Flatliners* (Joel Schumacher, 1990), *Dragonfly* (Tom Shadyac, 2002) and *White Noise 2: The Light* (Patrick Lussier, 2007)? Is Blackmore's assumption that only a materialistic world-view holds sway challenged or reinforced by cinematic forays in this area?
- According to Henry H. Price, if there is to be any personal survival beyond death, it is our memories that are to play an instrumental role in that process. To what extent might a film such as *What Dreams May Come* (Vincent Ward, 1998) be said to comprise a cinematic analogue of Price's paradigm of a memory-oriented, mind-dependent world?
- With reference to 'realised eschatology', are there any examples in cinema where future, supernatural language has been successfully appropriated in the context of terrestrial existence?
- To what extent is there any mileage in the assertion that the this-worldly dynamics of *Working Girl* (Mike Nichols, 1988) and *The Shawshank Redemption* (Frank Darabont, 1994) are no less terrestrial-based than what we find at the heart of Jewish and Christian scriptural teachings on heaven?
- Is there a degree to which filmmakers have meaningfully contributed to our cultural or theological understanding(s) of hell?
- To what extent do cinematic treatments of hell as a place or state in present existence have any theological value?

These questions are not exhaustive (nor are their answers), but my aim in the pages that follow is to at least give them a hearing, with a view to facilitating further interdisciplinary research in this area.

1

MAPPING THE AFTERLIFE IN THEOLOGY, ESCHATOLOGY AND FILM

The problem of death

From the outset, we are faced with a paradox. Why is it that the depiction of the afterlife – despite being, as Tom Ruffles puts it, 'a perennial topic in cinema' (Ruffles 2004: 1) – should be such a relatively unexamined field of enquiry within film studies? One possible answer is that this may have as much to do with questions concerning the aesthetic quality of those movies which depict life after death as with the more general scepticism which has tended to prevail in some corners of academia about the suitability of looking at work which carries spiritual or theological connotations.[1] Indeed, the films themselves are often treated as lightweight and flimsy products by critics and reviewers, unworthy of serious intellectual scrutiny. Upon its release in 1978, Warren Beatty's directorial debut, *Heaven Can Wait* (Warren Beatty & Buck Henry, 1978), a remake of the 1940s celestial fantasy *Here Comes Mr Jordan* (Alexander Hall, 1941), was dismissed by Richard Combs in the *Monthly Film Bulletin* as 'cottonwool fantasy' and 'antique whimsy' (Combs 1978: 201), while Paul Hogan's follow-up to *Crocodile Dundee* (Peter Faiman, 1986), the supernatural-themed *Almost an Angel* (John Cornell, 1990), was written off by Nigel Floyd in the same publication in 1991 as no more than 'a slight, sentimental tale consisting almost entirely of con-trived set-pieces and smart one-liners' (Floyd 1991: 38). Veteran director Blake Edwards similarly fell foul of *Sight and Sound*'s Philip Strick in 1992 when his gender-crossing reincarnation comedy *Switch* (1991), starring Ellen Barkin as a man trapped inside a woman's body following an arrangement between God and the Devil, was castigated as a film which, even 'within the laws of its own magic', was 'glibly eva-sive' (Strick 1992: 53). Moreover, according to Vincent Canby in the *New York Times*, 'Any movie that depends on the presence of either the Devil or God is asking for trouble, and *Switch* has them both' (Canby 1991: <http://movies.nytimes.com/movie/review?res=9D0CE7D8113CF933A25756C0A967958260>). These reviews not being unrepresentative, it is hardly surprising that research conducted in this area has been so sporadic. The fact that afterlife-themed films are also often associated by critics with sub-literary forms such as Gothic and horror literature, horror films and comics – a point made by Ruffles at the beginning of *Ghost Images: Cinema of the Afterlife* (Ruffles 2004: 1), a rare venture by a film studies scholar[2] into the terrain of eschatology – only serves to underscore the point: this is simply not fruitful academic material and should be broached at the scholar's own peril.

At the same time, however, death itself is the least flippant or trivial of all subjects, which makes its often unsophisticated and unchallenging treatment in films particularly incongruous. Indeed, death is the one incontrovertible certainty in life – 'Death is the one inevitable human fact. We all have to die at some time' (Badham & Ballard 1996: 1). In Ferrell's words, 'There is no other moment when man is closest to nature than when he recognizes his mortality. This is the element of truth that underpins all myth' (Ferrell 2000: 191). According to a survey from the mid-1970s, 27 per cent of a nationwide sample of Americans reported having had contact with the dead, a situation which was most common among those who were elderly, women, black, poor or widowed, as well as those who believed in the existence of life after death in the first place (Lester 2005: 161). Furthermore, according to a study published by Ross and Joshi in 1992, 5.2 per cent of the American population – not counting those who had experienced child abuse or who suffered from mental illness, among whom the figures were higher – claimed to have had contact with ghosts, 4 per cent claimed to have knowledge of living a past life, and 0.6 per cent believed that they had been possessed by the spirits of those who had died (in Lester 2005: 161). According to one 1986 survey, 20 per cent of people also reported having been the recipients of after-death communications, in the form, for instance, of hearing the presence or voice of the deceased, smelling a fragrance associated with them, and seeing them while asleep, in visions, in so-called out-of-body experiences, or simply when doors were being opened or closed (in Lester 2005: 162). Irrespective of whether or not these statistics are to be taken seriously – and there is no doubt that the parameters of this discourse are far from definitive, as when Singer and Singer in a survey from 1990 noted, though without being convinced themselves, 'that some people believe imaginary playmates to be spirits and, certainly, the concept of spirits could account for the phenomenon of imaginary playmates' (in Lester 2005: 166)[3] – these are particularly striking claims.

If there is any scepticism surrounding such figures, it comes down, arguably, to the same reason as to why afterlife-themed films are given such short shrift within the academy. In his *Theology, Death and Dying*, Ray Anderson identifies the problem thus:

> [Our western culture] has lost its fundamental connection with death itself. The individual no longer presides over his or her death, as was common in the biblical practice and continued in many ways through the medieval period. The family no longer participates in the ritual of dying. These rituals have now become restricted to monitoring bodily functions, administering chemical substances and connecting with artificial life support systems, all under the

supervision of medical professionals. Death has become institutionalized and professionalized.

(Anderson 1986: 19)

In such terms, a dichotomy may be said to have been set up between the realm of the living and that of the dead and dying, from whom the former are physically excluded. Indeed, in Andrew Edgar's words, the living are increasingly 'denied the language to express their feelings or their support for the dying, precisely because there are no longer the cultural resources available that will allow most people to feel secure in the face of death' (Edgar 1996: 164). This concern has been reinstated by Peter Stanford, whose *Heaven: A Traveller's Guide to the Undiscovered Country*, published in 2002, concluded with the admonition that 'As a society, we have become ever more naked in our avoidance of death' (Stanford 2002: 348). Where we entertain thoughts pertaining to the afterlife, Stanford observes that this is not usually for very long – 'which may perhaps explain why so much of the thinking about afterlife has been confused, not thought out, simplistically earthbound and, often, plain banal' (Stanford 2002: 349). Not only, then, are films which deal with the afterlife accorded such limited scholarly attention, but the theme of the afterlife itself has been somewhat marginalised even within theology. Indeed, one of the reasons Chester gives for eschatology never having been 'as fully developed, profoundly reflected upon, or given as rigorous and imaginative intellectual probing, as were other areas of Christian theology'[4] is 'the embarrassment and difficulties that eschatology presents' (Chester 2004: 255). Stanford, likewise, makes the instructive point that, today, 'There is no mention of hell from the pulpits of the mainstream churches' and that 'Purgatory and limbo have been put to grass' (Stanford 2002: 20), even though, ironically, 'the assumption in most religious circles is that we are all bound for some sort of heaven' (Stanford 2002: 21).

The reasons for this retreat from discourse about death are very far from clear, however. Is it because, for many people today, the only reliable path to knowledge is believed to be provided by the 'objective' and 'rational' pursuit of science, along the lines espoused by Richard Dawkins for whom 'Natural selection not only explains the whole of life; it also raises our consciousness to the power of science to explain how organized complexity can emerge from simple beginnings without any deliberate guidance' (Dawkins 2006: 141)? If so, then it is the very mystery, capriciousness and irrationality of death that, like religion itself, stands at odds with life in a secular, technological age. In Stanford's words, 'The secular answer to the mystery of death is effectively to deny death an airing' and so to not talk or think about it: 'when we face death in our own backyard … amongst our family and friends, we sweep it under the carpet and instead grow ever more obsessed with our living bodies – new diets, health regimes and endless work-outs – in the hope that somehow we can arrest the march of time' (Stanford 2002: 21). Death on such an interpretation is thus something associated with failure – 'a failure to eat the right food, or exercise or avoid the sun' (Stanford 2002: 21) – and something which we thus have some kind of autonomy and responsibility over, so that as long as we look after our bodies and do not eat too much chocolate, drink too much alcohol or smoke any cigarettes we can in some sense postpone or even negate that which, in Christian terms, for example, might be deemed to be our ultimate destiny. A theist might be inclined to hold, indeed, that when it comes to questions of our rights, these are God-given rather than inherent possessions and so life should be viewed, rather, 'in the transcendent context of God-givenness' (Gill 2006: 431). Against this, Stanford makes the critical observation that 'even among the rituals of a Christian funeral, we refrain from pressing our noses against the smell of our own physical corruption, from seeing, touching or holding a dead body' and that we 'rely on undertakers and hospices to maintain a cordon around the unpalatable reality and save our most flamboyant grieving for those we know only through the media and therefore can't touch' (Stanford 2002: 22), the death of Princess Diana being an obvious case in point.

The argument being adduced here is that this is a society that attempts to evade death – by, as Paul Fiddes puts it, 'shutting it away in elaborate funeral arrangements, by not allowing space to grieve', and 'by pretending aging does not happen through the use of cosmetics and surgery' (Fiddes 2000: 12). We see traces of this in TV and film. In Robert Zemeckis' *Death Becomes Her* (Robert Zemeckis, 1992), a deft satire about the extremes people will go to in order to defy the ageing process, Meryl Streep's character, a former Broadway and Hollywood siren, discovers immortality through imbibing the elixir of eternal youth. This predilection towards staying young and remaining impervious to decay has also been something of an obsession on British television, with programmes such as Channel 4's *10 Years Younger*, in which, in the words of the show's web site, 'two women go head to head each week with one goal – to look younger' (<www.channel4.com/programmes/10-years-younger>), regularly showing in prime time. At the time of writing, a quick perusal at some contemporary news stories finds heated debates in the British press concerning whether female talent show judges are too old at 66 or women newsreaders at 57. Indeed, one headline on the *Guardian* web site in July 2009 read 'Strictly ageism? Row as Arlene Phillips, 66, is axed for a 30-year-old' (Holmwood 2009: <www.guardian.co.uk/media/2009/jul/17/arlene-phillips-strictly-come-dancing>), while in 2008, British newscaster Selina Scott sued TV channel Five for age discrimination (BBC News 2008 [b]: <http://news.bbc.co.uk/1/hi/entertainment/7764644.stm>), a comment echoed in 2006 by outgoing veteran newsreader Anna Ford who believed that, had she remained at the BBC, she would have been sidelined because of her age (BBC News 2006: <http://news.bbc.co.uk/1/hi/programmes/panorama/4892178.stm>). In another topical story, a former contestant, Niki Evans, on the British TV talent programme *The X Factor* was quoted in *The Scotsman* in September 2009 as saying that artists over the age of 25, who are placed in a separate category to their boy, girl and band counterparts under that age, are at a competitive disadvantage due to ageism: 'I will eat my hat if an over-25 woman ever wins *The X Factor*' (*The Scotsman* 2009: <http://news.scotsman.com/entertainment/XFactor-judges-accused-of-ageism.5667957.jp>). These controversies are, it must be said, as much about alleged sexism as ageism, but they do provide some ballast to the view that old age and death are somewhat out of kilter with what modern society, or at least the media, considers acceptable.

Nor is this predilection unique to Britain or America. In Germany, as the Protestant theologian Jürgen Moltmann attests, the number of so-called 'anonymous burials' has risen, and mourners have no public status anymore. In his words, 'In the great cities, the districts where people live and the cemeteries where the dead lie are now far apart, and families no longer live together in a single place, so the graves can neither be visited nor cared for' (Moltmann 2000: 254). Likewise, when it comes to pastoral care and counselling, Moltmann bemoans the fact that 'we ask less about what happens to the dead than about what is going to happen to the living after their loss' (Moltmann 2000: 254). This is all in marked contrast, according to Moltmann, with what happened in the past, both in the old village communities of Europe and in traditional societies of Africa and Asia, where there existed a cult of one's dead ancestors. As in the supernatural romance *The Ghost and Mrs. Muir* (Joseph L. Mankiewicz, 1947), where the ghost of a middle-aged, rambunctious sea captain, played by Rex Harrison, befriends a young widow and intervenes, from beyond the grave, to save and protect her from embarking upon a doomed affair with an already-married man, so Moltmann has in mind the way in which the dead were believed by the living to be spiritually present. Rex Harrison's character, Captain Daniel Gregg, may not have been a relative of Gene Tierney's headstrong widow, Lucy Muir, in Mankiewicz's film. Rather, he is merely a previous occupant of the Cornish coastal home, Gull Cottage, she has bought in order to escape from her unhappy past. But, Moltmann's illustration of how ancestors could 'torment their descendants through their unrest, or bless them through their peace' (Moltmann 2000: 253), and in which if the dead do not receive justice then they find no peace and, in turn, do not allow their descendants to live in peace, is mirrored in the events of this film. For, Gregg's ghost goes to extreme lengths to disrupt and re-arrange the seemingly serene new life that Lucy has found for herself until she is literally badgered and cajoled into seeing through the unscrupulous advances made by the rakish Miles Fairley (George Sanders). By the end of the film, so 'inexorably, eternally joined' are the deceased sea captain and the widow that 'When Lucy dies, the captain dies as well', since 'Lucy is the catalyst that brings the captain into existence and she alone fosters his immortality' (Kovacs 1999: 49). Kovacs' claim that 'With or without Lucy, the wonderful irascible ghost of Daniel Gregg is, in mid-20th century, the last of his kind' (Kovacs 1999: 49), is a very pertinent observation, squaring as it does with Moltmann's claim that, unlike in the past, in modern societies 'the dead no longer have influence on our lives in the same way – rather, the living have ascendancy over the dead' (Moltmann 2000: 253).

Even the constant representation of death in television news and on film somehow manages to evade its real impact. This is a point made by Fiddes, for whom 'Death has been packaged as virtual reality, as a media event' (Fiddes 2000: 13). The thinking, here, is that even though we are 'a society that views more simulated deaths on television in a few days than most of our ancestors confronted real deaths in a life-time' (Anderson 1986: 20), this is not the same as saying that we are able 'to face the fact of death' (Fiddes 2000: 12) and thereby confront and address the possibility of our own demise. There is a strong Heideggerean existentialist ballast to all of this, in that, for Heidegger, unless one is able to transcend the limitations and constraints of our being – which, as it stands, is caught up in illusory and fragmentary affairs – then there will be no deliverance from what presently amounts to an inauthentic existence (see e.g. Heidegger 1962: 277). Heidegger thought that an authentic relationship to death was required, in which we accept the fact that 'the very nature of our existence is characterized by death' (Edgar 1996: 160), at the moment of which 'all the worldly projects that have sustained us, and given meaning and purpose to our existence, crumble to nothing' (Edgar 1996: 159–60). It is only, then, by 'meditating on such limit-situations in life that we can be awakened to decision, to freedom, and, hence, to authentic existence' (Livingston 1971: 350), or else we run the risk of remaining transfixed and incapacitated in transitory and inauthentic concerns, together with the concomitant inclination 'to cling to them as secure indicators of what we really are' (Richardson 1991: 195).

So, although, in the modern day, we are only too familiar with the phenomenon of death through the media this does not mean that death has been squarely faced. In Hick's words, 'Children as well as adults see men being shot and otherwise deprived of life very frequently on films and TV' (Hick 1976: 86) – to the point, indeed, that according to a 1971 report from a meeting of the American Academy of Pediatrics by the time a child in America is 14 he or she can be expected to have seen on average the deaths on television of 18,000 people. But, to quote Hick, 'those 18,000 deaths on the screen simply trivialize death and make it unreal to the viewer', managing to 'turn the fact of death into part of the magic world of the screen which is unconsciously bracketed as unreal' (Hick 1976: 87). Anderson similarly adds that 'these same children will live, on average, for the next 40 years without experiencing the death or loss of an immediate family member', and that even at such a time 'they will be shielded from the death so that the living will disappear instantly, almost like the sudden departure of a character in a television drama' (Anderson 1986: 20). The fact that, when we do see death on the TV screen, it tends to take the form of those who have been killed in war or in some natural disaster only reinforces the point that, though it makes death visible, what we are seeing is 'death in exceptional forms', which is not the end that 'the ordinary person may expect' (Hick 1976: 87) to happen in their own life. This is all redolent of Heidegger's talk of how authenticity requires the stripping away of all the cosy security of that which we take for granted in our everyday life where death remains a distant threat in a secure and homely world (see Edgar 1996: 158). Otherwise, all we are really doing is evading confrontation with the world as it really is – namely, 'characterized by mortality and transience' (Edgar 1996: 160) – and failing to accord the fact of our deaths 'the most profound reflection', with the concomitant 'stripping away of every taken-for-granted presupposition of worth or value that I might have used to justify my existence' (Edgar 1996: 160).

Hence, notwithstanding the concern expressed by conservative commentator Michael Medved that every night on prime time American television the four major networks (Fox, CBS, ABC and NBC) feature an average of 350 characters, of whom seven will be murdered (see Deacy & Ortiz 2008: 129), the influence upon us of the mass media can actually inoculate and estrange us from taking death seriously. For the

New Testament scholar Rudolf Bultmann, moreover, the influence of the mass media, together with the monotony of everyday living and our passion for material things, have succeeded in alienating us from our true selves and have caused us to lose ourselves to the variety of outside pressures that try to deny our individuality and freedom. In Bultmann's words, 'Man exists in a permanent tension between the past and the future' and is confronted with one of two choices – 'Either he must immerse himself in the concrete world of nature, and thus inevitably lose his individuality, or he must abandon all security and commit himself unreservedly to the future, and thus alone achieve his authentic Being' (Bultmann 1972 [a]: 24–25). As things stand, in other words, we remain in bondage to death, and it is only when we face the reality of death (which he saw in terms of our creatureliness and mortality), as well as the nothingness of human existence, that we can more properly appreciate the fullness of the present moment and so live for the 'here and now' (see Livingston 1971: 350).

On such a reading, of course, the media could be construed as something of a barrier to 'doing' theology. If all the media does is to propagate illusion and fantasy, then it could be argued that it is particularly adept at allowing us to retreat from reality in the way Heidegger and Bultmann here envisage. Although Paul Tillich is often cited as a theologian whose work most enables a fruitful dialogue between theology and film to arise, in the light of his contention in *Theology of Culture* that neither the religious nor the secular realm 'should be in separation from the other' since both 'are rooted in religion in the larger sense of the word, in the experience of ultimate concern' (Tillich 1964: 9), Tillich's theology also underscores the dangers inherent in presupposing that so-called secular phenomena can lead to a fruitful conversation with theology. Despite being seen as someone for whom, in Lynch's words, 'any form of belief that genuinely provides the basis for a person's or community's life could be understood as "religious"', and that 'if religion is the search for and expression of "ultimate concern", then culture is itself a manifestation of this fundamental religious orientation' (Lynch 2005: 29), Tillich was also quite limited in his understanding of the parameters of this process. For, the mere fact that for Tillich 'Ultimate concern is manifest in the aesthetic function of the human spirit as the infinite desire to express ultimate meaning' (Tillich 1964: 8) and 'refers to every moment of our life, to every space and every realm' (Tillich 1964: 41) does not mean to say that all works of art are theologically productive *per se*. In *The Courage to Be*, Tillich undertook a psychoanalytical study of contemporary life and found that people often seek meaning in transitory and unfulfilling things which encompass only parts of life, rather than the totality:

> ... one is cut off from creative participation in a sphere of culture, one feels frustrated about something which one had passionately affirmed, one is driven from devotion to one object to devotion to another and again on to another, because the meaning of each of them vanishes and the creative eros is transformed into indifference or aversion. Everything is tried and nothing satisfies.
>
> *(Tillich 1979: 55)*

It thus follows that while in principle 'everything that has being is an expression, however preliminary and transitory it may be, of being-itself, of ultimate reality' (Tillich 2004: 210), not every manifestation or interpretation of popular culture bears witness to this dimension of depth. As when we accord ultimate worth to relationships, power and wealth, we will, argued Tillich, ultimately be let down because they will not satisfy our deepest spiritual needs: 'The anxiety of emptiness drives us to the abyss of meaninglessness' (Tillich 1979: 55).

Transient and ephemeral though much of the mass media may be, however, it does not straightforwardly follow from this that all films are indicative of an inauthentic approach towards death. Not everyone reads the same texts in the same way. Perhaps, indeed, films can provide us with a full and authentic awareness of the contingency of the world rather than necessarily inhibit us from doing so. The fact that 'No other narrative art can get as close as the cinema does to the variety, the texture, the skin of daily life' (Berger 1991: 16) does suggest that, say, Bultmann's or Tillich's dismissal of what the media can do provides only a partial picture. In the more realistic and, arguably, cynical and morally ambiguous world of *film noir*, for example, something more authentic has the capacity to take place, not least through *noir*'s unflinching confrontation with death and by exploring the seedy underbelly of human existence, than we find in works of escapism, where there can be no more than a fleeting reprieve from life's shortcomings. Indeed, as I have written elsewhere, 'it is the *noir* protagonist's intrinsic feasibility and authenticity, even when – or, perhaps, especially when – that entails the delineation of human existence lived out at its most *sub*human, at its most brutal, oppressive and capricious' (Deacy 2001: 102) that makes *noir* so open to a theological reading. It is true that many of the films that will be focused on in this book are tinged with escapism and tend to romanticise or simplify the boundaries between life and death. Binary oppositions between good and evil, heaven and hell are in abundance in everything from *Ghost* (Jerry Zucker, 1990) and *Flatliners* (Joel Schumacher, 1990) to *Bedazzled* (Harold Ramis, 2000) and *Little Nicky* (Steven Brill, 2000). But this fails to do justice to what amounts in many cases to quite subversive, mocking and challenging films to have come out of Hollywood and elsewhere in recent decades, and which have the capacity to put many contemporary theologians on the defensive.

Towards survival

While death itself may be a difficult, indeed a taboo, subject for many people to address, the attempt to evade (or, as happens in *Death Becomes Her* when Madeline Ashton [Meryl Streep] drinks the magic vial of rejuvenating potion, cheat) death is only one side of the eschatological coin. Many people may be disinclined to face death, but there are plenty of others (perhaps even many of the same people) who seem determined to study it. Concomitant with the Western obsession to defy the process of growing old through cosmetic surgery is what Arthur Berger identified, in his 1987 publication *Aristocracy of the Dead: New Findings in Postmortem Survival*, as the 'burgeoning interest in death and the possible post-mortem state on the part of academics of religion, philosophy and humanistic disciplines, theologians and the clergy, and workers in the fields of thanatology, sociology, psychology, medicine and nursing' (Berger 1987: 169). Concern with death is no longer limited, Berger continued, 'to people facing death or to widowers or widows' but has, rather, 'been uncovered and placed in the sunlight for examination by people in a wide range of disciplines', to the point, indeed, that 'Thousands of courses on death and dying are offered in high schools, colleges and universities and professional schools such as law, medicine, nursing and theology' (Berger 1987: 169). This has also been my own experience, from the time I pursued a Master's degree in this area in the mid-1990s. Irrespective of whether one is a theist or an atheist, a preoccupation with what amounts to 'the oldest manifestation of religious concern' (MacGregor 1992: 51) would thus seem to be very much in vogue. Indeed, concomitant with the readiness to embrace death in this fashion is the willingness to explore questions pertaining to immortality and the post-mortem condition. On one level, of course, this should come as no surprise. In the words of Collins and Fishbane, 'The quest for another world beyond this one, a world of spirits immune to death, is as old as recorded civilization, and attested in cultures East and West, North and South' (Collins & Fishbane 1995: ix). Moreover, this need not be seen as mere wish-fulfilment. In answer to the Marxist critique that, as expounded by Engels, religion 'is nothing but the fantastic reflection in people's minds of those external forces which control their daily life, a reflection in which the terrestrial forces assume the form of supernatural forces' (in Clarke & Byrne 1993: 142) – in other words, that religion is an illusion which, like opium, deadens the pain and discourages us from reacting against the status quo – belief in a life after death need not simply be seen as a deluded and fanciful hope that projects our attention away from the trials and tribulations of present existence. If it were, this would not make sense of why some of the forms that belief in an afterlife take, most notably the concept of hell with its attendant connotations of pain, suffering and damnation, are no less prominent in literature and film, as well as theology, than the utopian or 'pipe dream' consolation of heaven. Quite simply, it is the very mystery and inscrutability of death that makes it such fertile territory for theologians, filmmakers and others to interrogate.

Even for those who are certain of a belief in eternal life, however, Stoeger makes the instructive point that, in Christian terms, there is no sidestepping the fact that 'the death and dissolution we experience and which the natural sciences predict is real and will occur' (Stoeger 2000 [a]: 20). Accordingly, when we speak of salvation and redemption these are somehow to be 'realized precisely through these disconcerting events – in a way that we do not yet fully understand and on which we have only a partial analytical purchase' (Stoeger 2000 [a]: 20). In other words, we may look forward to what the future has in store but it does not thereby follow either that our passageway from this life is going to be easy or without cost. Nor is the specific make-up of the next life known to us in any concrete or definitive way. As Stanford puts it, indeed, even for those who believe in the existence of the soul – 'that invisible but integral part of us that is above the messy business of physical death' (Stanford 2002: 10) – it remains the case that, notwithstanding its enduring popularity, 'a heavenly hereafter for the souls of the faithful departed has been officially declared by the mainstream churches as being beyond our imagination' (Stanford 2002: 10).[5] What therefore comes to the fore in any discussions pertaining to the afterlife is that, even among theists, there is no uniformity or unanimity afoot concerning the form or nature of the post-mortem condition. Even if one is vehemently convinced that there is an afterlife – on the grounds, for example, that it is impossible to suppose that a God who has 'so lovingly guarded and guided me through the earthly pilgrimage that we call earthly life, will end by extinguishing the object of his incomparable solicitude and love' (MacGregor 1992: 49) – what may not be so clear-cut is the time scale of the process.

Does immortality kick into being immediately at the point of death, in the form of a particular or personal judgement, or can the deceased expect to look forward to a future Day of Judgement when all the good and bad deeds of all those who have ever lived will be weighed, followed by a future destiny to be spent in either heaven or hell? Or is there some sort of 'sojourn in purgatory' (Stanford 2002: 5) first, during which, in traditional Roman Catholic terms, one's sins will be cleansed, during what amounts to an indeterminate period of continuous punishment, in order to make the deceased fit for heaven? Is the afterlife for everyone, or are only religious adherents the recipients of eternal life? In which case, is it only Christians, or only Muslims, who will be 'saved'? If it is, say, only Christians, is there a further distinction between Anglicans, Methodists, Russian Orthodox or Roman Catholic Christians? What, further, is the connection between the life after death and our present, mortal existence? Will there be a physical dimension to the afterlife, and, if so, will there be any scope for physical interaction with anyone else in the same (or in a similar) manner to that which we are accustomed to on earth? Or do we survive merely as some form of 'continuing consciousness' (Hick 1976: 21) without a bodily frame of expression, in which, though 'I' am extinguished, 'some effluence of me somehow persists, as a perfume lingers after its wearer has left the room or as smoke may persist for hours or even days after the fire is extinguished' (MacGregor 1992: 44)? Alternatively, does the afterlife merely take the form of 'me' somehow 'living on' in the memories of those who are left behind, or through the books, music, artefacts or ideas that I am able to bequeath? If the latter is the case, then does this mean that Jesus Christ, Joan of Arc, William Shakespeare, John F. Kennedy, Elvis Presley, Princess Diana or Michael Jackson are somehow more 'immortal' than most people because their legacy has managed to endure in spite of – even because of – their physical demise? Obviously, we do not know the answers to all of these questions, so that, maybe, the best we can do is 'wait and see – or, it may be, wait and not see!' (Hick 1976: 21).

Threat from science

Before we turn specifically to the way in which filmmakers have examined and depicted on screen issues pertaining to the afterlife, it is apparent that there are broader difficulties which eschatological speculations invariably engender and which impact on any such debate. John Hick presents the problem in stark terms: 'The firm assumption that this life is part of a much larger existence which transcends our earthly span is no longer a part of the thought world of today', in which 'Post-Christian secular man believes only in what he experiences, plus that which the accredited sciences reveal to him' (Hick 1973: 143). Since the afterlife falls outside of this domain then it is 'accordingly dismissed as a fantasy of wishful thinking' (Hick 1973: 143). Much the same position has been put forward from within astrophysics by William Stoeger[6] who writes that

> From all the indications we have from the neurosciences, biology, physics, astronomy, and cosmology, death and dissolution are the final words. There is no scientifically supportable foundation for the immortality of the soul, the resurrection of the body and the person after death, a transformed new heavens and new earth.
>
> *(Stoeger 2000 [a]: 19)*

When scientists thus predict that the sun will one day exhaust its fuel, thereby terminating life on earth, and the universe will either collapse in upon itself in a 'big crunch' or dissipate away due to infinite expansion (see Tanner 2000: 222) – even if this does not happen for trillions of years (see Stoeger 2000 [a]: 27) – this does not exactly square with the eschatological hope envisaged by many theologians. Indeed, Watts writes that the latter could be said to belong 'to a completely different world from the impersonal predictions of cosmology' (Watts 2000: 48). We see traces of this conflict in Robert Zemeckis' film about the possibility of extra-terrestrial communication, *Contact* (1997), in which one of the underlying themes addressed is that of how science has 'wrested control of cosmic cataclysm away from religion' (Ostwalt 2003: 177). Religious representatives in the film are portrayed either as apocalyptic terrorists, right-wing bigots or, in the case of Palmer Joss (Matthew McConaughey) – who identifies himself as 'a man of the cloth … without the cloth' – as 'compromised and unconvincing' (Ostwalt 2003: 177) due to the 'abstract, meaningless, and void' (Stone 1998: 6) nature of the faith he seems to represent in the film. There is an implicit suggestion in *Contact*, and which is true also of many popular films, that, in Bryan Stone's words, 'traditional religious faith is deeply untrustworthy and to be placed at the margins of culture if not rejected altogether' (Stone 1998: 10). When it comes to questions of eschatology, therefore, it does rather look as though 'religion is anachronistic (if not irrelevant)' (Ostwalt 2003: 177), thus suggesting that the sort of enterprise I am engaged in in this book is something of a stumbling block to the 'closed world' of modern science.

Indeed, on a superficial level at any rate, many filmmakers would seem to be deviating from the materialistic disposition of contemporary scientific as well as philosophical discourse. This, as expressed in Cartesian-Newtonian terms, explains death 'in terms of mechanistic and organic processes' (Anderson 1986: 24) and sees consciousness as the product of the brain, which necessarily ceases to function following biological death. MacGregor puts the problem as follows:

> ... my brain, including every one of its millions of cells, will have been totally atrophied at my death and the three pounds of matter in which it functioned will be either cremated with the rest of my body or else left to rot in a grave.
>
> *(MacGregor 1992: 16)*

In such materialist terms, after death there can be neither sensation nor self-awareness, and so the 'soul' − if it exists at all − must perish together with the rest of the body, since the idea of an incorporeal substance is a contradiction in terms (see Lorimer 1984: 94–96). We should only therefore believe in that which we can directly experience. This certainly ties in with Russell's claim that the most widespread dogma among educated people by the end of the twentieth century was physicalism − that is, 'the metaphysical belief that the only valid statements about reality (other than mathematics) are statements about physical objects, movements, and forces', such that 'there is no real world other than the physical world' (Russell 2006: 135). Doore similarly writes that with 'the spectacular rise of modern Western science from around the sixteenth century ... the materialistic worldview has gradually gained ascendancy, until today it commands enormous influence' (Doore 1990: 3). On such an interpretation, any theological or spiritual explanations about the soul or consciousness surviving death are necessarily superfluous to material and neurochemical processes in which the inner is now 'explained in terms of the outer, the subjective by means of the objective' and 'mind as a manifestation of the brain' (Lorimer 1995: 167). In a nutshell, '*nothing* survives after death because consciousness is merely a by-product of the physical brain and is therefore incapable of surviving the demise of that organ' (Doore 1990: 2). Although the philosopher Antony Flew did, in his latter years, change his position on the possibility that a theistic world-view might have any merit,[7] back in 1950 he could not have been more dismissive of what, to a materialist such as himself, any talk of the possibility of an afterlife entailed: 'the news of the immortality of the soul would be of no more concern to me than the news that my appendix would be preserved eternally in a bottle' (in Zaleski 1995: 402).

In Marxist and Dawkinsian terms, a thoroughgoing reductionism is, of course, in play, here, whereby any suggestion that there is any kind of transcendent or ultimate meaning or value to our lives, let alone any possibility of an individual or communal post-mortem destiny, is believed to be the result of wishful thinking (see Stoeger 2000 [b]: 67). Heaven and hell are deemed to comprise nothing other than supernatural fantasies, on this reading, a point articulated by Nicholas Lash, for whom the future hope is a mythological fantasy and belief in paradise is equivalent to belief in fairyland (see Badham & Badham 1984: 51). Such thinking has, unsurprisingly, had a huge impact on the way in which theology has been conducted over the course of the last century or so. One of the most popular undergraduate courses I teach is called 'Death of God? Christian Theology and the Modern World', in which one of the areas of focus is on the so-called 'Death of God' theologians, such as William Hamilton and Thomas Altizer, from the 1960s, according to whom 'The death of God abolishes transcendence, thereby making possible a new and absolute immanence ... freed of every sign of transcendence' (Altizer & Hamilton 1966: 137). For such thinkers,

'Every trace of a truly and finally transcendent God has vanished, and this vanishing is the realization of a pure and total immanence' (in Fiddes 2000: 246).

I assume that Hick had this school of thought in mind when he wrote a decade later that radical theologians 'have been so embarrassed by the traditional christian [sic] hope that they have tried either to suppress the eschatological element within Christianity altogether or else to present it without the scandalous affirmation of personal life after death' (Hick 1976: 93). This is not to say that traditional ideas about resurrection, judgement, heaven and hell are no longer believed any more. But, Badham is quite right in his claim that 'Talk of life after death seems strangely remote from our everyday thinking' and that 'although most Christians will say they believe in it when asked in an opinion poll' (Badham & Badham 1984: ix), they will also be quite secular in their world-view. Writing in 1992, Geddes MacGregor illustrated the point as follows: 'Today, a worker in Manhattan who lives in one high-rise building and works in another day after day in a world of computers, telephones, typewriters, and fax machines' (to which we could also add, today, e-mail, iPhones, broadband and Blu-Ray technology) 'is so estranged from the realm of the spirit that he or she can hardly be expected to understand biblical language' (MacGregor 1992: 110). More recently, Stewart Hoover, one of the most influential voices in the current Religion and Media field, has argued that in a world where the media 'play a central role in providing the symbolic resources through which we make meaning of our social worlds' (Hoover 2006: 56), it is not surprising that a profession such as journalism should have 'a problem with religion' (Hoover 2006: 57). The grounds for this are that 'religion has always claimed to be about things beyond the rational sphere of the "here and now" – the natural turf on which most journalists see themselves working' (Hoover 2006: 57). In such a context, it is not surprising if the mainstream churches today are 'wary of providing any directions for, or details of, landmarks in the afterlife', and that, when pressed, will 'talk simply and without enthusiasm of experiencing God's love in a more perfect way on earth and treat heaven as a metaphor that has a confused past and which has now all but passed its sell-by date' (Stanford 2002: 297).

However, even when filmmakers touch on the subject of the 'end', as in the case of *Contact*, they are not necessarily envisaging a future life after death – clearly a stumbling-block to a scientific world-view – but, rather, a new and improved present order of existence.[8] The simple fact that filmmakers are inclined to draw upon the subject of eschatology in their work does not thereby mean that such enterprises are, by definition, affirming a belief in discredited, scientifically obsolescent phenomena.[9] Moreover, there is also the important consideration that the debate cannot be seen in such black-and-white, 'progressive science' versus 'superstitious religion', categories in any case. John Polkinghorne, who resigned his Chair of Mathematical Physics at Cambridge in 1979 in order to become a Church of England priest, is a prime example of a modern day scientist for whom science need not exercise such a tyrannical hold over the way in which questions about death and eschatology are undertaken. Polkinghorne's position is that, however satisfying science can be, 'it is not enough by any manner of means' (Polkinghorne 1995: 9) and that 'its impersonal approach will never touch more than the periphery of our human experience' and that all 'those things that touch us in our inner being lie beyond its grasp' (Polkinghorne 1995: 59). Drawing on the Anthropic Principle – the concept of the fine-tuning of the universe, whereby scientists have identified a number of special conditions in the structure and evolution of the universe which have enabled intelligent life on earth to have come about and which, were any of these to be altered by an infinitesimal degree the delicate balance of physical and cosmological constants would be destroyed and life could not exist – Polkinghorne holds the line that one could 'call the universe's intelligibility a signal of transcendence, an intimation that there is more to understand than has met the scientific eye' (Polkinghorne 1995: 38). In such terms, that which has happened in the twentieth century is what he calls 'the death of a merely mechanical, deterministic, atomized account of the physical world' (Polkinghorne 2000: 34). Perhaps, then, in view of such factors, the coherence and credibility of eschatological hope need no longer be subject to what contemporary scientific discourse alone deems acceptable or not. Impressive though a scientific account of the world may be, Polkinghorne queries whether the laws of nature are by themselves sufficiently intellectually satisfying or self-explanatory to constitute an adequate foundation on which to build our understanding about how the universe functions (see Polkinghorne 1995: 3–4).

Of course, this is a far cry from saying that films have all the answers, but when Polkinghorne writes of how there lies deep within us 'an intuition of hope and human significance, despite the manifest transience of life in this world' (Polkinghorne 1995: 59), it does seem somewhat churlish to suppose that works of human creativity and imagination, such as that found across the arts, can offer no insight into questions of death and the afterlife. Irrespective of whether or not films correspond to the latest scientific paradigms, there is little doubt that, provided often artificial dichotomies between subject areas ('science' vs. 'religion', for instance) are removed, then the 'secular' medium of film might be found to comprise a surprisingly rich repository of eschatological activity, and which, moreover, has the capacity to challenge and re-orient the way in which debates in both contemporary theological and scientific discourse are framed. According to the revised correlational model approach that was outlined in the introduction, a 'complex conversation' is valued 'between the questions and insights of both religious tradition and popular culture, and allows for the possibility that both religious tradition and popular culture can be usefully challenged and transformed through this process' (Lynch 2005: 105). In keeping with this model, so it is my intention, here, to show that rather than dismiss afterlife-themed films as a throwback to a pre-scientific way of thinking, such movies can shed new light on the way in which religious, theological and philosophical themes are being conducted in a 'secular' setting. To put it starkly, eschatology cannot simply be seen as the preserve of theologians alone (see Watts 2000: 49). Accordingly, when Fraser Watts makes the instructive point that, with respect to Marxism, Christian eschatology cannot reasonably 'continue oblivious of this recent wave of secularized eschatology; it is necessary at least to engage with it' (Watts 2000: 50),[10] so I want to argue that this applies no less cogently to the medium of film.

Death, immortality and film

That eschatological questions are central to many contemporary movies is an important starting-point to our discussion. In the past I have been critical of 'movies which facilitate little beyond superficial, escapist, entertainment value to audiences' (Deacy 2005: 23), whereby 'a short-term success or advantage in the film narrative symbolically resolves and liberates the characters (and by extension the film audience) from the pain and suffering of human existence' (Deacy 2005: 25). However, there are many instances of films of a wish-fulfilment sensibility having the capacity to shed new light on the way in which theologians have conceived of the afterlife. *Field of Dreams* (Phil Alden Robinson, 1989) is one such example, in which the estranged father of an Iowa farmer, Ray Kinsella (Kevin Costner), is 'magically reincarnated' in 'the earthly mythic site beloved by Hollywood' of 'the baseball field' (Martin & Ostwalt 1995: 70), and in which Kinsella sees 'eternity in a night baseball game played in a converted cornfield by ghosts from the past' (Ferrell 2000: 157). Injudicious though it may be to 'read' the film as conforming to the Christian vision of the Kingdom of God (there is no suggestion that this was ever the filmmakers' intentions), which is, arguably, more dramatic, cosmic and social in scope than Kinsella's almost Gnostic vision which can be discerned only by a chosen few in his Iowa cornfield, Marsh attests that the themes of forgiveness and reconciliation that lie at the film's heart are nevertheless 'compatible with thinking about what participation in the Kingdom of God entails' (Marsh 2007 [a]: 152). Accordingly, for Marsh, *Field of Dreams* 'brings to the screen an imaginative presentation of what it means to live according to a vision' (Marsh 2007 [a]: 152). Others have been more emphatic about the film's eschatological constitution. This is a movie which, in the words of evangelical commentator Greg Garrett, 'knits together life after death, the granting of wishes, the reconciliation of a son with his dead father, and, ultimately, a visit to heaven' (Garrett 2007: 10–11). Ferrell similarly identifies 'a kind of afterlife, a form of myth that exists within every civilized culture', whereby it is thought that 'at some point in time, the individual, the culture, and the world will attain eternal paradise' (Ferrell 2000: 158). According to Stephen Brown, further, the film's baseball players can be seen as 'the Spiritual Community representing the company of heaven' (Brown 1997: 230).

Some will, of course, see this as mere pie-in-the-sky idealism. It could be said, for instance, that the transitoriness and inauthenticity that Heidegger spoke of corresponds to the somewhat comforting and idyllic images of *Field of Dreams* 'in which the problems of the present are symbolically resolved in a past that not only did not, but could not exist' (Collins 1993: 257). This is, after all, a film in which baseball is associated with pre-1960s America and a rural wholesomeness about which the audience is expected to feel nostalgic and sentimental, even though it is a past that lies beyond historical and chronological time. This is undoubtedly pure wish-fulfilment – 'the attempt to recapture the elemental simplicity of childhood delight in a magical state that yields its perfect resolutions of the otherwise impossible conflict' (Collins 1993: 262–63). Not surprisingly, it accords with Tillich's claim that the condition of existential disappointment, namely, the feeling of emptiness and insecurity, can cause some people to frantically seek some new ground of assurance and purpose in life, often in the form of some sort of 'retreat from reality' (in Livingston 1971: 358). The kind of manufactured positive visual insights of the world that are on display in *Field of Dreams*, though entertaining, will always therefore amount to something of a diversion in which we find ourselves attending to the 'reel' rather than to the 'real' world.

Ultimately, however, there is something unknowable about the structure, content or form of the afterlife, which makes its rich and varied treatment in film difficult to completely reject as false or mistaken. In Stanford's words, 'As, it would seem, we cannot try it out and report back any feelings of disappointment, it remains nothing more than a glorious but untried promise, utterly open to the wiles of our imagination' (Stanford 2002: 5). When Garrett thus suggests that *Pulp Fiction* (Quentin Tarantino, 1994) – which, he argues, contains '[o]ne of the great stories of redemption in recent American film' (Garrett 2007: 86) – has an eschatological dimension to it we can see just one of the more unusual, and inventive, ways in which life and death questions have the capacity to be played out on screen. Garrett has in mind, here, the way in which, due to the film's non-linear chronology, it brings one of the characters, a hit man, Vincent (John Travolta), 'back to life in the movie's final section even though he's just been filled full of lead in the section preceding' (Garrett 2007: 87). More conventionally, perhaps, horror movies can also be seen to be a potentially rich site of eschatological concern. Writing in a recent article, Douglas Cowan observes that 'Throughout its history, cinema horror is in fact replete with religion' (Cowan 2009: 405), not least by the way in which, to give two examples, 'Satan has shown himself a cinema horror staple' (Cowan 2009: 406) and ghost stories are 'predicated on the possibility of life after death and the disposition of the soul or spirit' (Cowan 2009: 405). Referring to a study of British horror movies, Cowan also writes that two-thirds of them rely on the supernatural in some form (Cowan 2009: 406). Across a diverse range of genres it would not, then, be at all wide of the mark to see questions pertaining to death and the afterlife as foundational. Paul Fiddes goes even further, writing in his 2000 publication *The Promised End: Eschatology in Theology and Literature*, that for literary critics also 'the basic nature of texts is eschatological, and that this dimension is too important to be left to the minority interests of science fiction and disaster novels' (Fiddes 2000: 5). Fiddes' premise is that 'All texts are eschatological, both in being open to the new meaning which is to come to them in the future, and also in being "seriously" open to the horizon which death gives to life' (Fiddes 2000: 6). In a sense, this appeal to eschatology as the basic mood of both theology and literature should come as no surprise. After all, the Christian idea of the last things is located in a story (namely, the death and resurrection of Christ) and is dependent on literary sources, principally those of the New Testament, while in Fiddes' opinion literary critics also are concerned not just with the text but with questions about human existence, human society, human hope and the threat of death (see Fiddes 2000: 6). Fiddes' thinking, here, is that if 'all created things live in the presence of a self-revealing God, then they will make a response to this revelation in a way which is appropriate to their particular place in the world' and that 'the images and stories of creative writers on the one hand, and the concepts of theologians on the other, are *all* responses to the creativity of God' (Fiddes 2000: 191). While not everyone may be inclined to subscribe to Fiddes' quite sacramentalist position – it is hard to see all literary critics sharing the view that 'the forms of both imagination and doctrine are responses in their own way to the self-giving of the triune God' (Fiddes 2000: 191–92) – where he is not wrong is in seeing ideas about death and the afterlife as being elementary human concerns rather than the exclusive province of the theologian.

A further theological underpinning to this way of thinking is provided in the work of the twentieth-century theologians of hope, Jürgen Moltmann and Wolfhart Pannenberg, for whom eschatology cannot simply be relegated to questions of our future, biological demise. Rather, there is something inescapably eschatological about our whole structure of being. In Moltmann's words, 'From first to last, and not merely in the epilogue, Christianity is eschatology, is hope, forward looking and forward moving, and therefore also revolutionizing and transforming the present' (Moltmann 1967: 16). Moltmann's thinking, here, is that the future is not simply determined by the present in the way that our chronological understanding of time would suggest. Rather, it is the future that determines the present. For him, the future is 'ontologically prior' (Miller & Grenz 1998: 111) to both the present and the past, and, rather than rise from the present, it would be more accurate to see the future as drawing the present forward into totally different forms of reality. The new possibilities of God's future thus have a power, for Moltmann, which, as Fiddes puts it, 'works back into the present, as hope for the new creation sets the old creation in a new light' (Fiddes 2000: 173). In Moltmann's own words, 'the future-made-present creates new conditions for possibilities in history' (Moltmann 1996: 20), and in which eschatological redemption entails

> a movement which runs from the future to the past, not from the past to the future. It is the divine tempest of the new creation, which sweeps out of God's future over history's fields of the dead, waking and gathering every last created being.
>
> *(Moltmann 1993: 303)*

This understanding of a future eschatology is reiterated by Pannenberg, who sees the future as transcending each moment within history, including our present lives (see Miller & Grenz 1998: 139). Important though the focus therefore is on the end of life, it is significant that in a number of films, also, the need to revolutionise and transform the present in the light of that future hope are pivotal themes. Frank Capra's Christmas classic *It's a Wonderful Life* (1946) is taken to be just such a case in point by Stephen Brown, who comments that the whole film, which has been shot from a heavenly point of view ('the angelic throng bending near the earth to touch their harps of gold'), 'depicts a world ultimately under the reign of a good God', and in which the suggestion is that 'God's reign, even if hidden, has begun' (Brown 1997: 232).

The lesson, here, Brown continues, is that 'Humans cannot effect their own trans-formation by themselves' (Brown 1997: 232). Rather, this 'present life can only be wonderful if we believe in God's promise through the risen Christ to be with us to the end of time, working with us' (Brown 1997: 232). In terms which would not be an anathema to Moltmann and Pannenberg, Brown thinks that the terms 'Kingdom of God' and 'eschatology' can be appropriated vis-à-vis Capra's film to demonstrate that 'life is not a totally meaningless and random existence if looked at from the point of view of the end' (Brown 1997: 232).

A similar dynamic is afoot in the reincarnation comedy *Switch* (Blake Edwards, 1991), in which a male chauvinist, Steve Brooks (Perry King), is given the chance to enter heaven on the condition that he first finds a woman who likes him. Despite the intervention of the Devil, who convinces Steve (while he is trapped in a woman's body) that his fate is sealed and that no such woman exists, the ending, in which Steve/Amanda (Ellen Barkin) gives birth to a baby daughter whose love for him/her enables the protagonist to pass through the pearly gates, does not simply follow the conventional route of seeing the future as determined simply by what one does in the present. His/her old creation, as an irredeemably sexist and manipulative male, is cast in a new light by the gender reconfiguration, which leads to empathy and reciprocal love between two people. S/he may not have been awakened and gathered from the dead in the way Moltmann anticipates, but talk of a new creation is definitely afoot, here. The protagonist has not simply come to some kind of inner, spiritual or moral transformation in his/her present life by having been afforded a 'second chance' of sorts. Rather, the film is told from a heavenly vantage point, in a manner not dissimilar from that of *It's a Wonderful Life*, in which, though now in heaven, Steve/Amanda is told by a heavenly chorus that s/he can still 'watch [his/her baby daughter] grow up' on earth and is to 'Take your time; you have all eternity' to 'decide whether you want to be a male or a female angel'. None of this, of course, lends itself to as sophisticated a theology as we find in the eschatological writings of Pannenberg and Moltmann whose work hardly lends itself to lightweight and unde-veloped musings about angelology. But, patchy though the film is – the *Variety* reviewer called *Switch* 'a faint-hearted sex comedy that doesn't have the courage of its initially provocative conclusions' (in Elley 1994: 888) – the film does link with their thinking in one other respect. Both theologians are critical of power and hierarchy, preferring to emphasise the importance of fellowship, equality and interdependence, to the point that, for Moltmann, the future Kingdom should not be construed in terms of a hierarchical monarchy but as a harmonious fellowship between humans and God: 'In the experience of freedom, we experience ourselves as God's servants, as his children, and as his friends … ' (Moltmann 1981: 221). Mutuality, rather than lordship, is thus the key. For Pannenberg, similarly, it has been detrimental to theology to say that, in Trinitarian terms, the Son and Spirit are subordinate to the Father. The model Pannenberg prefers is one of mutual dependence, in the respect that in sending the Son into the world the Father has made his lordship over creation dependent on the Son's completion of his mission (see Miller & Grenz 1998: 134).

While *Switch* may offer little scope for dialogue with theologians on the question of the Trinity, this model of mutuality is very much in keeping with the way *Switch* concludes. Whereas the Devil in the film is portrayed as a misogynistic manipulator – and thus an extension of the male incarnation of the protagonist at the start of the movie – the voice of God in the film contains both male and female parts that complement one another and speak in unison. Like Pannenberg's talk of how, at the consummation, God's unity will finally be shown (though with the difference that, for Pannenberg, at the eschaton there will be no new experiences as such [see Fiddes 2000: 213]), at the movie's consummation the protagonist's female incarnation, Amanda, is heard weighing up the equally attractive merits of becoming either a male or a female angel. What is more, for neither theologian nor for the filmmakers is death something to be feared. Moltmann's talk of how when we die we enter upon an intermediate state in which the life that was cut short can develop freely, and in which God's history with a human being can come to its flowering and consummation (Moltmann 2000: 252), is mirrored by Steve/Amanda's enlightened post-mortem condition, in which s/he can both 'watch [his/her baby] grow up' and contemplate, for an eternity if need be, how s/he can be best fitted for future moral and spiritual growth. The fact that, under Moltmann's schema (unlike Pannenberg's), when the final transformation takes place by God's grace the individuals concerned are awake and receptive agents of that transformation, rather than passive, and that even interhuman reconciliation would seem to be possible (see Volf 2000: 271), does suggest that, for all its flaws, *Switch* bears witness to an albeit surprising working-out of core Moltmannian teachings.

Methodological questions concerning the use of film

The attempt to pair Moltmann and Pannenberg (who are themselves in disagreement over whether there will be any new experiences at the *eschaton*) with the work of a comedy director such as Blake Edwards, perhaps best known for the series of *Pink Panther* films starring Peter Sellers, presents an obvious methodological problem. Tempting though it may be to find points of correlation between the themes of a cinematic product and that of two distinguished twentieth-century 'theologians of hope', there are, invariably, points of divergence which are no less compelling. In the case of *Switch*, Steve/Amanda succeeds in entering Heaven at the end because s/he successfully finds one person who loves him/her. But, this has nothing at all to do with the way theologians have traditionally approached the question of the afterlife, where their specific focus has been on the form and nature of resurrection, immortality and eternal life. In Christian terms, for instance, Russell Aldwinckle writes that it is 'well to admit frankly' that if one 'believes that he will "be" in some sense real after death, he does so on the basis of his faith in the power of God to secure his continuance in existence' (Aldwinckle 1972: 84). Quite simply, according to Aldwinckle, the believer puts his or her 'confidence in the God who raised Jesus Christ from the dead' (Aldwinckle 1972: 84–85). Outside of Christianity, analogous dynamics are at work, as when in Zoroastrianism 'the savior Saoshyant breathes life into the lifeless bodies of all humanity' or, in the case of Islam, 'when the individual souls are called to the final day of judgment' (Smith 1989: 90). In marked contrast, it is unusual in films – even those which purport to deal with an afterlife – for there to be any strong doctrinal or philosophical point of view which accords with any one tradition (as the conclusion, which explores the commingling of Christian and Buddhist motifs, will show). It is especially pertinent in this regard that when Clive Marsh draws upon a case study of three films in his section on 'The end' in *Theology Goes to the Movies*, he notes that none of these movies – *Jesus of Montreal* (Denys Arcand, 1989), *Truly, Madly, Deeply* (Anthony Minghella, 1990) or the aforementioned *Field of Dreams* – 'necessitates any clear, single conviction about life beyond physical death' (Marsh 2007 [a]: 145). In so doing, Marsh continues, they could be seen to 'reflect contemporary caution about believing anything concerning what lies beyond death' (Marsh 2007 [a]: 145).

Superficially fascinating though it therefore is from a theological perspective to see that death and immortality are being addressed in the cinema, and notwithstanding the fact that there is a certain convergence at work in that such films are calling to mind 'a range of questions with which Christian theology has long dealt' (Marsh 2007 [a]: 146), it is questionable that the parallels hold up to close scrutiny. After all, the films often celebrate ambiguity, as illustrated by the diverse range of interpretations that have been ascribed by commentators to *Field of Dreams* alone. This is a film which has been viewed as a story about heaven (Garrett 2007: 11), reincarnation (Martin & Ostwalt 1995: 70), religion as therapy that has more to say about this world than the next one (Marsh 2007 [a]: 152), and 'a fable about redemption and reconciliation that uses the mythos of baseball as an organizing metaphor' (Elley 1994: 292). For Roger Ebert of the *Chicago Sun-Times* this is, further, a 'movie about dreams', a film which 'leaves the viewer wondering what the borderlines are between reality, fantasy and madness', a 'fragile construction of one goofy fantasy after another', as well as a picture about baseball as religion (Ebert 1989 <http://rogerebert. suntimes.com/apps/pbcs.dll/article?AID=/19890421/REVIEWS/904210302/1023>). Theological doctrines, in contrast, tend to be more about fixing meaning and reducing images and stories to concepts – a point succinctly made by Fiddes, according to whom 'literature tends to openness and doctrine to closure' (Fiddes 2000: 7). The Council of Chalcedon, for example, which was the attempt by the Church Fathers in 451 CE to resolve, or at least hold together, conflicting positions on the human versus divine natures of the person of Christ, may be regarded, in McGrath's words, 'as laying down a controlling principle for classical Christology, which has been accepted as definitive within much Christian theology' (McGrath 2001: 367). Notwithstanding the fact that films often tend to have contrived, fixed, 'happy' endings – one of the problems I have had in the past with escapism, for example (Deacy 2005: 25) – which tend to be preferred by the studios, it is hard to reconcile the 'fixed doctrine' of, say, Chalcedon with a movie such as *Field of Dreams*. For, this is a film which, in Ebert's words, 'depends on a poetic vision to make its point' and in which the baseball players from the past 'come back from the great beyond' not to make 'any kind of vast, earthshattering statement' but 'simply to hit a few and field a few, and remind us of a good and innocent time' (Ebert 1989 <http://rogerebert.suntimes.com/apps/pbcs.dll/article?AID=/19890421/REVIEWS/904210302/1023>). In stark contrast to the subtle and sophisticated theological nuances of the Nicene Creed (which endeavoured to affirm Christ's full humanity against the Arian relegation of Christ's status to that of creature) or the Chalcedonian Definition, Rita Kempley of the *Washington Post* sums up the indistinctness of *Field of Dreams* sharply: 'This is the myth of peanuts and Cracker Jack, ball play as next to God, and Shoeless Joe Jackson as archangel' (Kempley 1989 (a): <www.washingtonpost.com/wp-srv/style/longterm/movies/videos/fieldofdreamspg kempley_a09fb9.htm>).

Another methodological problem, which also frustrates any attempt to forge straightforward links between a cinematic and a theological eschatology, concerns those films which represent the absence, or dissolution, of life. In *Sunset Boulevard* (Billy Wilder, 1950), *Reversal of Fortune* (Barbet Schroeder, 1990) and *American Beauty* (Sam Mendes, 1999), voice-over narration is provided by the protagonists, and the narratives comprise a flashback covering the period leading up to his or her death. This raises the question, as Ruffles sees it, 'of how an individual can be so organized to be able to project a coherent personality, with memories, desires and regrets, in the absence of bodily organization' (Ruffles 2004: 62). In the case of *Sunset Boulevard*, for example, Joe Gillis' (William Holden) voice 'is able to co-exist with the image of his corpse floating in the swimming pool' (Ruffles 2004: 63). Similarly, in *Reversal of Fortune*, based on the real-life case of Claus Von Bülow's trial in 1982 for the attempted murder in Rhode Island of his wealthy, socialite wife, Sunny, we hear Glenn Close's voice-over reminiscence of her character's past while the figure we see before us lies comatose in what she herself explains is a persistent vegetative state. What is it exactly that constitutes these characters so that, as Ruffles puts it, 'an entire person can be inferred from a voice-over' (Ruffles 2004: 63)? Since a person cannot be both alive and dead simultaneously (though in Sunny's case this is debatable in view of her irreversible brain damage) then the specific nature of their existence is difficult to ascertain. Should we take their voice-over to be a 'sign of omniscience that depends on the continuation of life after death' (Ruffles 2004: 63)? Indeed, are the films implicitly postulating a life after death, in a way that is explicit in the case of *American Beauty*, whose protagonist, middle-aged magazine publisher Lester Burnham (Kevin Spacey), who has become withdrawn from his sham marriage and job, says in voice-over mode, while surveying the final year of his mortal existence: 'I'm forty-two years old. In less than a year, I'll be dead. Of course, I don't know that yet … '? The film also concludes with the tantalisingly eschatological forewarning to audiences: 'You have no idea what I'm talking about, I'm sure. But don't worry … You will someday'.

Beguiling though such talk is, however, a number of theological problems present themselves. Once the initial fascination has passed that filmmakers are treading on theological territory, there is no suggestion in these films that anything especially challenging is really taking place. Though writing with regard to the inadequacy of much current thinking among Christians concerning the nature of the afterlife, Badham's concern that many people today believe on the one hand that we will be re-embodied or resurrected in heaven but 'that the question of the whereabouts of heaven is either totally ignored, or answered with the assertion that heaven has no location' (Badham 1976: 92) can equally apply to the content of afterlife-themed films. Even if one takes the line that, due to the cosmological discoveries of the seventeenth century, heaven has been somewhat internalised, realised and spiritualised 'into describing a state of being, rather than a future dwelling place' (Badham 1976: 92), Badham is correct that such a position overlooks the fact that these two currents of thought are incompatible with one another. For, an 'immortal soul can be thought of as existing without location in a non-located heaven. But a resurrected body requires to live somewhere' (Badham 1976: 92). Accordingly, when a film such as *American Beauty* hints at a future life, the fact that the very content and form of that post-mortem condition is nebulous and unformulated tends to close down, rather than open up, serious theological dialogue. Has Lester Burnham been resurrected or is his soul simply immortal? The film does not tell us, but, in theological terms, such questions matter. Paul Coates similarly writes that 'There is no indication where Lester is speaking from' and 'no indication of how it might relate to traditional Western conceptions of the afterlife' (Coates 2003: 183). He continues that the best indication 'for a concrete equivalent of so unclassified a condition would, of course, be Purgatory, which is inherently intermediate – containing the flames, like Hell, but redirecting them to divine ends – but any such categorization would be as irre-levant as it would be speculative' (Coates 2003: 183). All we can do is surmise as to what the filmmakers' intentions may have been.

To be fair, it is not as though theologians have all of the answers, either. To give one example, when St Paul, in his first letter to the Corinthians, is emphatic that the resurrection body will be our own body and not merely a strange or new body (1 Corinthians 15: 42–50), Ray Anderson responds that St Paul 'does not answer the question as to precisely what this resurrection body will look like or how the embodied existence of the resurrection can be understood in terms of our present embodied state' (Anderson 1986: 120). Such ambivalence may be sufficient to scotch any suggestions that theologians have all the answers and exclusively control the contours of the debate. But it also remains the case that, while filmmakers may have fresh and innovative ideas to offer on the theme of the afterlife (this has never been in question from my point of view), there is something inherently barren and unsophisticated about what they can teach theologians about death and eschatology *per se*. Quite simply, there may be a superficial resemblance between *American Beauty* and St Paul over the fact that a person's life does not come to an end upon physical death, but they also differ on the fundamentals. From the early days of Christianity, death was believed to have been conquered by the resurrection of Christ and only from that non-negotiable starting-point does post-mortem existence have any meaning. In French's words, 'After death, the true Christian, according to St. Paul, can expect to survive in a celestial body and look forward to deathlessness, eternal life in Heaven' (French 1997: 48). But, *American Beauty* does not tell us anything about how the life of a person continues or is reconstituted following Lester's homicide. The audience, if it is so inclined, can only surmise. Lester may 'live on', but, in

Pauline terms, the only meaningful account of death is a decidedly more concrete one than the spiritual, immortal and soul-surviving intimation of post-mortem survival that we have in Mendes' film, which does not seem to 'involve anything potentially disturbing' and which is devoid, moreover, of what Coates calls 'religious otherness and judgement' (Coates 2003: 184). Indeed, Lester's final voice-over in which he reflects that

> ... it's hard to stay mad, when there's so much beauty in the world. Sometimes I feel like I'm seeing it all at once, and it's too much, my heart fills up like a balloon that's about to burst ... and then I remember to relax, and stop trying to hold on to it, and then it flows through me like rain and I can't feel anything but gratitude for every single moment of my stupid little life

would seem to comprise nothing more profound than 'a stream of apparently banal moments seen in the true light of transcendence, earthly beauty become sublime' (Coates 2003: 184). Rather, for Paul, anything non-bodily in nature is theologically inadequate: 'For Paul, we are bodies. First terrestrial and then, by the will and grace of God, celestial, but always bodies. He does not talk about souls' (French 1997: 49). To be fair, there is a strong bodily dimension to Lester's existence, but this only applies to his mortal, rather than immortal, condition. As Coates puts it, 'The emphasis on body-building and on remembrance establishes an almost Proustian sense of recollection in the body' (Coates 2003: 184). But, this is hardly sufficient to generate any meaningful parallels.

Moreover, the fact that there are other films in which the characters giving the ostensibly post-mortem narration turn out to be alive after all simply exacerbates the difficulty of seeing film as an intrinsically constructive site of eschatological significance. In Scorsese's *Casino* (1995), the very first scene consists of a shot of the protagonist, gambling expert Sam 'Ace' Rothstein (Robert De Niro), turn on the ignition of his car which we then see explode, followed by his descent back to the ground against a backdrop of flames. The clear implication is that Rothstein has been killed, a point emphasised by his voice-over which refers to a time 'before I got blown up', as well as the use of a flashback structure (see Ruffles 2004: 63). We later discover, however, that Rothstein has survived, and, in Ruffles' words, 'Surprisingly we realize that the narration has been provided by somebody who is alive' (Ruffles 2004: 63). To underline this, another character (the mobster Nicky Santoro, played by Joe Pesci) also supplies a voice-over during the film, only this comes to an abrupt end, mid-sentence, when we see him beaten to the point of death and buried in a shallow grave. When the boundaries between life and death are so malleable and fluid, it is not clear that such films are as insightful to the theologian as the initial subject matter may suggest.

A cursory examination of the western genre also demonstrates just where the differences lie between a cinematic and a theological sensibility vis-à-vis the question of an afterlife. From the outset, it is clear that 'Death is the predominant element of the westerner's world view' (French 1997: 3), in the respect that in westerns are displayed the conflicts that occur when those who care about the existence of God, the immortality of the human soul, obedience to divine moral commands, familial human relationships and the like confront those who could not give a damn about the existence of God, deny the immortality of man, have no interest in whether or how they will get on in a future eternal life, have invested themselves in a moral code that regards the commands of Judeo-Christian ethics as senseless, and care more about friendship relationships than marriage or familial relations

(French 1997: 11)

Peter French has made a rich contribution to this area of study in his 1997 publication *Cowboy Metaphysics: Ethics and Death in Westerns*, where the point is made that in contrast to an afterlife, in westerns the 'sting of death is very real', and whose 'victory is the victory of ending a person's existence and all that person ever was or will be' (French 1997: 49–50). Whether we are talking about Clint Eastwood's tortured and three-dimensional protagonist William Munny in the revisionist western *Unforgiven* (1992), or John Wayne's gunfighter J.B. Books in the final film he made, *The Shootist* (1976), who is (like Wayne in real life) dying of cancer, and who we see committed to making one last stand against three enemies of Carson City, French is correct that 'All westerners have something inside that has to do with death, and it is not just because they live and die by the gun' (French 1997: 47). Rather, it is 'because the westerner cares about death, his own death. It is extremely important to him. It focuses and frames his world view and the ethics to which he is committed. Death, in no small measure, is what his life is all about' (French 1997: 47). But, crucially, the western hero does not characteristically tend to hold out hope for an afterlife – indeed, he[11] categorically rejects all hope of salvation. Death is understood, rather, as 'the utterly inevitable annihilation of a life' where there is no promise or hope of a post-mortem existence – 'Death brings it all to a close' (French 1997: 49). In *The Shootist*, indeed, Books tells Mrs Rogers (Lauren Bacall), who runs the lodging house where he has come to spend his final days, that he will not accept her invitation to accompany her to church because his church has always been the wilderness (see French 1997: 136). In French's words, 'The wilderness is the one thing with which the westerner seeks identity' (French 1997: 136). A perfect illustration of this process can be found with regard to the opening shot of Sergio Leone's spaghetti western *The Good, the Bad and the Ugly* (1966), which consists of an empty and desolate environment that could be said to epitomise

Leone's vision of the West as the landscape of death. Yet hardly is that vision established in the eye of the spectator before it is interrupted by a face that swings up into the frame. This face offers an obvious human parallel to the background from which it appears to emerge. The eyes are cold, and the contours of the face rough and jagged like the Spanish terrain in which Leone shot the scene.

(McGee 2007: 179)

What matters in westerns is how the deceased lived rather than 'that he has a soul or spirit that is precious in itself and worthy of divine or human consideration' (French 1997: 53). Indeed, the only component that lives on after the person has died is 'the memories the living have with the deceased' – memories which are, moreover, framed in 'purely nonspiritual terms, in terms of the actions and the attitudes of the deceased while alive' (French 1997: 57). Whereas, then, in Christian terms death is the gateway towards eternal life, in the western it is construed as annihilation. *Unforgiven* encapsulates the genre's approach to death well when retired gunslinger and bounty hunter Will Munny (Clint Eastwood) tells his protégé, the Schofield Kid (Jaimz Woolvett), 'It's a hell of a thing to kill a man. You take away everything he's got … and everything he's ever going to have'. There are, of course, other perspectives afoot, as when Patrick McGee wrote in 2007 that violence in the western is justified 'through an appeal to transcendence', and that any forgiveness on display in such films 'is the gift of transcendent authority' (McGee 2007: 199). But, despite talking of transcendence, there is no suggestion from McGee that there are any post-death dynamics at work. Rather, any retribution or justice that is administered has a strongly this-worldly dimension. Although McGee refers to death as being a good thing 'because it is the passage to another world' (McGee 2007: 200), and notwithstanding Peter Krapp's point that 'the deadline of the last judgement whose instrument Clint Eastwood's protagonist once again plays is that very due date when all deferrals cease and all debts come true' (in McGee 2007: 199), all the dynamics are nevertheless played out *in this world* of space and time. The instruments, moreover, of this eschatological process are not divine or supernatural. They belong, simply, to 'those capable of the violence retribution requires' (McGee 2007: 199) here on earth, usually involving guns and bullets. This is quite fervently (and flamboyantly) encapsulated by the shoot-out at the end of *Unforgiven* in which Eastwood's Munny shoots dead a number of unarmed men as vengeance for the brutal murder of his partner, Ned Logan (Morgan Freeman). Again, it is not obvious that a theological and a cinematic eschatology amount to the exact same thing.

There are other reasons why a cinematic eschatology cannot easily be formulated. In horror movies, for example, one of the most popular motifs is that of the Antichrist, with such pictures as *The Omen* (Richard Donner, 1976), *The Seventh Sign* (Carl Schultz, 1988), *End of Days* (Peter Hyams, 1999) and *Lost Souls* (Janusz Kaminski, 2000) featuring race-against-time scenarios in which the likes of Gregory Peck and Arnold Schwarzenegger go to great lengths to prevent Satan from inhabiting the body of an otherwise innocent child. Such films often receive a critical mauling. Indeed, Neil Smith wrote a review for the BBC of *Lost Souls* upon its release in Britain in 2001 in which he argued that 'The Devil may have all the best tunes, but he's not so lucky when it comes to scripts', and that 'Lucifer has been poorly served by Hollywood's current penchant for Satanic shenanigans' (Smith 2001: <www.bbc.co. uk/films/2001/01/10/lost_souls_2001_review.shtml>). Yet, they undoubtedly have a strong cultural resonance. On 6 June 2006 I received a telephone call from a local radio station in Kent asking me to give an interview about the theological significance of the date – 6/6/6 – in the light of the release that day of John Moore's somewhat lacklustre re-make of *The Omen* (2006), starring Julia Stiles and Mia Farrow. Among students of theology and the Bible, also, such films have a certain appeal, as shown by Conrad Ostwalt's recent claim that when he was teaching a class on the New Testament twenty years ago it soon became apparent that more students had seen *The Seventh Sign* than had read the Book of Revelation, and that 'much of what the students knew about the Christian Apocalypse had been informed more by *The Seventh Sign* than their reading of the Bible' (Ostwalt 2008: 35). As a result, Ostwalt continues, 'We had to do some serious unpacking before we could discuss the book in class, but I believe in some ways the students continued to see the apocalyptic text in terms of the movie' (Ostwalt 2008: 35). All this is very elucidating since there is no figure called the Antichrist in the Book of Revelation. Rather, as such passages from the New Testament as 1 John 2:22 ('Who is the liar but he who denies that Jesus is the Christ? This is the antichrist') and 2 John 1:7 ('For many deceivers have gone out into the world, men who will not acknowledge the coming of Jesus Christ in the flesh; such a one is the deceiver and the antichrist') indicate, the Antichrist denotes someone who denies that Jesus is the Messiah. In other words, the term refers to those who subscribe to a false or defective doctrine concerning the Person of Christ. In *The Seventh Sign*, in marked contrast – an apocalyptic thriller that ostensibly draws on Revelation and ancient Jewish mythology – Demi Moore's character is due to give birth to a child without a soul, thereby initiating the events of the end-time. As Mary Ann Beavis puts it, 'The idea that the birth of a soulless child will be the end of the world is ... not a biblical doctrine, but an obscure bit of Jewish folklore, which teaches that when the number of the pre-existent souls of the righteous (the *guf*) is exhausted, the messiah will appear' (Beavis 2003: 12). Similarly, in *Lost Souls*, at the start of the film a prophecy appears on screen from Deuteronomy 17 about a man of incest becoming Satan and bringing about the end of the world. In Beavis' words, however, 'the quotation bears no resemblance to anything in the fifth book of the Pentateuch, or to any other part of the canon' (Beavis 2003: 13).

The difficulties in seeing films as mere purveyors of biblical or theological themes and teachings, or as somehow 'bearing witness' to what is contained in ancient manuscripts, particularly comes to the fore in the case of *Stigmata* (Rupert Wainwright, 1999), a horror film made by an atheist about a Pittsburgh hairdresser who is afflicted by the five stigmata wounds of Christ. Upon its release at the beginning of the millennium, the film provoked much controversy due to its account of the 'missing' fifth Gospel – the Gospel of Thomas – which, the film indicates, has been suppressed by the Catholic Church over the last two thousand years because of the threat that it poses to the Church as a result of its anti-institutional teachings. Moreover, the film suggests, there are actually 'dozens of ancient Gospels in addition to the four canonical ones, and that the Roman Catholic Church has systematically suppressed them because of their revolutionary implications for Christianity' (Beavis 2003: 21). If we take the film at face value, we would form the impression that the 'truth' about Jesus can be found not in the Gospels of Matthew, Mark, Luke and John but in the non-canonical, apocryphal writings. Of course, the Gospel of Thomas does exist, and it may even contain some genuine words of Jesus, but it is not exactly a widespread view among biblical scholars that Thomas is the most authentic text, nor has the Vatican been hiding it away. The film concludes with a title card explaining that the Gospel was denounced by the Vatican in 1945 as a 'heresy', prompting Roger Ebert to write in his review – which condemns the film as a 'storehouse of absurd theology' – that 'the filmmakers have a shaky understanding of the difference between a heresy and a fake' (Ebert 1999: <http://rogerebert.suntimes.com/apps/pbcs.dll/article?AID=/19990101/REVIEWS/901010302/1023>). Douglas Cowan is thus correct when he writes that filmmakers 'can use fabricated scripture as a plot device' because they are able to 'count on the gravitas these references lend without worrying unduly that too many people will point out the obvious fakery', since the majority of audience members will be insufficiently conversant in biblical criticism 'to know where the line between fiction and reality is drawn' (Cowan 2009: 414). Beavis similarly argues that despite being, as a biblical scholar, 'delighted by the postmodern playfulness of these invented scriptures', she finds that 'the imaginary apocrypha' of so many horror films 'evidence a horrifying lack of knowledge of the basic contents of the Bible on the part of their intended audiences, and/or their willing suspension of disbelief when it comes to the Bible and horror' (Beavis 2003: 29).

Such problems also arise with particular regard to horror films which specifically deal with questions of death and the afterlife. In *The Others* (Alejandro Amenábar, 2001), Nicole Kidman plays a Catholic mistress in a secluded Victorian country house at the end of the Second World War in which she quarrels with her children over Bible stories and in which the accuracy of the biblical account of the afterlife is challenged. Despite being taught about the three words for hell that appear in the Bible (Sheol, Gehenna and Hades, about which more will be said in Chapters 5 and 6), it transpires at the end of the film that all of the characters are actually dead, and that the ghosts that we are led to believe are haunting the 50-bedroom mansion are living human beings. Not only does the film deal with the themes of 'guilt and fear of judgment and the afterlife' (Bradshaw 2001: <www.guardian.co.uk/film/2001/nov/02/nicolekidman>), but, moreover, the suggestion is that its teachings are actually wrong – the 'biblical hells do not exist; nor does the Christian heaven' (Beavis 2003: 23). Although *Ghost* (Jerry Zucker, 1990) is not a horror film as such, there is a clear implication in this picture that hell is a very real place – it is, after all, where those who commit evil acts, like the homicidal Carl Bruner (Tony Goldwyn) are quite literally dragged for all eternity by a pack of mauling demons. The film may suggest that divine justice lies at the kernel of the universe, but theologically a number of problems arise, here. Notwithstanding the fact that the film's protagonist, Sam Wheat (Patrick Swayze), seems to be in some sort of limbo for a time, which must also be factored in to the theological equation, Aldwinckle made the instructive point back in 1972 that 'whether any men die so corrupted and deformed by evil that even at the end of this life, the possibility of change is non-existent, is something which we simply do not *know*' (Aldwinckle 1972: 139). Even if it is the case that the dead go screaming off to hell, as in many supernatural-themed films, Aldwinckle is here counselling that, when it comes to matters of detail, a better position is one of agnosticism. Irrespective of whether or not, as he says, evil persists, 'we cannot anticipate God's final judgement by drawing up a named list of those who would be in this category'. Quite simply, 'we cannot "know" this in any detail or with certainty' (Aldwinckle 1972: 139). Visually impressive, and perhaps, even, for some viewers morally edifying, though it may be to see such a clear-cut dualism between good and evil as happens in horror movies, in a theological sense such scenarios are often quite unsophisticated and hollow, thus making them quite unsuitable dialogue-partners with mainstream liberal theology.

To put it starkly, films do not always tend to allow the same degree of subtlety and nuance that theological reflection is able to engender. Aside from the entertainment value of seeing film characters bound for heaven or hell, for many theistic traditions it is the case that, rather than a destiny that awaits them at the point of death as in a film such as *Ghost*, immortality is, rather, something that is bestowed upon individuals at the Last Day and as, moreover, a gracious act of God.[12] As Mark Fox puts it, 'The belief of many within such traditions is that life after death proceeds by way of *resurrection*: the raising to life by God of an embodied – albeit transformed and glorified – self prior to judgement' (Fox 2003: 238). In Augustinian terms, there is a clear and ontological relationship between sin and mortality, whereby, building on St Paul's talk in Romans 6:23 that 'the wages of sin is death', it is believed that human beings have been born into sin and so warrant eternal torment, and can only be saved from this fate by 'faith in the redeeming blood of Christ, shed to avert the divine condemnation' (Hick 1976: 208). This is not simply down to individual autonomy. Without denying that there are some areas of modern Christian theology in which such a position is defended (for Methodists, Pentecostalists and Quakers after the Protestant Reformation what was believed to matter was the character of each individual human individual in the redemptive journey), in traditional terms it is believed that redemption lies exclusively within the jurisdiction of God (see Deacy 2001: 72). The situation is even more complex in terms of (the later) Augustine's teaching on predestination, in which it is believed that 'God has arbitrarily chosen some to be saved' (Lorimer 1984: 77). There is a certain paradox afoot, here, in that if it is believed that there are only a certain number of, as it were, free berths in heaven (the total amount having been settled upon before the beginning of the human race) then it is not possible even to affirm that by the grace of God we may escape from the impending judgement (see Hick 1976: 207).

None of these considerations tend to arise in afterlife-themed movies, where immortality might almost be construed as some kind of autonomous possession. A good illustration of this is in *American Beauty*, where, as we have already observed, Lester Burnham concludes his post-mortem voice-over narration with the words: 'You have no idea what I'm talking about, I'm sure. But don't worry … You will someday'. There is no talk, here, of only the elect being predestined to some form of paradisiacal or heavenly condition. Rather, the film seems to be saying, we may have to wait, but we too 'will someday' see things from the enlightened vantage point that, at present, Lester alone occupies and which is, for the time being at any rate, hidden, disguised and camouflaged from us in some Gnostic-type scenario. Is this really compatible with the Christian, Jewish and Islamic belief that there will be a judgement on the Last Day whereupon the whole of humankind will be separated into two groups? We learn from Revelation 21:8 that the category of the damned – which consists of cowards, liars, the faithless, the unclean, those who have murdered, fornicated, practised sorcery or worshipped false idols – will receive God's curse and 'their lot shall be in the lake that burns with fire and sulphur'. Together with the devil and his angels, the damned are to be 'tormented day and night for ever' (Badham & Badham 1984: 59) – an account, which, as Badham points out, 'was taken for granted by most of the Christian tradition for 1900 years' (Badham & Badham 1984: 59). In films, in marked contrast, we are used to seeing characters being translated instantly either to a life of endless bliss or everlasting torment, as the respective trajectories in *Ghost* of Sam and Carl may be seen to typify.

Methodological questions concerning the use of theology

In line with the revised correlational method which I am utilising, however, it is not sufficient to state that films necessarily fall short when compared and contrasted to the seemingly more sophisticated and erudite discipline of theology. Nor is it especially fair to try to equate an intellectual and scholarly discipline, practised in university and ecclesiastical institutions, with what is primarily an entertainment medium. The one prides itself on intellectual rigour, the other has a penchant for delineating a manu-factured, illusory and escapist worldview, but this does not make the former superior to the latter. All too often, however, this kind of tendency has been allowed to hold sway, as when David Jasper contended in his contribution to Marsh and Ortiz's *Explorations in Theology and Film* in 1997 that film is only effective insofar as 'it seems to offer the viewer the power to understand without the need seriously to think or change' (Jasper 1997: 243) and is simply 'there to help us through the tedium of inactivity' in what, at root, amounts to 'an art of illusion' (Jasper 1997: 235). In contrast, Jasper sees theology as a much more creative and 'two-edged' entity which 'emerges from more problematic and disturbing material than Hollywood dare show', and which offers 'the viewer a commodity which can be consumed without fear of significant change or disturbance' (Jasper 1997: 244). But, even if we agree with Jasper that, in view of its intellectual nature, theology is 'ironic, difficult and ambig-uous' (Jasper 1997: 244) in a way that film, as an industry, could never be, revolving as it does around 'money and profit' in which celebrities – who 'all too often fall from their dizzy heights as dramatically as they climb to fame' – are 'paid enormous sums of money' (Jasper 1997: 235), it nonetheless remains the case that, when it comes to questions of death and eschatology, theology does not exactly comprise a settled, consistent or coherent area of discourse. As Chapter 4 will show, for example, there are quite wide differences of emphasis between present and future forms of eschatology, to the point that the same terminology is often expected to accommodate both the quest for an afterlife and the search for transcendence within present existence in this life on earth.

Such inconsistency can even be found, moreover, within the work of the same individual. In the case of St Paul, in Romans 8:18 we learn that 'the sufferings of this present time are not worth comparing with the glory that is to be revealed to us', and that, according to Romans 8:22, 'the whole creation has been groaning in travail together until now'. The implication, here, is that the future is to be seen in apocalyptic terms as the birth of a new age. However, in Paul's letter to the Galatians, the suggestion seems to be that the end has *already* taken place, for there Paul writes about freedom from the law and how Christ 'gave himself for our sins to deliver us from the present evil age' (Gal. 1:4). He similarly identifies eschatology as a present phenomenon in 1 Corinthians 1:18, where we learn that 'the word of the cross is folly to those who are perishing, but to us who are being saved it is the power of God'. In the case of St Augustine, we have even greater forms of inconsistency. Despite, in his earlier days, preaching a theocentric, God-centred heaven, in his later writings the emphasis was much more on a strong social dimension, including the enjoyment of physical beauty (see Stanford 2002: 17), to the point that in 'later life, Augustine looked forward to lunching in heaven with his old friends' (Stanford 2002: 102).[13] Indeed, whereas he had once been dismissive of the body, as when in *The City of God* Augustine explicitly rules out the re-creation in heaven of household bonds and family ties, as this was to be a world in which the spirit was dominant – 'How wonderful will the body's condition be, when it will be in every way subject to the spirit, by which it will be made so fully alive as to need no other nourishment' (Augustine 1998: 1165–66)[14] – he later came to believe that heaven would be replete with risen bodies, albeit with all of their defects taken away (see Stanford 2002: 101). In Chilton's words, 'Enfleshed humanity was the only genuine humanity, and God in Christ was engaged to raise those who were of the city of God' (Chilton 2000: 94).[15]

Similar ambiguity arises in the case of Augustine's understanding of the Last Judgement, where there would appear to be both an individual resurrection at the point of bodily death, which Augustine construed as a spiritual resurrection consisting of the rising to faith of those souls who believe in Jesus, and a universal judgement at the end of time, which he thought would be a literal bodily event (see Hick 1976: 197).[16] Yet, the idea of there being two judgements – an individual one at death followed by a universal judgement at the end of history – is a 'somewhat uncomfortable combination, since there would seem to be no room for these two judgements to give different verdicts for the same individual' (Penelhum 2000: 40). Added to this is the consideration that, for Aquinas, although the individual judgement necessarily has priority, the total effects of all our evil actions will not be known until the end of time (see McGinn 1999: 389) – which would thus allow for the possibility that, when viewed from the vantage-point of the End, the individual judgement could be reversed. The matter is not helped by turning to Scripture for advice or clarity. For, in the Book of Daniel, we learn that judgement is to take place *after* the resurrection of the dead. This can be seen in Daniel 12:2 where we learn that 'many of those who sleep in the dust of the earth shall awake, some to everlasting life, and some to shame and everlasting contempt'. However, in Pharisaical Judaism more broadly, the implication is that the wicked, whose souls are condemned to eternal punishment or imprisonment, will be denied resurrection altogether (see Segal 2000: 18). This itself raises the moral and practical question of why a beneficent God would raise a person only to destroy them.

It is also not clear whether, assuming judgement takes place at all, the process is conducted solely and unilaterally by God or whether we have any input in the process. According to Greene and Krippner, in *The City of God* Augustine wrote in relation to the concept of the Book of Life that is identified in Revelation 13:8 that a certain divine power is present in the human soul which becomes activated during judgement (see Greene & Krippner 1990: 73).[17] What this effectively means is that the light of God's presence 'infuses souls of the deceased with a higher spiritual illumination that enables them to observe the whole life with a marvelous rapidity', and the 'knowledge absorbed from this vision then either excuses or accuses that soul's conscience' (Greene & Krippner 1990: 74). This is quite significant,[18] as it seems to suggest that, in line with the anthropocentric orientation of redemption that has come to the fore in post-Reformation thinking, whereby what particularly matters is the character of each individual human person in the redemptive journey (see Deacy 2001: 72), it is possible for one to play an active part in earning his or her own passage either to eternal damnation or eternal salvation. This line of thinking is similar to how in Zoroastrianism, in addition to the school of thought which holds that the individual is judged before crossing the Chinvat Bridge which lies across the abyss of hell and which leads at the far end to the realm of bliss, it is also the case that 'one really brings upon oneself the bliss of heaven or the misery of hell … as surely as if there were no formal judgment' (MacGregor 1992: 102). In more traditional Christian accounts, however, the emphasis is exclusively on Judgement as an objective, divine activity, whereupon Christ, in accordance with the Father's will, will return in glory to judge both the living and the dead (see 1 Corinthians 15:20–28). In addition, he will sit on a royal throne (see Romans 14:10; 2 Cor. 5:10) where he will judge all the nations, both the just and the unjust. Even so, we still do not know the time nor the place of the Judgement, and as to precisely how Christ will appear in judgement. Will it, for instance, be in the form of a glorified servant? Nor do we know the manner of Christ's decree of Judgement. Will it be spoken or communicated mentally (see McGinn 1999: 388)? We are also unclear as to precisely how God's mercy and justice, not to mention questions of free will versus predestination, are able to be reconciled.

In view of this ambiguity in the record, it is not surprising that, throughout history, many Christians have tended to simplify the process, so that, at the point of death, it is thought that one is immediately bound for either Heaven or Hell. On such a picture, there is a concomitant lack of either an intermediate state or, indeed, a corporeal body (see Penelhum 2000: 40). This, of course, is the picture presented in most afterlife-themed films, though, to be fair, not in all, as can be seen in the case of *The Heavenly Kid* (Cary Medoway, 1985). This picture has the distinction of introducing the concept of purgatory through the metaphor of a subway train that the protagonist must ride in order to move from 'midtown' to 'uptown', thus suggesting that films have the capacity to be more creative and even challenging than many theological accounts. It is not really appropriate, therefore, to criticise filmmakers for a lack of theological sophistication when it is often theologians and religious adherents themselves who have formulated and promoted quite crude and one-dimensional representations of eschatology. Even when the opposite is the case, and theologians are engaged in more nuanced and complex musings, it does not follow from this that theologians always have the upper hand – no matter how persuasively Jasper argues that movies are unable to portray the nuances of everyday life in the way that theology is so inclined and able. A case in point is the way that heaven has been conceptualised by different theologians (an area that will be examined in more depth in Chapter 5). For Paul Tillich, for instance, heaven was neither a place nor a state of being, and to paraphrase Jeffrey Burton Russell's reading of Tillich in this regard, 'we are not in a position to say *what* it is; we share in it, but how we do is unclear' (Russell 2006: 120). For Karl Barth, similarly, it is very difficult to pinpoint where he stands vis-à-vis the concept of heaven, with his talk of heaven being 'unitary but not formless, collective but not without individuation, total but not uniform or monotonous' (Barth 1961: 447), as well as 'invisible and therefore incomprehensible and inaccessible, outside the limits of human capacity' (Barth 1961: 424), quite unhelpfully opaque. As Russell thus puts it, 'The difficulty in a view of heaven as diffuse as Barth's was that without some definition, meaning leaks out onto the sand' (Russell 2006: 122).

Nor does it help when scholars contradict one another when writing about the same theological topic. In the case of Augustine, for example, Bruce Chilton thinks that Augustine subscribed to belief in the resurrection of the flesh (Chilton 2000: 94). In contrast, in their comprehensive account of historical perspectives on the afterlife through the ages, *Heaven: A History*, Colleen McDannell and Bernhard Lang indicate that, at least in his earlier days, Augustine 'gave clear preference to the angelic mode of existence' and 'took great care' to liberate 'the term "body" (*corpus*) from all its material connotations' (McDannell & Lang 1990: 58). After the resurrection, our bodies would thus 'lose their material quality' (McDannell & Lang 1990: 58). Quite simply, in McDannell and Lang's words, 'There can be no fleshly dimension to the next life. Everything must be spiritual' (McDannell & Lang 1990: 58). Further, whereas McDannell and Lang write that 'Augustine's spiritual heaven' (McDannell & Lang 1990: 59) was the complete opposite of the fleshly teachings of the second-century apologist Irenaeus, Chilton takes the line that Augustine revived the tradition of Irenaeus concerning God's embrace of his own creation (see Chilton 2000: 94), and that, in relation to St Paul's teachings in 1 Corinthians 15 concerning the necessity of a 'spiritual body', Augustine was categorical that flesh was nevertheless involved. There is certainly a foundation for this. In his *City of God*, Augustine wrote that although the flesh will be 'subject to the spirit' it 'will still be flesh and not spirit' (Augustine 1998: 1152).[19] But, it is difficult to find any real consistency on the matter.[20] The problem is exacerbated when we take into account the work of Jean Delumeau, whose *History of Paradise: The Garden of Eden in Myth and Tradition* was published in English in 2000. There, Delumeau acknowledges that, for Augustine, the earthly paradise should be understood 'sometimes corporeally and at other times spiritually' (Delumeau 2000: 18). But when Delumeau attests that he finally leaned towards allegorism, thinking that we can see in the account of creation all the figurative meanings we desire, this does not fit at all with the more materialist trajectory outlined by Chilton. Imperfect though many cinematic renderings of the afterlife may be, one charge that cannot be levelled against them is that, *per se*, they 'fall short' when compared to the ostensibly more coherent, reasoned and well-structured deliberations of theologians.

Even outside theistic traditions, we find similarly inconsistent perspectives in play concerning afterlife teachings. In Yoga schools of Buddhism, the aim is isolation of the newly liberated soul from any contact with matter. A similar belief is held in Jainism where it is taught that, since the soul's embodiment in matter in this life is attributable to karma, the aim is release from both karma and matter 'into *Nirvana*, at the top of the universe, where there are many blessed and omniscient souls which are called "isolated"' (Parrinder 1973: 96). This is very different from Vedantic Hinduism, however, where the souls do not exist in isolation but are, rather, 'joined to or identical with the Cosmic Spirit, Brahman or a personalized Godhead' (Parrinder 1973: 96) in what amounts to 'a merging of the self into the universal but conscious Self, which is Being-Consciousness-Bliss' (Parrinder 1973: 96). In terms of the time scale of the process, there are similar differences of emphasis to that found in Christian teachings concerning the individual and universal judgements. In the Pali tradition, it is believed that no time elapses between the point of death and the new embodiment. Quite simply, death and rebirth follow one another without any break in continuity, though for some in this tradition nothing of the previous life continues into the next one (see Neumaier-Dargyay 2000: 91). In Mahayana Buddhism, in marked contrast, there is both an intermediate state and a belief that the being who lives there is tantamount to a clone of the deceased, and can even relive some of the experiences of that individual (see Neumaier-Dargyay 2000: 93). There is even diversity among Buddhists living in the same community, as observed by Charles Hallisey, who writes that

> it is common throughout the Buddhist world to assume that beings experience more than one life and are reborn again and again, but some Buddhists, especially in the twentieth century, have seen little reason to affirm this assumption, even as they recognize that some of their Buddhist neighbors accept it as truth.
>
> *(Hallisey 2000: 4)*

Indeed, for some Pure Land, or Shin, Buddhists, there is no belief in the transmigration of souls – it is maintained, instead, that when this life comes to an end so does the cycle of birth and death (see Hallisey 2000: 4).

In the light of such ambivalence, it is my aim in the pages that follow to provide what has, to date, been conspicuously absent from the vast corpus of literature that has been produced in theology over the years: that is, a critical and dialogical conversation between theological and cinematic representations of the afterlife. While there have been publications in this area before, there has been insufficient attention accorded to the degree to which both partners in the two-way exchange have the potential to be challenged or changed by the other. To this end, it is my aim in the rest of this book to juxtapose eschatological perspectives from within Christian theology with critical readings of a number of filmic texts that address questions of death and the afterlife.

2

RESURRECTION OR IMMORTALITY?

The body and the soul in theology and film

As will particularly come to the fore in Chapter 4, when correlations will be adduced between debates in realised eschatology and cinematic representations of Heaven, Hell and Purgatory as metaphors of present human experience, it is not only films that explicitly delineate an afterlife that comprise a potentially rich site of eschatological activity. Supernaturally-tinged though a movie such as *Ghost* (Jerry Zucker, 1990) may be, in view of the way it bears witness to a traditional dualistic framework wherein the just ascend to a tunnel of light that reaches into the sky while the unjust are literally dragged off to hell by packs of savage and demonic beasts, there is no attempt to depict or document what life in heaven (or in hell) is actually like. Only at the film's denouement is Sam Wheat (Patrick Swayze) ready to embark on the next (whether it is final the film gives us no clues) stage of the post-mortem journey. Hitherto, the film's focus has been on the protagonist's attempt to wreak vengeance on those who were responsible for his premature death while at the same time endeavouring to save his earth-bound fiancée, Molly (Demi Moore), from undergoing a similar fate. There is an inescapably reductionistic dimension at work, here, in which the supernatural is more of a means to an end – resolving problems that have been engendered on earth – than the 'end' in itself. At first sight, indeed, it seems something of a cop-out when films ostensibly about the afterlife prove to be preoccupied with the continuation of this-worldly relationships and in which human, rather than divine, agency is paramount. While this may appear theologically problematic, it is my aim in this chapter to explore how eschatological language, even when couched in its most traditional forms of expression, is not always so inflexible or non-malleable that it cannot relate, with equal cogency, to both pre-mortem and post-mortem existence. Whether explicitly or implicitly, it is clear that even those films which deal with questions of personal identity formation on earth are eschatologically very important. Cases in point are *Big* (Penny Marshall, 1988), *Vice Versa* (Brian Gilbert, 1988) and *Face/Off* (John Woo, 1997), in which two individuals (an adult and a young boy in the case of the first two examples) find, whether through accident or design, that their minds have transferred into the other's body. For, in such instances of bodily transfer, to which we could add the more anarchic example supplied by Steve Martin in the Carl Reiner-directed *All of Me* (1984) in which two persons actually come to share the same body simultaneously, it is hard not to see traces of exactly the same questions that have beset theologians and philosophers over the centuries concerning the requirements and logistics of belief in the resurrection of the flesh or the immortality of the soul. After all, as Paul Badham puts it, 'if we concede that in imagination, or dream, I can identify my selfhood with another name, body, and life-style' then it is not 'meaningless to envisage the possibility that I could also identify my selfhood with another and different embodiment after death' (Badham & Badham 1984: 9). Badham continues that 'I could still be "I" though clothed with a new and different body, provided only that this new body was suitable as a vehicle for the expression of my distinctive thoughts, feelings and self-awareness' (Badham & Badham 1984: 9).

Such thinking has huge implications for belief in life after death. For, if the identity of a person is not, by necessity, connected with the persistence of that person's bodily frame over time, then the logical barriers towards seeing a person as surviving the death of his or her body are thereby removed. When the likes of *All of Me* or *The Man With Two Brains* (Carl Reiner, 1983) thus give rise to the possibility that it is not bodily identity but memory and personal identity that endures, then this inevitably impacts upon theological and philosophical debates around how, in Penelhum's words, 'it might be that a disembodied person might be said to be the same as some pre-mortem person because he might remember events and actions in his previous existence' (Penelhum 1970: 14–15). Penelhum, writing in 1970, did not draw any analogies from filmic representations of mind–body transfer. But when he illustrated his argument with the example of two people with differently shaped bodies – the one fat and short, the other tall and thin – having switched bodies because the characteristics of the one can be found in the other, it is possible to draw an analogy with the scene in *Prelude to a Kiss* (Norman René, 1992) when Alec Baldwin's character, Peter Hoskins, finds that the soul of the young woman, Rita Boyle (Meg Ryan), he has married has transferred into the body of an old, terminally ill widower, played by Sydney Walker. Such films, it must be admitted, often fail to take their inventive and resourceful premise to a particularly challenging or erudite conclusion. In his *Time Out* review, Geoff Andrew dismissed *Prelude to a Kiss* as 'maudlin hokum' (Andrew 2001: 920), while *Vice Versa*'s role-reversal scenario, in which a workaholic father swaps places with his eleven-year-old son, was mauled by Andrew in the same publication on the grounds that 'both script and direction are instilled with a numbing predictability' (Andrew 2001: 1247). Such difficulties notwithstanding, these pictures tie in well with Penelhum's reference to those 'imaginary situations in which we would be correct in saying that the identity of some particular person had transcended that of some particular body' (Penelhum 1970: 16–17). Badham similarly writes that 'few seem to find any difficulty at all in following the plots of fairy tales and of science fiction stories which involve bodily transfer' and that if 'the meaning of self were identical with the meaning of body, this would be impossible and such stories would simply be unintelligible' (Badham & Badham 1984: 9). The fact that there is no shortage of movies which address, albeit clumsily and unconvincingly, the theme of bodily transfer does suggest that when it comes to such issues as whether we prefer resurrection of the body or the immortality of the soul, there is a rich repository of creative material from which theologians and philosophers can draw.[1]

Resurrection of the flesh

Before exploring in detail how filmmakers have wrestled with the different claims of 'immortality' versus 'resurrection', it is important at this juncture to scrutinise some of the competing ways in which such language has traditionally been understood in the Christian tradition. From the outset, it is apparent that these two terms were used interchangeably in Biblical writings without there being any indication on the part of the authors of an incompatibility between them. Indeed, as Hick puts it, for the early Christians 'a material and earthly picture of the resurrection existed in tension with a more spiritual and heavenly picture' (Hick 1976: 187). We see traces of this in 1 Corinthians 15 where St Paul could not, on the one hand, be more emphatic about the importance of belief in resurrection. This is betokened by his claim that 'if Christ has not been raised, then our preaching is in vain and your faith is in vain' (1 Cor. 15:14) and that 'in fact Christ has been raised from the dead, the first fruits of those who have fallen asleep' (1 Cor. 15:20). Paul's premise, here, is that since for there to be existence there needs to be a body then, by implication, if we are to survive death there must be a resurrection body. On the other hand, even while arguing for resurrection, Paul arguably comes close in this passage 'to speaking of the immortality of the soul or spirit' (Marsh 2007 [a]: 148). Indeed, as to the actual form that such a body takes, Marsh is right to say that Paul 'flounders' (Marsh 2007 [a]: 148) in that his talk of a 'spiritual body' in 1 Corinthians 15:44 ('It is sown a physical body, it is raised a spiritual body. If there is a physical body, there is also a spiritual body') amounts to the not entirely seamless attempt to hold together both concepts at once. To be fair, the modern day distinction between resurrection and immortality was unfamiliar to the biblical authors, many of whom, at least as far as the Old Testament is concerned, subscribed to more this-worldly forms of expression – to the point, in fact, that the hope of life after death 'took much longer to develop than in surrounding cultures' (Fiddes 2000: 67–68). As Fiddes points out, to receive God's blessing tended to manifest itself in 'physical forms such as good health, prosperity, freedom from enemies and a large family, as well as the spiritual gift of fellowship with God in the Temple' (Fiddes 2000: 68). If there is a promise of immortality in the Old Testament it is 'basically implicit' with 'only occasional explicit citations' (Anderson 1986: 59). An example of such and exception is Daniel 12:2 where we learn that 'many of those who sleep in the dust of the earth shall awake, some to everlasting life, and some to shame and everlasting contempt'.

It is within this context that Anderson is able to write that in the Bible there is no concept of an immortal soul. This is because although the word 'immortal' appears three times, as in 1 Corinthians 15:53, the immortality is attributed not to the soul but to the risen Christ and the embodied person in the new age to come (Anderson 1986: 57). MacGregor similarly attests that *resurrection* is nowhere narrated in the New Testament in that what is proclaimed is not a particular form of rising from the dead but, rather, the conquest of death itself, that is, to paraphrase Paul in 1 Corinthians 15:54–57, the idea that death has 'lost its sting' (MacGregor 1992: 156). Quite simply, as MacGregor observes, 'We look in vain in the New Testament for any clear enunciation of what precisely we are to understand by resurrection' (MacGregor 1982: 16), a situation that is not helped by the fact that St Paul even discourages speculations of this sort on the grounds that they are corrosive of true faith. We see this from 2 Timothy 2:18 where Paul writes that those who deviate 'from the truth by holding that the resurrection is past already' are 'upsetting the faith of some'. What MacGregor seems to be reading into this passage is that, for Paul, any unorthodox teaching should be strictly dismissed rather than interrogated and dissected. Lorimer goes even further and suggests that, not only are the New Testament texts hard to unravel, but they 'may well have been tampered with in order to favor a literal or spiritual interpretation' (Lorimer 1990: 104). He has in mind the fact that, on the one hand, we read in the Gospel of John that Thomas was actually able to touch the body of Jesus (John 20:27), while, on the other, in the garden, he instructs Mary not to touch him (John 20:17), he is not instantly recognised by his disciples in Luke's Gospel ('While they were talking and discussing together, Jesus himself drew near and went with them. But their eyes were kept from recognising him' [Luke 24:15–16]), and he seems to be capable of materialisation and dematerialisation ('And their eyes were opened and they recognised him; and he vanished out of their sight' [Luke 24:31]).[2]

It may well have been the case that for biblical authors the language of resurrection and immortality was used interchangeably, but this is of limited help in the present day when we are accustomed to viewing both of these terms in contrasting and divergent ways. It is true that, if one holds that there is an interval in time between death and resurrection, then it is possible to hold together both resurrection and immortality language, such as by positing an interim period during which the soul may survive in anticipation of a future, corporeal resurrection (see Penelhum 1970: 4). But, the concepts also carry connotations which cannot be so easily conjoined. In the case of resurrection, it is important to note that, as far as the New Testament writers and early Church Fathers were concerned, the concept involved the re-collection of our physical particles. We can trace this line of thinking back to the earliest apocalyptic literature we have to hand, from the second century BCE, when the messianic age was believed to comprise an unending kingdom of God on earth in which the righteous who had died were presently deemed merely to be 'asleep', and who could look forward to being raised and revivified *in the flesh* (see Hick 1976: 182). We see the same sort of ideas in the writings of Tertullian from the turn of the third century, though here the resurrection body was believed to lie in a future, heavenly environment. For Tertullian, we will, at the resurrection, 'have a body identical to the present one', the grounds for this being that if 'the resurrected body is not our own earthly body, there is no point in the resurrection at all' (in Russell

1997: 68). Tertullian thought that our bodies, no matter how mutilated, will recover their perfect integrity in the resurrection and that we 'will lose nothing essential in our corporeal identity' (in Russell 1997: 68), retaining such characteristics as gender. If there was no resurrection of the physical body then, argued Tertullian, we could not be judged at the Last Day as a whole, and the damned would not be able to experience the fires of hell in their most palpable form (see Lorimer 1984: 76).

For Augustine, similarly, 'Nothing will perish at the resurrection ... , for every part of the body's substance will be restored to it, but altered in a way which is in keeping with the various parts of the body' (Augustine 1998: 1148).[3] Accordingly, for Augustine, 'those martyrs who have had limbs hacked off and taken away will not lack those limbs at the resurrection of the dead ... the limbs which were cut off will not be lost, but restored' (Augustine 1998: 1150).[4] Proceeding from the assurance given by Jesus that not a single hair on the heads of those who are granted eternal life shall perish,[5] Augustine came to the view that at the time of the resurrection of the flesh 'the body will have that size which it either attained in the prime of its life or would have attained had it achieved the pattern implanted in it' (Augustine 1998: 1151).[6] It was, without doubt, our earthly bodies which would be resurrected: 'Whatever has perished from the living body ... , or from the corpse after death, will be restored ... it will rise again' (Augustine 1998: 1152)[7] – the only difference being that the resurrected body, unlike its earthly counterpart, will be incorruptible. Even children or foetuses, who had died before being able to reach their full potential, would rise perfected at around the age of 30 (the template for this being Christ who died on the cross at this age while in his prime). As Anderson puts it, '[f]etuses will be mature, monsters made normal' and 'unsightly blemishes and deformities corrected' (Anderson 1986: 119). Likewise, in Russell's words, 'The resurrection bodies of the saved will be perfect and entire, with all their limbs and organs, and only what is ugly, deformed, or superfluous will disappear' (Russell 1997: 87).

It is questionable, however, as to whether any of this overly materialistic account of the resurrection, wherein our flesh will be re-constituted – albeit in a more glorious manner – holds sway in the modern world. For, in scientific terms, as Fiddes puts it, 'our knowledge about transfer of energy and the constant replacement of cells in our bodies through time makes the problems of re-assembly even more tortuous than the Fathers imagined' (Fiddes 2000: 80). Ironically, the extreme continuity ascribed to the resurrection body by Augustine, and later by Aquinas, does not entirely square with the New Testament record itself, where we learn from Paul's teaching in 1 Corinthians 15 concerning the term 'spiritual body' (1 Cor. 15:44) that Jesus' transformed body was as much discontinuous as continuous with its earthly counterpart. After all, 'what is sown is perishable' while 'what is raised is imperishable' (1 Cor. 15:42). In the modern world, where the constituent particles of our physical bodies can be re-configured and re-assembled for all manner of health or cosmetic reasons by the likes of plastic surgery (liposuction, face lifts, breast implants), pace-makers, artificial knee joints, prosthetic limbs, false teeth, blood transfusions or the fruits of stem cell research, it is hard to subscribe to a literal reading of the doctrine of the resurrection of the flesh. Badham sums up the situation thus:

Do limbs amputated years ago grow again during the process of healing? What about the thalidomide victim whose limbs never grew? What about the Siamese twin who died eighteen hours before his brother to whom he had been joined for all his life? Did he wait for his brother before being re-created? … Were the twins re-created in the joined-together state they were in when the first twin died, or were they re-created as the separate entities they were when the second died on the following day?

(Badham 1976: 76)

The problem is only exacerbated when we take into account current technologies involving the cloning of organic matter.[8] In the Arnold Schwarzenegger sci-fi movie *The 6th Day* (Roger Spottiswoode, 2000), birth–life–death is no longer the natural order of things. Rather, we are presented with a world in the ostensibly not-too-distant future in which 'if you're fed up with your girlfriend you can get a virtual one instead' (Wilkinson 2001: 1065) and in which medical laboratories are suffused with cloned human organs for transplants. When the protagonist, Adam Gibson (Arnold Schwarzenegger), is accidentally cloned and comes home from work one day to find another version of himself having sexual intercourse with his wife, all manner of ethical questions necessarily arise (even if the film itself addresses them in only a brusque fashion). The situation is made even more complicated by the revelation towards the film's denouement that the replica is actually the 'original' Adam and that the 'real' Adam is a clone, and that all the memories, thoughts and feelings of the last 40 or so years have been implanted following an illicit surgical procedure. If, as happens in the film, we can even postulate multiple clones being created of one person, does Tertullian's account of the fleshly resurrection lead us to suppose that they are each to be resurrected, or is it just the original that is to be raised? What happens, further, if each of the clones proceed to procreate and have children, and in turn grandchildren, of their 'own'? There is also the consideration that, in contrast to Tertullian, for whom we were made in the image of God, when it comes to questions of human cloning the flesh concerned is a human, engineered construction, manufactured in the image of 'man'.

Even if one considers the example of cloning a rather fanciful and hypothetical proposition, we still have the difficulty, when taking seriously belief in the literal resurrection of the flesh, over whether we would be the same person in the next life if our sexual nature did not play as equally fundamental and pervasive a role as it does in this one. Hick makes the point, for example, that if we are to remain the same person from this life to the next then we must continue to be sexual beings with an appropriate bodily structure to allow for reproduction, in which case 'presumably children are born into the next world' (Hick 1976: 419). Such a scenario is actually played out in what amounts to one of the more sophisticated and less predictable afterlife movies to have come out of North America, namely Canadian director Alan Rudolph's *Made in Heaven* (1987). In the words of Tom Milne, in his *Monthly Film Bulletin* review from November 1987, this is a picture which 'disappoints genre expectations, turning instead into an exploration of possibilities, of the thesis that love is the ultimate grail, eternally sought and eternally veiled by the vagaries of human endeavour' (Milne 1987: 336). In the film, we learn that heaven consists of an environment in which 'anything that can be imagined exists, and will eventually find its way to Earth, including future inventions and as yet unborn souls' (Milne 1987: 336). In quite a departure from the usual films of this genre, which, as in *Here Comes Mr Jordan* (Alexander Hall, 1941), are 'rather uncomfortably tinged with the fey archness which so often came over Hollywood when envisaging an afterlife' (Milne 2001: 501), here we find the protagonist, Mike (Timothy Hutton), a young, unemployed man from small town Pennsylvania who dies trying to save a family from a car accident, incredulous that people can actually make love in heaven. The woman he falls in love with, Annie (Kelly McGillis), was even born in heaven, as was her brother. In a reversal of Tertullian's understanding that the earthly body will be reconstituted in the next life, in Rudolph's film we learn that Annie, though herself 'unborn', will be reincarnated on earth, where, 30 years later, she will 'find' her soul-mate, who is himself originally of *earthly* descent. This fusion of earthly and celestial 'souls' falling for one another and eventually finding fulfilment on earth could not be more discordant from traditional Christian accounts where the goal is heavenly, rather than terrestrial, (re-)embodiment.

Towards the immortality of the soul

With such difficulties in mind, it is not surprising that, both in Christian theology and in many cinematic accounts of the afterlife, the emphasis has been on immortality rather than resurrection. Indeed, in Platonic terms, the soul has tended to be seen as the essence of the person, with the body seen merely as a vehicle for the soul in its manifold incarnations. Such thinking has permeated much of Christian thinking to the extent that, for Aquinas in the thirteenth century, even though everything other than God was deemed, in Aristotelian terms, to consist of 'form' and 'matter', the 'form' of the human being is comprised of the soul.[9] Since the soul cannot subsist on its own – it has to be embodied in some way, though it can exist temporarily without the body – a bridge to the doctrine of the resurrection of the body was thus developed. In seeing the soul as the information-bearing pattern of the body, it is not really surprising that most contemporary Christians have abandoned belief in a literal bodily resurrection in favour of seeing our identity from the life of this world to the life to come in terms of 'being clothed with a new and glorious body for a totally new mode of life in heaven', where an 'altogether more glorious and resplendent mode of being' (Badham 1995: 122) can be envisaged. On this reckoning, there is rather more to 'resurrection' than the idea of mere physical resuscitation. In Badham's words, resurrection should be seen to refer to 'the continuity of our self-hood through bodily death' (Badham & Badham 1984: 27). Going much further than Augustine who saw the resurrected body as a more perfect version of the exact same fleshly body we presently possess, this subtle shift towards the language of immortality allows for the possibility that the 'spiritual body', to paraphrase St Paul, that we will possess is nonetheless ontologically different from our present fleshly incarnation. Referring neither to 'the same bodies … we now inhabit' nor to any 'glorified and transformed versions of these bodies' (Badham 1976: 85), it would be more appropriate to envisage the afterlife as consisting of 'quite different bodies' in which 'the only bond of unity between our present and future bodies is that they will be "owned" successively by the same personality' (Badham 1976: 85). This way of thinking would certainly account for the Gospel accounts of Jesus' resurrection appearances to the disciples, which Aldwinckle categorises as 'veridical visions' (Aldwinckle 1972: 57).[10] Badham is thus correct when he observes that of Christian authors who 'have a positive doctrine concerning a future life the overwhelming consensus favours the view that our personalities will be clothed with new bodies in heaven', and that it is only those who still subscribe to an anachronistic, pre-scientific, biblical world view 'who still wish to affirm a real material link between our present and future bodies' (Badham 1976: 88).

There are, of course, detractors from this position. In contrast to Badham's talk of how the soul's immortality constitutes 'the link which provides for personal continuity' (Badham & Badham 1984: 27) between pre-mortem and post-mortem embodiment, Fiddes is less enthusiastic about the possibility that we could survive in a disembodied state. For him, the fact that the soul may be a distinct self with thoughts, feelings and actions which is not reducible to the body does not thereby establish that the self is potentially disembodied. As he sees it, 'Paul Badham's argument that the spiritual experience of God does not come to us through the sense and neural pathways is an attack on person–brain identity', but, Fiddes continues, 'it does not in itself establish (as [Badham] thinks) that this openness to God that we may well call "soul" can exist *without* the body' (Fiddes 2000: 90).[11] However, to my mind, Aldwinckle is spot on when he designates his preferred choice of language as 'immortality in an "embodied form"' (Aldwinckle 1972: 88). The clear implication here is that, as outlined by Gregory of Nyssa in the fourth century, resurrection does not entail the same body in the sense of a literal resuscitation or reconstitution of the same minuscule fragments of matter (which, in contrast to the stability and unbroken continuity of the *eidos* or form, changes continually). At the final resurrection, Gregory taught that the soul will imprint upon our resurrected body the same *eidos* that it previously possessed on earth. Whereas, in theological terms, we presently 'experience the material world and our own material bodies solely in a fallen state', such that 'it lies largely beyond the power of our imagination to conceive the characteristics that matter will possess in an unfallen world', there is scope, in terms of the Christian hope, for looking forward to 'the transparence and vivacity' and the 'lightness and sensitivity' with which 'our resurrection body, as once material and yet spiritual, will be endured in the age to come' (Ware 1995: 40). Similarly, for Origen in the third century, the body that is resurrected is continuous with the physical body in *principle* rather than in *substance*. In his words, in *On First Principles*:

> … although the bodies die and are corrupted and scattered, nevertheless by the word of God that same life principle which has all along been preserved in the essence of the body raises them up from the earth and restores and refashions them, just as the power which exists in a grain of wheat refashions

and restores the grain, after its corruption and death, into a body with stalk and ear.[12]

(Origen 1973: 141)

There is of course a major distinction between what Origen is talking about, here, and the way in which filmmakers have often conceptualised the afterlife. For Origen, and other Christian thinkers, any immortality that exists can only be understood in the context of the specific will of God in allowing an individual to rise from the dead. As he says in *On First Principles*, only those 'who shall be counted worthy of obtaining an inheritance in the kingdom of the heavens' (Origen 1973: 141)[13] can expect the body to be so refashioned in the future. There is, in short, no such thing as a natural immortality. Quite simply, the 'command of God' is required to refashion 'out of the earthly and natural body a spiritual body, which can dwell in the heavens' (Origen 1973: 141).[14] In marked contrast, in the absence of any theistic dimension the implicit suggestion in most afterlife-themed films is that immortality is an intrinsic quality of each human soul. In *Heaven Can Wait* (Warren Beatty & Buck Henry, 1978), for example, there is no suggestion that the central character, Joe Pendleton (Warren Beatty), an ageing footballer desperate for a chance to play in the Super Bowl, is destined to spend the afterlife in heaven as a result of anything remotely akin to that envisaged by Origen or any of the Christian Fathers. From what we can glean from the opening scenes of the film about Pendleton's personal and professional relationships, his outlook on life is, to all intents and purposes, secular in form. We have no reason to suppose that he subscribes to any particular theological or spiritual principles, dogma or creed. Even when Pendleton finds himself at a celestial way station, following a heavenly blunder in which we learn that he has been prematurely whisked off to the 'next world' several decades ahead of schedule, where he must wait until a new earthly body can be found for him so that he can return to earth and continue his footballing pursuits, there is not even a vague hint of any belief in God. Nor is Pendleton especially interested in that which lies beyond this mortal coil. Rather, his only motivation is to return to earth to complete his earthly goals and fulfilments. He could not be any less interested in what the life of the world to come may have in store, and he is even indulged to this end by the heavenly entourage around him whose sole raison d'être seems to be that of ensuring that he is compensated, following his return to earth, with a new and suitable bodily frame.

We see a similar dynamic at work in *What Dreams May Come* (Vincent Ward, 1998), in which Chris Nielson (Robin Williams) finds himself in heaven following his death and chooses to undertake a journey, along the lines of Orpheus in Greek mythology, to the depths of hell in order to rescue his damned, suicide-stricken soul mate, Annie (Annabella Sciorra). Yet, the film's reincarnationist denouement suggests that the ultimate goal in life is not the beatific vision but a thorough-going physical and corporeal life on earth where the two soul mates will meet again, albeit in a different bodily form. The continuation of this-worldly relationships is presented as intrinsically superior to an endless paradise in heaven. In this schema, heaven and hell are but means to a reincarnationist end, and where, once experienced, heaven is no doubt better than hell (from which Annie is eventually rescued) but grossly inferior to the pleasures of falling in love all over again as children. The divine is nowhere in view on this interpretation. The closest Ward's film comes to delineating the transcendent is when God is referred to by Nielson's spirit guide as being 'up there. Somewhere … shouting down that He loves us, wondering why we can't hear him'. Theologically fascinating though it is to see a film in which the content of the afterlife is given such dazzling and imaginative artistic treatment – the film deservedly won an Academy Award for Best Visual Effects – it is a pity that the film's handling of theological ideas is so jumbled and unfocused. As Peter Matthews wrote in his review of *What Dreams May Come* for *Sight and Sound* in January 1999, the film's theology amounts to 'So you can take it with you after all, and there's no pesky God around to horn in on your personalised nirvana', not to mention 'the interesting heresy that souls may choose to be reincarnated – as Chris and Annie do, just in time for one of the ickiest fade-outs in cinema history' (Matthews 1999: 61). There is nothing objective, or divine-oriented, about the afterlife in which Nielson finds himself situated. Instead, he dwells in a realm that is inherently subjective in nature, and in which human agency alone plays a role in shaping and structuring his post-mortem world. 'Heaven' though this may be, the environment he finds himself in exists in a state of flux where each soul creates his or her own subjective paradise. All boundaries between physical, exterior reality and inner, subjective reality are dissolved in this film, where the suggestion is clearly that heaven is merely a mental projection of whatever one wishes and imagines (see Deacy & Ortiz 2008: 190), and in which travel takes place on the basis not of an actual movement in space but simply the wish or desire to be at a certain place.

The immortality of the soul is, as we have seen, intrinsic to the way in which the afterlife is formulated for many thinkers throughout Christian history, from Gregory of Nyssa and Origen in the Patristic age to Aldwinckle and Badham in the twentieth century. But it is difficult to find many Christian theologians who would share the film's somewhat Gnostic vision that so distinct are our minds and bodies that thought is real but the physical is an illusion, and that what makes us human is that part of ourselves that is not in any way equivalent to the brain or organic flesh (see Deacy & Ortiz 2008: 190). How do we square any of this with how for both Old and New Testament writers what ultimately matters is not each person's individual immortality but 'the fact that the universal fact of death has no power at all in the face of the living God' (Anderson 1986: 44)? Indeed, as Anderson puts it, 'The central issue is not whether man has an essence that survives death (natural immortality), but whether the God in whom he believes has the power and moral integrity to "make good" with the life he himself has called into existence' (Anderson 1986: 45). There is a non-negotiable starting-point in Christian perspectives on life after death that, aside from the particulars over exactly how it is to be interpreted, Christ's death and resurrection is primary – the template, indeed, for all Christian hope concerning the afterlife. Outside of any belief in Christ's resurrection the only reasonable expectation is that of extinction. In Pauline terms, indeed, 'the wages of sin is death' (Romans 6:23), but for those who 'have been set free from sin' by the gracious gift of God 'the return you get is sanctification and its end, eternal life' (Romans 6:22). However it is understood, Christian teaching on eschatology is that humans are God's creatures and, without qualification, totally dependent on God as Creator. Since everything is thus subject to the will of the sovereign God, it is hard to see how Chris Nielson's reincarnationist odyssey can be seen as in any sense bearing witness to a Christian eschatology where the soul is anything but immortal by its own nature and where only those who 'truly adhere to Christ' will attain salvation 'in the resurrected state of the hereafter' (MacGregor 1992: 125).

Significantly, even in films where the resurrection of Christ is itself depicted, in the genre of biblical epics and Jesus films, there is often a similarly secular and subjective dimension at work which stands at variance with the more transcendental and devout perspective that lies at the heart of the Christian tradition. A case in point is Nicholas Ray's *King of Kings* (1961), which, as I have written elsewhere, is in any event interested more in the humanity, rather than divinity, of the person of Christ (see Deacy 2001: 84). In the words of Edward O'Connor, 'Not once in this film is Christ shown claiming divinity, and some scenes are so constructed that he seems to be disclaiming it' (in Baugh 1997: 20). This is a film, indeed, where the miracles are downplayed (we only see two being performed and even then they take place in silence and in which all we see is Jesus' shadow) and Jesus' preaching is limited to the Sermon on the Mount where the emphasis is very much on Jesus as the Son of *Man* rather than the Son of *God* (see Deacy 2001: 84). Indeed, the Sermon is staged not as an unbroken monologue by a static Jesus, as is the case in George Stevens' overly pious *The Greatest Story Ever Told* (1965), but we see a more human Jesus on display, who freely wanders through the crowd that has gathered to hear him and who espouses a message that makes no predictions concerning the resurrection of the dead or of eternal life. The film as a whole also seems more interested in first-century political issues, such as the economic situation of the region and the land and people of Palestine at the time of Roman aggression. As Geoff Andrew wrote in 1991, 'It is not necessary, therefore, to be a member of the Christian faith in order to become involved in the emotions on view', in a film where 'Ray's Christ, Barabbas, Judas and Lucius have their counterparts in the modern world; their hopes and fears are universal and timeless' (Andrew 1991: 184). With this in mind, it is not, perhaps, surprising that, in Mahan's words, *King of Kings* 'struggles with how to compellingly suggest the idea of resurrection' (Mahan 2002: 20). While the Resurrection is portrayed at the end of the film, all we are given is a series of 'brief images from different perspectives', culminating in a huge shadow of the risen Christ falling across the landscape and 'forming a cross as it lies across a rolled fishing net' (Mahan 2002: 20). Though undoubtedly 'pious in intent', Mahan nevertheless sees it as 'unconvincing' (Mahan 2002: 20), and he refers in his article to a review of the film, from the time of its original release, which suggests that the resurrection is presented as though 'it might have been an hallucination' (in Mahan 2002: 20).

As with *What Dreams May Come*, therefore, there are plenty of instances in films that address issues pertaining to eschatology and the afterlife where a substantially human-oriented and even subjective dynamic is at work. There are, of course, exceptions to this, as when in *The Greatest Story Ever Told* Stevens repeatedly affirms Jesus' divine and messianic status, not least during the 'Hallelujah' chorus which accompanies the Resurrection at the end of the film. As Pope attests, the Jesus of this film 'is the incarnate Word and his death, when it comes, can be pronounced to be salvific for the forgiveness of sins, because he is the divine logos, veiled in flesh' (Pope 2007: 81). This is an exception to the general trend, however – and the fact that Stevens' epic, with its use of big Hollywood stars (most prominently John Wayne's cameo as the Roman centurion who bears witness that 'Truly, this man was the Son of God'), elaborate set design and ever-swelling musical score was a commercial failure, making an overall loss in its theatrical distribution of $18 million (see Wall 1970: 52), only serves to illustrate just how far the goalposts have moved. In place of overly reverential treatments of theological topics, one of the more innovative and critically acclaimed films of this genre is *Jesus of Montreal* (Denys Arcand, 1989), an Oscar-nominated picture from Canada about a troupe of actors who stage an updated version of the Passion Play, with tragic results. The Passion narrative is interwoven within a contemporary narrative which offers, in addition to an adroit satire on political and ecclesiastical hypocrisy, materialism, media hype and advertising, a rich and subversive take on the concept of resurrection. Significantly, the film does not posit an afterlife. Rather, there is a discernibly this-worldly and realised eschatology on display in this film, in which 'resurrection is interpreted in relation to this present life' (Marsh 2007 [a]: 149), specifically with respect to the way in which, following the death of the lead character, Daniel (Lothaire Bluteau), whom we see towards the end of the picture lying in a hospital bed with his arms outstretched in cruciform pose, it is implied that others will be afforded the possibility of new life as a result of his organ donation – 'his organs are harvested and sent forth giving new life to others' (Mahan 2002: 39) – as well as by the indication that the acting company will continue in his name. This quite reductionistic approach to resurrection, though at odds with a traditional Christian picture of the resurrection of the flesh, is nevertheless very much in keeping with the language of realised eschatology, to which we shall turn in Chapter 4. This is because, in Marsh's words, 'If there is nothing beyond physical death, then we really must be wholly concerned about the present, knowing that there is no appeal to future judgement, or to heaven and hell, to enable us to shape contemporary decision-making' (Marsh 2007 [a]: 149). Indeed, as Marsh sees it, 'Heaven and hell may be tenable as no more than imaginative pictures' (Marsh 2007 [a]: 151).

The language of resurrection is certainly invoked in *Jesus of Montreal*. To this end it is worth adding that in the film's final moments we see the camera track 'up, through the earth, until it breaks forth on the hillside past the empty crosses of the play, and on up into the rainy but star light sky as a new day begins to dawn' (Mahan 2002: 38) in what amounts to a none-too-subtle visual encapsulation of Christ's own triumph over the fate meted out to him at Calvary. But, its point of reference is such that a new type of theology is going on, here. What is significant is that it is not one which simply and slavishly endeavours to correspond to a particular theological paradigm along the lines of Stevens' lavish, but ultimately rather empty, spectacle. Instead, it is filmmakers who are calling the shots – to the point, indeed, that, according to

Babington and Evans, Arcand's somewhat more sophisticated treatment amounts to 'the only postmodernist resurrection available' (Babington & Evans 1993: 98). It may have been George Stevens' belief that 'the awesome salvific event of Jesus the Christ, the narrative of universal human redemption through the extraordinary intervention of the incarnate Son of God, clearly the greatest story ever told' (Baugh 1997: 26), warranted a cinematically faithful and uncritical rendering which would both warrant and inspire religious devotion, or at least deferential respect, on the part of the audience. But, rather than illustrating or bearing witness to theology in this manner, it is apparent that filmmakers are changing, or at least have the capacity to change, the contours of theological debate around questions of resurrection and immortality, in line with the revised correlational model I am espousing throughout this book. Accordingly, both film and theology have the capacity to be challenged and critiqued by the other, even to the point that the way theologians have understood eschato-logical language, such as that pertaining to immortality and resurrection, needs to be re-visited as a result of some of the cinematic endeavours highlighted in this chapter. In the same way, filmmakers would do well to learn from Stevens' sincere, but misguided, assumption that a religious film simply entails the straightforward application or representation of religious subject matter on to the cinema screen.

3

NEAR-DEATH EXPERIENCES AND MIND-DEPENDENT WORLDS IN THEOLOGY AND FILM

Up to this point, the focus has been on those films which address the non-empirical question of what happens beyond the point of actual physical death. As we have seen, both theologically and cinematically, all manner of speculations have been rife concerning the nature of the 'body' that we may expect to inhabit in a post-mortem environment, and as to whether such representations accord with teachings that can be adduced from scriptural, creedal, doctrinal and other religious texts and formulations. *What Dreams May Come* (Vincent Ward, 1998) is a case in point. This is because the film's delineation of heaven as an inherently subjective environment where each soul creates his or her own paradise can only stand or fall on assumptions about the nature and form of the afterlife that have been arrived at from philosophical and theological musings which, no matter how erudite or intellectually satisfying, correspond to the very objection that Immanuel Kant espoused in the eighteenth century concerning whether we can ever attain knowledge of the ultimate realm. For Kant, it is impossible for humans to know about the world as it is in itself (the *noumenal* world); we can only speak of the world as it appears to us through the senses (the *phenomenal* world), inasmuch as the only possible ground for knowledge is that of our sense-experience (see Kant 2007: 258–62). The focus in this chapter will be on those attempts that have been made, particularly within the last century or so, to buck this epistemological trend, by interrogating through the latest scientific advances whether we can glean anything about the next world, if there is one, from the findings of so-called out-of-body and near-death experiences. This will be followed by a discussion of the no less fraught and contested, particularly in academic (including theological) circles, testimony pertaining to séances, mediumship and telepathic communication and what they may have to say about the veracity of so-called 'mind-dependent worlds' along the lines of that proposed in the 1950s by the philosopher and parapsychologist Henry H. Price.

Near-death experiences

It was in the mid-1970s, following the publication of *Life after Life* by philosophy professor-turned-psychiatrist Raymond Moody, that NDEs first received widespread attention. The data here, while in no way conclusive, is at least compatible with the question of survival, and has been the template for a number of cinematic works that envisage the possibility of some sort of resurrection, immortality or eternal life. Examples of this include *Flatliners* (Joel Schumacher, 1990), *The Frighteners* (Peter Jackson, 1996) and *White Noise 2: The Light* (Patrick Lussier, 2007). The empirical dimension that has so far in our discussion been so elusive lies at the very kernel of NDE discourse, where we learn that people who have been pronounced clinically dead have nevertheless been able to accurately observe their bodies from a different vantage point in physical space to that which would ordinarily be possible, and which medical personnel have been able to corroborate. According to one survey, around 5 per cent of Americans (amounting to approximately eight million people) have experienced an NDE (Feinstein 1990: 256). This figure was upheld by Bailey and Yates in *The Near-Death Experience: A Reader*, published in 1996, who refer to a Gallup poll from 1982 according to which 1 in 20 Americans have survived an NDE (Bailey & Yates 1996 [a]: 7). So pervasive is the interest in NDEs that, as Kenneth Ring, a Connecticut psychologist who has produced some of the most meticulous research on the subject, has written, it 'has achieved the status of a *cultural* and not just a clinical phenomenon' (Ring 1996: 181), to the point that

> Not only have hundreds of radio and television talk shows featured discussions on the subject in addition to countless articles about it in the print media, but also one can scarcely find anyone who has not encountered such an experience in a Hollywood film, a television soap, a short story or novel, or even in a cartoon of a fashionable magazine.
>
> *(Ring 1996: 181)*

To this end, we should not underestimate the extent to which media accounts of NDEs do not merely reflect, but actually shape, theological and religious accounts of the afterlife, a point suggested by David Lester in his 2005 publication *Is There Life After Death?: An Examination of the Empirical Evidence* (see Lester 2005: 83). Indeed, a film such as *Flatliners* is more likely to influence a contemporary understanding of what happens after death than, say, biblical teachings and perspectives which may be very far from homogeneous or consistent. Quite simply, as Ring attests, NDEs are 'a salient fact of our time and one which continues to exert a very powerful hold on our collective consciousness' (Ring 1996: 181–82).

Before we proceed, however, it is worth pointing out that there is nothing monolithic or universal about the characteristics and forms that NDEs take. As indicated by Mark Fox, whose *Religion, Spirituality and the Near-Death Experience* was published in 2003, they can be accommodated within a diverse range of philosophical and religious world views. According to Fox, many NDEs appeal to quite 'divergent scriptures and traditions ranging from Mysticism, Eastern Orthodoxy and Conservative Christianity through to Orthodox Judaism, Gnosticism and Tibetan Buddhism' (Fox 2003: 339). It is therefore difficult to reconcile such a heterogeneous assortment of teachings into anything resembling an all-encompassing interpretative framework without diluting or compromising the individuality and integrity of each particular tradition. The inclusion of NDE phenomena in a number of films only exacerbates the problem in that such films rarely, if ever, subscribe to a particular religious framework. In *Flatliners*, for instance, there is a discernibly Buddhist dimension to the way that the medical students, who endeavour to induce NDEs by using their medical knowledge to temporarily stop their hearts until the lack of vital signs show up on the EEG and EKG monitors as flat lines, find that each person is responsible due to their actions and behaviour in this life for the type of afterlife they go on to receive. As the different characters face up to the way they have treated others in the past – by inflicting psychological damage on others by being a school bully, as in the case of David Labraccio (Kevin Bacon), or bringing pain to adult relationships by pathological adultery and womanising, as typifies the irresponsible and care-free lifestyle of William Baldwin's character, Dr Joe Hurley – this corresponds to the way in Buddhism in which 'under the law of karma a bad action produces a like result, just as a good action produces a good result' (Hallisey 2000: 14). The fact that the students who 'flat line' all atone in some way for the pain they have inflicted on others suggests that, rather than wait until their 'real' deaths before confronting the traumas of their past, they can expedite and short-cut the process now and so ensure that a more advanced, and less negative, karmic retribution awaits them in the future. Yet, the film blurs the boundaries somewhat by bringing in an explicitly theistic dimension to the karmic law in operation, as when we witness Bacon's character, David Labraccio, 'railing against the heavens, fists and feet flying' (Maude 2001: 394) towards the end of the picture, when it looks as though one of his colleagues, the conceited and (at least in his youth) sadistic Nelson Wright (Kiefer Sutherland), is not going to return from his (karmically appropriate) negative and traumatic NDE.

The scene in question is one in which we see Labraccio shouting out to an unseen deity juxtaposed with the sight of Nelson Wright being tortured and victimised, in a reversal of the original sequence of events, by the young boy whose life he himself prematurely brought to an end by an especially malicious act of childhood bullying. Without detracting from the aesthetic and visual flair of this scene – and to this end it is notable that in her *Time Out* review Colette Maude refers to the 'flamboyant visuals' and 'other-worldly atmosphere' (Maude 2001: 394) conjured up in the film by the director, Joel Schumacher, and production designer, Eugenio Zanetti, which undoubtedly lends a polished and impressive visual facet to the proceedings – it is difficult to avoid the conclusion that its underlying theology is inescapably, even terminally, muddled. Of course, this is not to say that the film has no religious or spiritual value. Indeed, there is an insightful parallel between Wright's experience in *Flatliners* and the real-life story of Dannion Brinkley, a self-confessed angry and violent youth who later, in Vietnam, became involved in clandestine government operations, specialising in sniping and demolition work. Brinkley's case study is outlined in Chapter 4 of Bailey and Yates' *The Near-Death Experience: A Reader*. Brinkley was struck by lightning one day and underwent an NDE in which he says he was made to re-live all the pain and grief that his victims and their families suffered. In his words:

> The Being of Light engulfed me, and as it did I began to experience my whole life, feeling and seeing everything that had ever happened to me. It was as though a dam had burst and every memory stored in my brain flowed out. This life-review was not pleasant. From the moment it began until it ended, I was faced with the sickening reality that I had been an unpleasant person, someone who was self-centered and mean.
>
> *(Brinkley 1996: 64)*

The first thing he saw was an angry childhood – 'I saw myself torturing other children, stealing their bicycles or making them miserable at school' (Brinkley 1996: 64). Referring to one particular incident, he says:

> At the time I thought I was funny. But now, as I relived this incident, I found myself in his body, living with the pain that I was causing. This perspective continued through every negative incident in my childhood, a substantial number to be sure. From fifth to twelfth grade, I estimate that I had at least six thousand fist fights. Now, as I reviewed my life in the bosom of the Being, I relived each one of those altercations, but with one major difference: I was the receiver.
>
> *(Brinkley 1996: 64)*

Brinkley says this was not in the sense of feeling the punches that he had thrown – 'Rather, I felt the anguish and the humiliation my opponent felt' (Brinkley 1996: 64). The parallel with *Flatliners* is very strong, yet this does not disguise the fact that, theologically, the filmmakers' blending of reincarnationist and theistic ingredients is, at least intellectually, problematic.

It is one thing to say that, as Fox puts it, NDEs 'cannot unambiguously be used as apologetic tools for the propagation of any one particular religious or spiritual tradition or be somehow fitted into any one tradition to the exclusion of all others' (Fox 2003: 339), but quite another to suppose that the malleability and heterogeneity that filmmakers often bring to the task of delineating NDEs on screen has any intrinsic theological or pedagogical utility. Any suggestion that films which delineate NDEs, as in the case of *Flatliners*, can be used to illustrate or corroborate previously held theological or spiritual beliefs pertaining to the survival of the individual after death is invariably going to run into difficulties. For, notwithstanding Badham's claim that NDEs are 'highly relevant to the question of survival for they seem to point, if only for a moment at the brink of death, to a real separation between the self and its normal embodiment' (Badham & Badham 1984: 118), cinematic treatments of NDEs tend, almost without exception, to disclose much less about the possibility, let alone the actual shape, of an afterlife, than about the meaning or impact that such representations have upon present existence in the here and now. Indeed, it is questionable that *Flatliners*, despite its ostensible subject matter, is really about the afterlife at all. What the medical students undergo 'is not the sense of an impending new life (reassuringly full of light and welcome, to judge from published case histories) but a form of self-analysis stemming from unresolved events in their past' (Strick 1990: 321), such as (as has already been outlined) childhood bullying or a series of infidelities. Rather than a journey *per se* into the afterlife, Ruffles rightly observes that the characters are forced to 'confront their failings and past traumas, so that flatlining becomes a kind of extreme therapy' (Ruffles 2004: 129). It is this life, rather than an afterlife, which is being affirmed, with death nothing more than a portal or conduit for providing ethical lessons about how to behave on earth. Instead of affording us a glimpse into the future, what we actually have on display is an inescapably reductionistic dimension in which the supernatural subject matter is less an end in itself than a means to an end, namely, the moral lesson that we should behave better to others and make amends for the suffering we have inflicted. None of the characters actually die in spite of their flat EEGs, and they come back from the brink of death to recount the experience. When Kevin Bacon's character launches into a diatribe against God, the charge is not that death is, in itself, a bad (or for that matter a good) thing; he is angry for the simple reason that he is not yet ready to be separated from his friends. This-worldly relationships are, simply, too satisfying to merit any kind of foray into the unknown, even if the consequence of death is the experience of immortality.

Indeed, it is significant in this regard that *Flatliners* does not countenance the possibility of extinction. The worst case scenario is that the afterlife will be a negative, menacing environment where we will be punished for the pain and suffering we have caused other people, but it will be an afterlife nevertheless. Paradoxical though it may be, the implicit assumption is that the afterlife is real. Ruffles endorses this claim, as when he writes that, because the medical students all have flat EEGs, the experiences that take place must necessarily be 'extrapolated to the post-death state' rather than to brain activity, and the 'experience, given that it supports dualism, acts as evidence for the Afterlife within the film' (Ruffles 2004: 129). Ironically, the filmmakers are going even further in this respect than many of those professionals who specialise in NDE research. As Ruffles points out, it is not clear from the psychical research literature that exists 'to what extent NDEs can be seen as precursors to a post-mortem existence' inasmuch as there is 'no reason why the state reported by survivors should be identical to that pertaining after death' (Ruffles 2004: 125). It also tends to be the case that scientific reports that have been amassed on the subject of NDEs do not extrapolate on the basis of their findings the possibility that there may be a life after death – this is, simply, outside of their remit – and nor do they 'acknowledge that further inquiries into near-death experiences could contribute to the evidence bearing on this question' (Stevenson & Greyson 1996: 205). In films, in marked contrast, NDEs categorically suggest evidence of an afterlife.

In addition to *Flatliners*, a case in point is *Vanilla Sky* (Cameron Crowe, 2001), which, while not explicitly delineating an NDE, does have as its protagonist, David

Aames (Tom Cruise), someone who, in typical NDE terms, is immune to the laws that circumscribe the physical body. Rather than inhabit a physical world as such (his body has been cryogenically frozen for the last century and a half), Aames is living in an environment where some sort of dualism of soul and body has taken place. He can travel at speed between different states of consciousness and even backwards and forwards in time, and characters enigmatically swap identities and appear and disappear from one moment to another (see Deacy & Ortiz 2008: 193). Aames may, of course, only be dreaming, and, as I have noted elsewhere, the director, Cameron Crowe, has deliberately kept all options open as to the film's meaning (Deacy & Ortiz 2008: 194), so it would be injudicious to read too much into the idea that, while his body is comatose, Aames' 'self' or 'soul' is being afforded a glimpse of some kind into the realm of immortality. However, while such a film in no way proves the existence of a final or ultimate state, and does little more than support the possibility of belief in resurrection (in view of the teaching adduced at one point in the film that medical advances have enabled Aames to be 'resurrected to continue your own life as you know it now'), *Vanilla Sky* actually takes us further than research into NDEs by the likes of Raymond Moody and Kenneth Ring, to which we shall now turn, is able to take us.

From the outset, it is apparent that all five of the characteristics of modern accounts of NDEs that Moody identifies (in Collins & Fishbane 1995: x) are consistent with Aames' experiences in *Vanilla Sky*. The first of these is that there will typically be an experience of being separated from one's own body. In the film, Aames' body is in a comatose state while he is living in some kind of mind-dependent dreamscape that does not operate according to physical laws, as when the identities of his two lovers, a model and a dancer, blur and constantly cross-reference and shadow one another (see Deacy & Ortiz 2008: 193). The second feature is an encounter with a being of light. In *Vanilla Sky*, Aames' visual faculties are constantly put to the test and he is exposed to extremes of translucent, white light. It is significant to this end that he has spent the last 150 years of earth time as a client of the enigmatic Life Extension Corporation which is in the market of selling Lucid Dreams, so that, as he learns at one point, 'Your life will continue ... with the romantic abandon of a summer day'. Thirdly, Moody identifies a review of one's life. With respect to the film, Aames' world is being fashioned and induced by the memories, fantasies and traumas of his previous earthly existence, wherein he is haunted, and has to re-visit over and over, the guilt that he is responsible for the death of one, or even both, of his girlfriends, and he seeks to refashion the sequence of events that transpired on earth that led to his disfigurement and her/their death. Number four on Moody's list is a strong attraction to the afterlife. Vis-à-vis the film, this is more ambiguous, but the fact that Aames has opted to have his body cryogenically frozen does suggest that he is hankering on some level for immortality, though he may not have anticipated the mental experiences he is having while his body is comatose, expecting only, akin to the Woody Allen character in *Sleeper* (Woody Allen, 1973), for his physical life to simply re-commence on earth once the body has been defrosted. Finally, Moody posits a reluctant return to the body. In the film, if not quite a case of returning to the body, we do at least see Aames descending to his (second?) death by plunging from the roof of a high-rise building at the film's denouement.

Of course, to seek a perfect correlation between Moody's account of the characteristics of NDEs and the narratives and imagery of Crowe's film would be to stretch the point somewhat. After all, in choosing at the end of the film to sever all links with Life Extension Corporation, it would be more fitting to see, not a return to the body (reluctant or otherwise), but Aames' quest to escape both from his body and from the cycle of (immortal) life altogether. He no longer wants to live out for an eternity a mind-dependent dreamscape in which he can neither reconcile his conflicting feelings for the two women in his life, Sofia (Penélope Cruz) and Julianna (Cameron Diaz), nor his trauma at having been responsible for the death of one or other of them. In place of either immortality or a return to the body as such, Aames chooses extinction – a characteristic unusual, though not unprecedented, in NDE research where positive emotional feelings, such as an overwhelming experience of peace, joy and bliss, tend to hold sway (see Fenwick & Fenwick 1996: 134). Whereas NDE accounts normally entail the experience of a brilliant white or golden light at the end of a tunnel which acts like a magnet, drawing the person towards it, and having a quality of warmth (Fenwick & Fenwick 1996: 134), this is far removed from Aames' experience. Despite being informed that 'Upon resurrection, you will continue in an ageless state, preserved, but living in the present with a future of your choosing', he finds such an experience wanting. One of the characteristics of an NDE, as described by Carol Zaleski, is that of an immersion in light and love, with a profound sense of security and protection (Zaleski 1995: 391). Fenwick and Fenwick refer also to how, according to one survey, 82 per cent of those who have had an NDE feel calmness and peace (Fenwick & Fenwick 1996: 142). Yet, for David Aames, the experience is more akin to the accounts of negative NDEs which though less common than their positive counterparts do show up in some NDE literature. It may be the case that, as Fox puts it, 'most *reported* cases are overwhelmingly positive in nature' (Fox 2003: 259). But in a 1994 article in the *Journal of Near-Death Studies*, Kenneth Ring identified negative NDEs as 'inversions of positive ones, in which the individual finds it difficult to let go of his or her ego, creating fear and leading to the negative experience' (in Ruffles 2004: 195). Although Ring refers to the film *Jacob's Ladder* (Adrian Lyne, 1990) as a good example of such a type, *Vanilla Sky* also fits the criteria. This is because Aames' landscape has been moulded by the experiences of his earthly life, and, whether he likes it or not, he cannot escape the fact that he is the spoiled, selfish and hedonistic playboy son of a business tycoon whose lifestyle becomes too dispiriting and facile for him to want to re-live for an eternity, to the extent that he finally chooses annihilation from the cycle of life (see Deacy & Ortiz 2008: 196).

When a 1985 study of NDEs in both Britain and America thus defined a negative NDE as characterised by feelings of extreme fear or panic, emotional or mental anguish, desperation, intense loneliness and desolation (in Greyson & Evans Bush 1996: 213), it is not difficult to see why a film such as *Vanilla Sky* might be thought to comprise a potential repository of NDE activity. Even though, as David Lorimer sees it, negative NDEs provide recipients with 'opportunities to face their demons and overcome them' (Lorimer 1995: 168), Aames' shallow existence is such that there is limited room for moral or spiritual growth, and becoming dissatisfied with the world he has fashioned for himself, Aames' redemptive journey, if we can even call it that, has come to a tragic, though perhaps inevitable, terminus (see Deacy & Ortiz 2008: 197). Before we go down the path, however, of affirming that, because an eschatological theme has been identified in a film, this automatically constitutes a normative reading of that picture, it would be worth pausing to take on board the consideration that *Vanilla Sky* does not completely conform to a specifically Christian or theological schema. Indeed, one reading would be that, far from closure, at the end of the film Aames has merely entered into the next, and by no means final, stage of his post-mortem odyssey. After plummeting to his 'death', he hears the same words that appeared at the opening of the film, 'Open your eyes', suggesting that, despite his intentions to the contrary, his consciousness has not been annihilated and the cycle of life–death–rebirth continues. A similar motif appears at the end of David Fincher's *The Game* (1997) in which a middle-aged business tycoon, Nicholas Van Orton (Michael Douglas), commits suicide by plunging from the top floor of a hotel, albeit this time while he is still alive (although we do in an earlier scene see Van Orton buried alive in a Mexican cemetery) rather than in some sort of post-mortem state, only to find that 'new life' is the only possibility open to him. This is betokened by his amenability to embrace those that he had hitherto rejected in favour of self-absorption and to embark on a new relationship in the film's final scene that, for once, is not navigated or negotiated solely on his own terms. In another non-specifically eschatological film, Jane Campion's *The Piano* (1993), in which a mute Scottish widow travels to New Zealand in the 19th century to execute an arranged marriage with an oppressive and jealous landowner, Ada's (Holly Hunter) close brush with death, when she nearly drowns, could likewise be said to mark the death of her former, enslaved self and her affirmation of life.

   The fluidity and malleability of language pertaining to NDEs is remarkable inasmuch as it is not only films that specifically delineate an afterlife, along the lines of *Flatliners*, that have generated insightful eschatological discussion. In the case of *The Piano*, Marsh even goes so far as to say that 'As a consequence of [Ada's] near-death experience, and the surprising exercise of her will to live, she (literally) finds her voice and is able to relate to others in a new way' (Marsh 2007 [a]: 119). As with the protagonist in *The Game*, the language used here is somewhat reminiscent of that employed in NDE discourse, as when Lorimer writes that practically none of those who have had an NDE 'now fear death, while almost all … are convinced that they went through the first stage of the death process and are equally convinced that they will survive the transition' (Lorimer 1995: 170). Lorimer is referring explicitly to those individuals who have been pronounced clinically dead but have been brought back to life by medical and surgical resuscitation procedures, whereas in *The Piano* we are not privy to the consciousness of the protagonist and so are in no position to ascertain whether death, as opposed to the threat of death, has actually occurred. But, when Ada says, in voice-over mode, 'What a death! What a chance! What a surprise! My will has chosen life', the confidence and new zest she feels for living, following an encounter with mortality, is in line with Fenwick and Fenwicks' observation that to

> come near to death and then escape it must be one of the most profound human experiences, with or without an NDE. Anyone who has ever been in a situation where death seemed imminent or inevitable, but who then survives, feels to some extent reborn. It is as though one has been given a second chance, that one is somehow 'special' to be alive when one might so easily have died.
>
> *(Fenwick & Fenwick 1996: 148)*

Irrespective of whether the experience is positive or negative, it is clear that both can have transformative effects on the individuals concerned.[1] In Ada's case, moreover, the experience was such that, to cite again from her voice-over, 'It has had me spooked and many others besides'. It would be injudicious to draw too strong a correlation between Ada's experience and Lorimer's attestation that those who have had an NDE 'certainly think that they have caught a glimpse of the afterlife' (Lorimer 1995: 170), or indeed Fenwicks' claims that 'The NDE certainly tends to confirm belief in some form of afterlife' and that 'Most who have had an NDE have a strong conviction that some important part of them – their consciousness, their soul – can exist quite independently of their body, and may continue to do so after death' (Fenwick & Fenwick 1996: 149). Quite simply, the film itself affords us no clues. But, in both a number of films and in NDE literature, numerous parallels do seem to exist, not least the concept of a life review, whereby an encounter with death 'is typically taken as an occasion to evaluate one's life and how one has lived' (Walls 2002: 153), with the attendant opportunity for growth and change – the very antithesis, of course, of Aames' trajectory in *Vanilla Sky*.

On one level, it is not surprising that such a correlation can be drawn. Even before the term NDE was first coined, the concept of a drowning man seeing his life flash before him[2] was already familiar (see Zaleski 1995: 394). In theological terms, further, the idea 'could be understood as God's call to accountability, along with encouragement to accept his transforming grace in those areas of one's life that need reformation and renewal', such that to 'accept such transformation is to draw closer to God and the life of heaven in all of its fullness' (Walls 2002: 153–54). Neither in *The Game* nor *Vanilla Sky* is any such theistic framework even suggested. But what such films do share with many of the world's religious traditions is the expectation that either upon or following the point of death each person can expect to have him or herself and his or her deeds rendered transparent, scrutinised and judged, whether by an external deity or, as is the case in these films, by the judgement one brings on one's self. In terms of this latter perspective, Lorimer calls this the Higher Self or Witness Consciousness, namely, an impartial and all-knowing awareness (Lorimer 1995: 169) through being confronted 'with ourselves *as we really are*' (Deacy & Ortiz 2008: 196). Outside Christianity, of course, this motif has appeared in numerous ways, such as, to quote Zaleski, 'the mirror of karma, the book of deeds, the personification of virtues and vices, and the weighing of deeds' (Zaleski 1995: 396). Regardless, then, of whether there is any kind of interrogation by a divine figure or presence, what we see at the end of *American Beauty* (Sam Mendes, 1999), for example, is the sensation of Lester Burnham's (Kevin Spacey) life passing before his eyes after he is shot and his concomitant inability to conceal anything. One of the most well-known examples of such a life review is that delineated by Charles Dickens in *A Christmas Carol*, which was first published in 1843 and has been adapted on celluloid more than a dozen times, most recently in a 3-D version, directed by Robert Zemeckis and starring Jim Carrey. By way of the visitations Ebenezer Scrooge receives by the Ghosts of Christmases Past, Present and Future, Greene and Krippner make the instructive point that he 'not only travels into his past but also experiences a "flash forward" in which he sees his own gravestone in a "possible future," a future that inspires him to transform his life in order to avoid the dismal fate he sees awaiting him' (Greene & Krippner 1990: 62). Without wishing to unduly widen the contours of what constitutes an NDE, it is significant that Tom Ruffles takes the line that 'The tours that Scrooge is taken on can be likened to the life reviews that sometimes accompany NDEs' (Ruffles 2004: 77).

A similar motif appears in *Jacob's Ladder* in which we see the protagonist, Jacob Singer (Tim Robbins), badly wounded in combat in Vietnam at the start of the film and dead at the end, with everything that happens in between taking the form 'of an unusually complex near death experience' (Ruffles 2004: 192) in which Jacob undergoes 'a life review made up of memories mixed with desires and fears' (Ruffles 2004: 193). What is not, however, clear is whether we are witnessing a 'flashback' or a 'flash forward'. The time frame is constantly shifting between past, present and future, to the extent that, in Ruffles' words, 'Competing interpretations are permissible, and the audience is forced to share the protagonist's confusion' (Ruffles 2004: 193). We are not aware, for instance, of whether the experiences are utterly subjective in form. Are they taking place, in other words, entirely within Jacob's traumatised and drug-enhanced consciousness in which all of the images and 'memories' are self-induced? Or are they objective, in the sense that he is being shown by some external agency facets of his actual or possible past or future with the concomitant opportunity for him to seek inner peace from his attachments to his earthly existence (and which are so strong that he does not even realise that he has died)? Whichever of these interpretations is held, it is significant that, at the end of the film, after his Meister Eckhart-quoting chiropractor, Louis (Danny Aiello), has counselled him that if he clings to life in fear of death the devils will come to tear him away, whereas if he accepts death then the devils are really angels helping him on his way (see Cho 2009: 175), Jacob is finally afforded the possibility of redemption and closure. This event is connected to the death of his young son whom we see accompanying the protagonist up the stairway, or ladder, at the top of which lies an incandescent, heavenly light into the auspices of which his post-mortem odyssey now takes him. This motif corresponds to the well-known staple in NDE testimony of a 'tunnel which links heaven to earth' (Stanford 2002: 320), which can itself be likened to Hieronymus Bosch's late-fifteenth-century painting *Ascent of the Blessed* in which we see the newly departed floating upwards through a tunnel towards the light on the other side.

Antecedents to and ramifications of NDEs

Theologically, of course, so much of what we know about NDEs is speculative. With few exceptions, such as the work conducted by Paul Badham and the Alister Hardy Society Religious Experience Research Centre, Fox is right in his claim, written in 2003, that there has been 'an almost total ignorance on the part of theologians and philosophers regarding the mass of research into NDEs that the last thirty years have produced' (Fox 2003: 5). He also writes that 'there are vast areas of research into the mystery and complexity of the NDE still to be done' (Fox 2003: 338). Even where research on NDEs has been conducted, it has failed to establish any universal paradigms or methodologies. Indeed, as Kenneth Ring puts it, such efforts have 'utterly failed to produce any kind of generally accepted interpretation, even among those who have spent years carefully examining it' (Ring 1996: 186). With this in mind, it would be wrong to assume that straightforward correlations can be drawn between trends in theology and the narratives and images of cinematic texts. However, long before the term 'Near-Death Experience' was first coined in the latter half of the twentieth century, there have been a number of antecedents to NDE discourse. The tenth book of Plato's *Republic*, for instance, might be said to comprise an early account of an NDE, as when we learn of Er the Pamphylian who was slain in battle and, after being in a coma for 12 days, recounted what he had seen in the other world, including the rewards and punishments that the dead could expect following judgement (Plato 1974: 447–55). Some have also alleged that there are traces of NDE-like elements in the Bible, such as Moses' call coming from the burning bush in Exodus 3:2 and the fire of light which led the Israelites towards the Promised Land in Exodus 14:20 (see Bailey & Yates 1996 [a]: 18). There is also a New Testament angle to this, namely, Paul's conversion on the road to Damascus in which we learn from Acts 9:3 that 'suddenly a light from heaven flashed about him'. In early Christendom, we find further accounts of otherworldly visions in the context of legends built around the great figures of the New Testament, as in the case of the third-century *Vision of Paul* in which St Paul was led by the Archangel Michael through hell, by way of fiery trees, blood, snakes, lightning, stench, ordeal bridges, pitch and sulphur (Haas 1999: 451). There are also reports of medieval 'out of body experiences' in which we learn how souls were led out of their bodies in order to walk the path of the dead through the underworld (see Haas 1999: 446). According to Peter Dinzelbacher, 'There are not only the eternally burning fire in ovens and seas of embers or the bites of immortal snakes, but also boiling kettles, fields full of eternal ice, automatically closing bridges, from which one falls into rivers of swirling sulphur', and other 'countless refined agonies which are to be administered to the soul under the watch of the most horrible demonic figures' (in Haas 1999: 446). The most famous example of a fictional otherworldly journey is Dante's *Divine Comedy* – a pilgrimage that Dante makes through hell and purgatory to heaven – which, in Haas' words, 'raised the otherworldly journey to the pinnacle of the genre' (Haas 1999: 461). While Haas is quite right to warn that, as regards content, 'it certainly is not a matter of simple comparisons if these medieval otherworldly journeys are held up to modern forms of out–of–body and near-death experiences', there is a case for arguing that, structurally, 'a schema does indeed appear that applies to both the medieval and modern variations' (Haas 1999: 446).

In Eastern traditions, there would likewise appear to be strong parallels between modern NDEs and ancient accounts of visionary experiences. According to Carl Becker of Kyoto University, the belief in Mahayana Buddhism that after death one will be born in the Buddha's Pure Land is actually dependent on death-bed and visionary narratives from the fourth to the seventh centuries (see Badham 2005: 40). NDEs may thus have played a role in the formulation of ideas on the Pure Land which lie at the heart of Mahayana Buddhism, and, as Badham points out, in Japanese doctrines about Amida Buddha greeting the dying person we can find similar claims, based on the visions and experiences of Japanese monks from the tenth to the twelfth centuries (see Badham 2005: 40). In the case of Hinduism, it has also been alleged that there is a correspondence between the descriptions conveyed by those who have had NDEs in the modern world, as disclosed in the work of Moody, and the characteristics attributed to the so-called 'subtle' body (see Rambachan 2000: 76). When the Upanishads 'suggest that the point of exit of the subtle body from the physical body at the time of death is determined by the nature of the individual's consciousness' and that 'the journey and destiny of the individual after the death of the physical body are also determined by the same factor' (Rambachan 2000: 77), Anantanand Rambachan makes the case that Moody's talk of the imperceptibility of the spiritual body, being composed of matter in a subtle form and thus inaccessible to the organs of the physical body, is simply a modern day version of the same philosophical teaching. Finally, when we turn to the Tibetan Book of the Dead, we find further affinities with reports of NDEs, such as, in the words of Eva K. Neumaier-Dargyay,

> the perception of brilliant light, the sensation of seeing one's old body, observing relatives and friends in their responses to one's death, and the feeling of being not confined by the materiality of a physical body while continuing to have a kind of bodily sensation.
>
> *(Neumaier-Dargyay 2000: 102)*

With such possible antecedents in mind, the distrust on the part of academics towards the paranormal, as with the scepticism outlined at the beginning of Chapter 1 regarding the efficacy of afterlife films themselves, does seem somewhat misplaced.[3] Although Fox is right that neither theologians nor philosophers 'have engaged at any length in discussion with each other over the phenomenon, and there are only a very few theologians who have evolved theories designed to explore the NDE in the light of recent discoveries about its nature and significance' (Fox 2003: 63), this might say more about the conservatism of many theologians than about the legitimacy *per se* of scholarly activity in this area. Such an attitude is illustrated by Zaleski's point that theologians feel more comfortable when treating testimony of otherworldly journeys in metaphorical or literary rather than literal terms – to the point, indeed, that they 'attentuate the visionary virus until it is so weak that it produces immunity instead of contagion' (Zaleski 1987: 184). Accordingly, as Fox puts it, 'far from constituting any systematic or dynamic engagement with NDEs, theology's few responses to them often stand alone, like a series of isolated islands showing little or no evidence of pattern, development or, indeed, history' (Fox 2003: 63). Of course, this is not helped by the fact that the NDE data we have to hand is fragmentary and incomplete. For instance, as regards his pioneering research in *Life After Life*, Moody himself admitted that of his 150 accounts no two were exactly the same and that no one person has reported every single feature that pertains to NDE testimony (Moody 1975: 23). Such characteristics include separation from the body (an out-of-body experience), a dark tunnel, a journey motif, an encounter with deceased friends or relatives, a life review, positive emotional feelings, an immersion in light and love, the presence of a being of light, a return to the body and transforming after-effects (see Zaleski 1995: 391 and Fenwick & Fenwick 1996: 134). Moody noted, for example, that some people saw the 'being of light' before, or at the same time as, they left their physical bodies 'and not as in the "model", some time afterward' (Moody 1975: 24).

Similarly, although in a 'typical' NDE 'people have the sensation of being pulled very rapidly through a dark space of some kind' (Moody 1975: 32), the language used to describe the sensation is not uniform. Moody calls this particular section of his book 'The dark tunnel', but not everyone who has claimed to have had an NDE has described the darkness as tunnel-shaped. One individual referred to 'moving through a deep, very dark valley', another as 'just floating and tumbling through space', while a third claimed to have entered a 'narrow' and 'very dark passageway' (Moody 1975: 32–33). Of the testimony contained in the Alister Hardy Centre, none contained all 15 of the features that were recorded in Moody's original model – the maximum number in any one account is 10 and the average number of elements in any one account was a mere 3.3 (Fox 2003: 289). These points notwithstanding, it does not follow from this lack of uniformity that the whole typology is flawed. By way of analogy, when it comes to attempts to construct Christ-figure correlations in films, the advocates of such an endeavour, such as Anton Karl Kozlovic, are not deterred even though it is difficult to find a single film that bears witness to more than half a dozen or so structural characteristics, yet a total of 'twenty-five structural characteristics of the cinematic Christ-figure' (Kozlovic 2004: 66) have reputedly been identified. Just as Kozlovic believes that 'innumerable Christ-figures and other holy subtexts are hidden within the popular cinema' (Kozlovic 2004: 5) even though one of the films he focuses on at length, *The Man Who Fell to Earth* (Nicolas Roeg, 1976), conforms to just four of the 25 structural characteristics he so painstakingly identifies, so it does not follow here that we should dismiss the veracity of NDE evidence simply because it provides us with nebulous, partial or inconsistent data.

To put it starkly, this is important territory for the theologian, and, in Fox's words, 'many of the claims that near-death experiencers ... have made in the last quarter-century are such that they may well be said to *demand* a response which goes to the very heart of the West's understanding of what it is to be human' and, indeed, of 'what it is for human beings to die' (Fox 2003: 5). The reticence of contemporary theologians to embrace that which pertains to the paranormal or supernatural stands in marked contrast to the openness, even optimism, that key figures in the field of religious experience showed a century or so ago towards the scholarly study of 'alleged phenomena such as telepathy and precognition' (Fox 2003: 5). Even William James, the Father of Modern Psychology and author of *The Varieties of Religious Experience* (1902) – about which Eugene Taylor wrote that 'There is no more influential book in the field of the psychology of religion' (Taylor 1996: 84) – was co-founder in 1885 of the American Society for Psychical Research. The Association's remit (in the words of the ASPR web site) 'has been to explore extraordinary or as yet unexplained phenomena that have been called psychic or paranormal, and their implications for our understanding of consciousness, the universe and the nature of existence' (<www.aspr.com/who.htm>). Rather than a 'trend which was to continue unbroken through subsequent decades', however, Fox is right to suggest that 'the rigorous academic investigation' of psychical phenomena 'now resembles a historical curiosity' (Fox 2003: 5). The marginality, not to mention the perceived eccentricity, of psychical data is the central theme in a recent film, *Dean Spanley* (Toa Fraser, 2008), based on the 1936 novel *My Talks with Dean Spanley* by Lord Dunsany, in which, as a result of the transmigration of souls, an Edwardian Anglican cleric, played by Sam Neill, is gradually revealed to be the reincarnation of a Victorian spaniel. At the beginning of the film, we are party to a lecture given by an Indian swami on the theme of transmigration, this being an era when, as Sam Davies wrote in his review of the film for *Sight and Sound*, 'attempts to investigate the occult and the unconscious were made with imperfect tools such as drugs, mediums, séances and hypnosis' (Davies 2009: 60). Here, it is intoxication by an obscure Hungarian wine called Tokay that facilitates the memory of a past life, and there is a quaint, old-fashioned and whimsical aura to this film – Davies calls *Dean Spanley* a well-crafted 'exercise in the warm and fuzzy' (Davies 2009: 60) – which, perhaps, reinforces the idea that its spiritualistic subject matter is nothing but inoffensive, belonging as it does to an Edwardian past that no longer holds sway.

An obvious criticism that could be levelled at the NDE, and indeed at spiritual and paranormal activity and testimony in general, is that such phenomena are primarily of interest only to those who either already have a religious or spiritual belief, or are looking to such phenomena for empirical verification in order to provide ballast to, and prop up, a faith that is fragile. In a world where, as was discussed at the beginning of Chapter 1, there is often a suspicion in 'secular' circles, as typified by the recent proliferation of books on the New Atheism by the likes of Dawkins and Hitchens, that discourse involving religion has any positive value, it is easy to see why interest in afterlife-themed films should have received such limited critical attention. Despite the implicit assumption in many such films, *Flatliners* and *Dragonfly* (Tom Shadyac, 2002) being obvious cases in point, that there is a God, it is significant that not all recipients of NDEs themselves subscribe to the view that there is anything intrinsically theological or spiritual about their experiences. In the work of Michael Sabom, published in 1982, for example, it was found that the religious background of the subjects was not a factor in whether or not they had an NDE, and that the testimony of religious, agnostic and atheist individuals all tended to coincide (see Fox 2003: 32). Notwithstanding the fact that NDEs tend to correspond to the cultural and, where applicable, religious background of the experients – so that Christians may see the Being of Light as Christ, Buddhists as the Buddha, while for an atheist it may appear as a ball of light (Ellison 1995: 178) – there are remarkable uniformities between reports from different cultures (see Stevenson & Greyson 1996: 204). It may be too great a stretch to see such data as 'suggestive of the possibility of another realm of existence into which we pass at death' (Stevenson & Greyson 1996: 204), but there would at least appear to be grounds for supposing that, if the NDE were a purely psychological phenomenon, 'one would expect it to be much more culturally influenced than it seems to be' (Fenwick & Fenwick 1996: 149).

One piece of testimony which has, perhaps, been overlooked is that, as a result of the NDE experience, there are few reports of conversions – in other words, agnostics do not become believers, Christians do not become Jews and Protestants do not become Roman Catholics (see Fox 2003: 33). There may be a deepening of religious commitment on the part of those who already have a religious faith, but the prior religiosity of an individual is unlikely to have any bearing on either the likelihood or the depth of that experience.[4] Added to this is Ring's consideration that experients tend to feel more spiritual than religious, in the respect that the formal, institutional and external aspects of religious worship will weaken in importance (see Ring 1996: 189). Rather than subscribe to a particular denominational or sectarian affiliation, such recipients are 'more likely to express an unconditional belief in "life after death" for everyone and to endorse the conviction that not only will there be some form of post-mortem existence, but that "the Light" will be there for everyone at death' (Ring 1996: 189), irrespective of the specific theological or doctrinal belief – or lack thereof – that they had previously entertained regarding what happens beyond death. If, moreover, NDEs were only efficacious in corroborating or confirming an already existing faith, it is significant that many NDEs fail to conform to traditional Christian teachings concerning the Last Judgement, Hell and eternal torment. Calvinism, for example, has traditionally highlighted the deep fissure between those who are pre-destined, or elected, to eternal salvation and those who would be consigned for an eternity to eternal damnation, such that the death of Christ merely takes away the penalty of sins of those who have been predestined to salvation rather than on the whole human race (see Deacy & Ortiz 2008: 59). There is no such exclusivity at work in NDE testimony. Rather, aside from the discussion earlier in this chapter concerning negative NDEs, Walls is right that 'encounters with the being of light are characteristically positive experiences in which the subjects feel loved and accepted, regardless of their religious beliefs or lifestyle' (Walls 2002: 153).

Response to NDEs

None of this is to say, of course, that the existence of NDEs proves that there is an afterlife. Indeed, when the first reports on NDEs came to prominence in the 1970s, Zaleski makes the important point that in an 'effort to stem the tide of sensationalism, experts came forward from several quarters eager to attribute near-death experience to the mind-altering effects of drugs and anesthetics or to conditions which are part of the normal physiology of dying' (Zaleski 1995: 391), such as oxygen deprivation in the brain. Indeed, in Stanford's words, according to detractors of NDEs, 'The dying brain is starved of oxygen, which, in its turn, causes neurons or brain cells to rush about to try and make good the deficiency' (Stanford 2002: 322).[5] This 'last-gap' activity creates a sensation of light at the centre of our visual field' and which could be said to account for 'the white tunnel to heaven or the aura of God that many report having seen' (Stanford 2002: 322), not to mention the sensation of one's life-time experiences flashing before one's eyes in the form of the 'life review'. Indeed, this could be put down to how 'stimulation of cells in the temporal lobe of the brain can produce instant experiences that seem like the reliving of memories' (Blackmore 1996: 294). Feinstein has similarly argued that the 'reported sense of going down a tunnel and seeing brilliant light that does not hurt one's eyes has been explained as resulting directly from phosphenes stimulating the visual cortex' (Feinstein 1990: 257).

One of the most well-known critics of the NDE is Susan Blackmore, a humanist and atheist whose doctoral research in the late 1970s was in the area of para-psychology. Her *Beyond the Body: An Investigation of Out-of-the-Body Experiences*, which was first published in 1992, and *Dying to Live: Science and the Near-Death Experience*, published in 1993, amount to some of the most sustained and challenging research that has been published on how NDEs should be explained in purely psychological terms. She accounts for the out-of-body experience that first attends an alleged NDE by arguing that 'if the normal eye-level model of reality breaks down it can be replaced by a bird's eye model from memory and imagination' (Blackmore 1992: 280) which will then replace the existing model of reality and thus seem extremely real to us. The fact that some people undergoing an OBE have been able to hear what is taking place around them can be accounted for by such a reading in the respect that 'Since hearing is the last sense to go in unconsciousness, it makes sense that people near death can hear what is going on and seem to see it all from above' (Blackmore 1992: 280). Rather than proof of survival, Blackmore thinks that the OBE is best seen as an altered state of consciousness – effectively an hallucination, albeit one predicated on real information and events – in which one's 'imagination is more vividly experienced than it is in everyday life' (Blackmore 1992: 243).

One of the best analogies is with that of hallucinogenic drugs in the respect that, in the early stages of intoxication, tunnels, spirals and lattices are common and – in a manner consistent with Wright's and Labraccio's experiences in *Flatliners* – sometimes episodes from one's childhood are re-constructed and experienced as if re-lived. Blackmore also takes the line that just as in normal circumstances we have no diffi-culty in distinguishing reality from imagination, so in an alleged NDE our brains have to decide which model of reality seems to be the most convincing. During the NDE it may be that 'the tunnel being created by noise in the visual cortex will be the most stable model' (Blackmore 1996: 293) and so will seem authentic. In Blackmore's words, 'Fantasies and imagery might become more stable than the sensory model, and so seem real' (Blackmore 1996: 293). In terms of survival, Blackmore is emphatic:

'Nothing leaves the body in an OBE and so there is nothing to survive' (Blackmore 1992: 251). The fact that not all of those who have had an NDE were actually dead only reinforces the suggestion that they should not be cited as proof of an afterlife. In her words, 'Many very similar experiences are recorded of people who have taken certain drugs, were extremely tired, or, occasionally, were just carrying on their ordinary activities' (Blackmore 1996: 287). Blackmore's own position is remarkably akin to the Buddhist idea that there is no soul, or real, permanent self – there are 'no substances or essences ... that provide islands of permanence in a sea of impermanence' (Neumaier-Dargyay 2000: 89). In her words, 'We all too easily assume that we are some kind of persistent entity inhabiting a perishable body' (Blackmore 1996: 296). The NDE thus has the capacity to show us that our bodies are no more than 'a lump of flesh' and that we are 'not so important after all' – a realisation that she takes to be 'very freeing and enlightening' (Blackmore 1996: 296). Technically, therefore, NDEs take place neither in nor out of the body, in the respect that, for Blackmore, 'neither experiences nor selves have any location' and it is 'finally death that dissolves the illusion that we are a solid self inside a body' (Blackmore 1996: 296).

The fact that all of those individuals who have had NDEs were resuscitated also goes some way towards showing that it is difficult to extrapolate too much from the testimony we have received from the likes of Moody and Ring. From within the Christian tradition, Hans Küng makes much of this lack of correspondence between empirical data and proof of survival. As he puts it, 'These were experiences of people very close to real death, who mistakenly thought they were dying, but eventually did not die', and that 'Close as they were to the threshold of death, they never passed over it' (Küng 1984: 35). Accordingly, questions of eternal life cannot be deduced from NDE testimony. For Küng, such accounts 'do not settle the question of where the dying person goes: into non-being or into new being' (Küng 1984: 36). Although he concedes that 'Moody and numerous like-minded people deserve respect when, as Christians, they advocate belief in an eternal life', Küng takes the line that, when considered more closely, 'their arguments ... are inadequate and refer only to the present time and not to eternity' (Küng 1984: 36). In his words, 'all the phenomena of light, however striking, do not amount to a proof or even to an indication of an entry into a bright eternal light' (Küng 1984: 36). Until or unless we therefore come to a firm definition of death, the jury is necessarily going to be out. As Robert Kastenbaum sees it, moreover, all we have at present 'is a set of competing definitions and views' in which the possibility can even be entertained that 'death might be considered to be a matter of degree', or that it 'might even take more than one form' (Kastenbaum 1996: 259). As things stand, the quantity of NDE data that has been amassed tells us little about the possibility of survival: 'Ten thousand reports are no better than ten reports if they are offered simply as further examples of the fact that some people believed they have died and come back to life, rather improved for the experience' (Kastenbaum 1996: 260). The fact that many people who return from a close encounter with death did not have an NDE further casts doubt about the meaning of the evidence, a problem compounded by the fact that, according to Kastenbaum, 'People who were actually close to possible death have been found less likely to report an NDE than those who were less endangered' (Kastenbaum 1996: 261). Consequently, it would be spurious to infer that those who die and do not return to recount their experiences have actually survived death; quite simply, 'NDE research has provided no evidence for this proposition' (Kastenbaum 1996: 261).

One possible naturalistic, reductionistic explanation for NDEs is that a process of depersonalisation has taken place. According to such a picture, when confronted with an environment that is unfamiliar to us and which is the antithesis of life, a person psychologically conceives of an afterlife state. Such a process 'might be mediated by the same neural mechanism whose function it is to help the organism deal with danger by intensifying alertness while at the same time inhibiting potentially disorganizing emotion' (Kastenbaum 1996: 262). In other words, a mental state is brought about which enables us 'to remain calm and effective in the midst of a crisis' (Kastenbaum 1996: 262). This state of affairs is realised on screen in Peter Weir's *Fearless* (1993), in which Max Klein (Jeff Bridges), a neurotic and nervous San Francisco architect, is psychologically transformed by experiencing a plane crash in which his business partner and many other passengers are killed when, in the seconds before impact, he realises that he no longer has a fear of death. In the words of one reviewer, 'even as he strides through the physical world, he somehow makes us believe he has transcended it' (Fox & McDonagh 2003: 232). In his *Time Out* review, Geoff Andrew specifically identifies Klein's experience as an NDE, and refers to him as 'reborn' and as 'afraid of nothing' (Andrew 2001: 377). Indeed, we see Klein, with self-assurance, walking across a busy road in front of oncoming traffic, standing on the top of a roof of a high-rise building, and eating strawberries despite hitherto being allergic to them (they would bring about life-threatening convulsions). Discovering this new heroic calm, Klein would seem to have entered 'an exalted state in which he feels that he has "passed through death" and believes that nothing can harm him' (Elley 1994: 290). Such a scenario would seem to tie in with Kastenbaum's claim that the 'experiential state that is known as an NDE tends to occur when the individual can do nothing directly to improve his or her chances of surviving the crisis', and in which the 'sense of serenity associated with an NDE serves to quiet the nervous system and conserve energy' (Kastenbaum 1996: 262). In short, as with Max Klein in Weir's haunting, mystical treatise on the possibility of transcending death, when we find that we are powerless to do anything in the midst of a life-threatening or dangerous situation, 'it is time to take refuge in a pleasantly tinged state of withdrawal' (Kastenbaum 1996: 262). Ruffles refers to a similar dynamic in the case of *The Wizard of Oz* (Victor Fleming, 1939), in the respect that, rather than a transcendent experience as such, Dorothy Gale (Judy Garland) undergoes an NDE induced by the perception of danger, in which, for example, the ball of light with which the Witch of the North comes and goes 'might elsewhere be seen as divine conveyance' (Ruffles 2004: 126). On such a naturalistic reading, it may be that the traumatic episode Dorothy witnesses stimulates the production of brain opiates known as endorphins, in which a morphine-like substance is released by the brain in order to alleviate distress.

Persuasive though such arguments may be, however, many theologians are nevertheless unimpressed by such reductionistic approaches, in which all aspects of the human consciousness are reduced to materialistic and biological explanations. For such theologians, NDEs have been experienced by individuals with flat EEGs – for whom, in other words, all brain activity has ceased – and if the experiences concerned were merely psychologically-induced phenomena then they would, necessarily, show up as brain-wave activity (see Stanford 2002: 322). Although, as Ring concedes, 'the idea of life after death no longer fits with our postmodern, secular view of things', the NDE has emerged in recent decades 'as a subject of serious scientific research' (Ring 1990: 205). One of the most recent such research projects has taken place at Singleton and Morriston Hospitals in Swansea by Penny Sartori, an intensive care nurse who has carried out the largest and first long-term clinical study in the UK of NDEs within an Intensive Therapy Unit. Sartori wrote up her findings for her doctoral work in Lampeter, subsequently published as *Near-Death Experiences of Hospitalized Intensive Care Patients*, in which she reports 15 accounts, mainly from heart attack patients, of NDEs, which include the characteristic features of out-of-body experiences (in which the individuals floated above themselves and were able to accurately report back on what they had observed in the room despite being unconscious and having their eyes closed), entering a tunnel at the end of which was an incandescent light, and meeting loved ones who had already passed away. Despite taking into account the effect of endorphins and other physiological explanations, Sartori concluded, in an interview for the BBC News web site in 2008, that 'All the current sceptical arguments against near-death experiences were not supported by the research' (BBC News 2008 (a): <news.bbc.co.uk/1/hi/wales/7463606.stm>). What is particularly striking in her research is that patients were able to supply a correct description of how they were resuscitated, whereas when she asked patients who had been resuscitated without having had an NDE how they thought they had been revived they had no idea and their proposed reconstructions were wide of the mark (see Sartori 2008: 212–15). Such research corroborates Tart's assertion that 'the experiments in parapsychology are generally far better quality experiments than in ordinary branches of science, because the criticism has been so intense that the methodology has gotten extremely good' (Tart 1996: 323). Ring also goes so far as to claim that the NDE is quite subversive in the respect that it threatens 'to undermine our hard-won secular and scientific worldview' (Ring 1990: 205).

The straightforward and uncritical assumption that only a materialistic world-view holds sway is thus challenged by NDE testimony. When filmmakers draw upon such themes as telepathy (*The Shining* [Stanley Kubrick, 1980]), clairvoyance (*The Gift* [Sam Raimi, 2000]), séances (*Séance on a Wet Afternoon* [Bryan Forbes, 1964]), precognition (*Minority Report* [Steven Spielberg, 2002]), telekinesis (*Carrie* [Brian De Palma, 1976]) and psychokinesis (*The Fury* [Brian De Palma, 1978]), even if it is the case that the question of surviving death is no more than peripheral to these pictures, the fact that psychic phenomena are being treated at all goes some way towards corroborating Doore's claim that 'the heyday of materialism seems to be waning' (Doore 1990: 3). It is also very much in keeping with Tart's conviction that there are grounds for refuting 'the claim of materialistic science that survival of consciousness after death is impossible in principle' (Tart 1990: 141). While Fox is quite right that, to date, despite what is now thirty years' worth of near-death studies, 'the question as to whether the NDE *does* prove some form of body-soul dualism has yet to be fully answered to everybody's satisfaction', and that 'no researcher has provided evidence for such an assertion of an acceptable standard which would put the matter beyond doubt' (Fox 2003: 340), we seem to have moved on a long way from the 1950s when, as Doore points out, 'virtually all reputable scientists and philosophers subscribed to a strictly materialistic worldview' (Doore 1990: 3). According to such a way of thinking, to 'profess a serious belief in the possibility of survival after death was, in effect, a form of heresy, a straying from the official dogma, and automatically relegated one to the status of crank' (Doore 1990: 3). The position of many naturalists such as Blackmore, despite the eloquence and rigour of their work, is in my view ultimately unsatisfactory, when one considers the lack of empirical evidence for their findings. As Lester sees it, in a recent publication, Blackmore 'presents no studies (methodologically sound or unsound) comparing the visions produced by opiates and endorphins with near-death experiences' and, in view of one of the physicalist arguments that she has adduced, 'presents no studies comparing the visual effects produced by disinhibition of the visual cortex and near-death experiences' (Lester 2005: 88). There is also something quite inconsistent about Blackmore's position, as when she attempts to explain away OBEs by saying that on the grounds that only an eye can perceive then the body on the bed must be using some form of extra-sensory perception, such as telepathy or clairvoyance, to be able to identify what is taking place. As Badham puts it, this supposes 'that the deeply unconscious physical brain of a dying person is somehow able to perform feats of ESP which far transcend the abilities of all the most famous ESP experimenters in good health' (Badham & Badham 1984: 77). And, of course, there is also the irony that ESP is antithetical to the very materialist position to which Blackmore subscribes, thus making her argument somewhat arbitrary.

At the same time, we must not allow ourselves to get carried away (one way or the other). Even Lester, who looks in detail at the empirical case for survival in his book *Is There Life After Death?: An Examination of the Empirical Evidence*, reaches what is ultimately an agnostic and non-committal conclusion. In his words, 'the research reviewed in this book fails to be convincing that there is a life after death' (Lester 2005: 214). The fact that the jury is still out suggests that, rather than close down the debate, Fox is right when he counsels that 'there is still a colossal amount of near-death research to be done by persons working within very many academic disciplines' (Fox 2003: 347). The disciplinary areas Fox has in mind include theology and religious studies, with particular attention to phenomenological approaches within the study of religion, which, he indicates, can help ensure that neuroscientific approaches restrict themselves to producing theoretical frameworks which do justice to actual peoples' experiences. He also has in mind such sub-fields as the psychology, sociology and philosophy of religion, in which the latter can, for example, test the epistemological accuracy and phenomenological cogency of the claim that a common core underlies the varieties of NDEs. There is no reason, however, why the field of theology/religion and film should not also be added to this list. Fox is undoubtedly right that 'sensible academic disciplines have long shown themselves to be wary of entering into contexts where parapsychological claims are at stake and are under investigation' (Fox 2003: 358). But, the fact that filmmakers are increasingly interested in exploring the phenomena of NDEs and the afterlife – at the time of writing in December 2009 one of the most anticipated films of the new season is Peter Jackson's *The Lovely Bones* (2009) in which a young girl who has been murdered watches over her family, as well as the man who killed her, from what she calls 'the blue horizon between heaven and earth' – does suggest that theologians and others have a responsibility to take such endeavours seriously.

Mind-dependent worlds

Another contested area of scholarship entails the relationship between posthumous personal identity and memory. If we are to survive bodily death then it is at least implicitly supposed that, although the brain has ceased to function, some form of memory from our previous lives has been, or is capable of being, carried over to the next life. Such a picture is akin to that of David Aames in *Vanilla Sky* for whom, while his body lies in a state of suspended animation, it is his memories of a former life that sustain and inform his new mind-dependent dreamscape. Underlying this way of thinking is the non-materialist premise that what ultimately makes me 'me' is not, as Badham puts it, 'my external appearance, to which I may be relatively indifferent, or even my characteristic behavioural patterns of which others may be more conscious than myself' (Badham & Badham 1984: 10). Rather, 'it is that I am the subject of the thoughts, feelings, memories and intentions of which I am aware' (Badham & Badham 1984: 10). In short, no matter how strongly disposed we may be to evaluate other people on the basis of external, physical appearances – their particular facial characteristics, the size or shape of their bodies, the cost or design of their shoes, their distinctive style of dress, whether they wear tattoos or have any body piercings are often the first things we look at when trying to form an impression of a person – this is not usually the way in which we tend to identify or adjudicate ourselves. It is our thinking, feeling and self-awareness that is more likely to constitute self-identity, to the point that 'if my memories, thought-processes and feelings were all taken away from my body I would not mind what happens to it' (Badham & Badham 1984: 11). Indeed, Badham continues, 'The flames of the crematorium will not torture "me" for "I" shall not be there' (Badham & Badham 1984: 11). As when in dreams it is sometimes possible for one to identify the self with a different embodiment or historical milieu – we might find ourselves in a dream as a pop star from the 1960s or as a composer from the nineteenth century, or even as a specific historical figure, such as Napolean Bonaparte, George Washington or even Adolf Hitler, even if, in our waking reality, the ability to sing, write music, or lead a nation or army (whether democratically or despotically), is not our most customary talent or trait – then so it is not unintelligible 'to identify the self with a different embodiment and a different historical setting in a life after death' (Badham & Badham 1984: 12).

Zaleski goes even further, here, and attests that memory is 'the key not only to identity but also to a sense of wholeness' (Zaleski 1995: 400). We can also cite

Augustine in this regard for whom in an otherwise fragmented existence, whereupon 'I have been severed amid times, whose order I know not; and my thoughts, even the inmost bowels of my soul, are rent and mangled with tumultuous varieties' (Augustine 1969: 228),[6] it is through the gift of memory that we are able to experience continuity. Memory thus has a salvific and healing dimension, on such a reading. Similar motifs can also be found in Judaism, where it is the memory of past sins (albeit in the context of the nation of Israel rather than the individual *per se*) that the redemption of the people can be facilitated, as when in the Book of Judges we learn that 'the people of Israel did what was evil in the sight of the Lord' (Judges 2:11) and needed to remember and learn from previous experience that 'going after other gods, serving them and bowing down to them' (Judges 2:19) would inevitably result in punishment, and, if not outright destruction, then at least the dispersal of the people of Israel (a forerunner to the Exile, indeed). In the Tibetan Book of the Dead, also – a post-mortem guidebook written by Tibetan monks for fellow monks and devout lay people to enable them to incorporate a lifetime of spiritual practice into and beyond death (see Levine 1990: 227f.) – the emotional response a dead person has to the memory fragments of their past life provides the foundation for the new life to come (see Neumaier-Dargyay 2000: 99). This is very similar to al-Ghazali's description in Islam of the next stage of our existence as the mind-dependent state of *Barzakh* which is shaped by our thoughts and feelings, in which we are enabled to reflect upon our past life before the Day of Resurrection (see Badham 1995: 121). Badham also likens the process to the ancient Hindu concept of a world of desire, *Koma Loka*, 'which is understood as a mind-dependent state reflecting our desires and memories' (Badham 1995: 121). In all these instances, it is our memories, thoughts and feelings, including an ability to reflect upon and learn from our past lives, that thus make us who we are, rather than bodily or fleshly continuity as such.

Such a perspective finds a strong expression not only in theological accounts but in the contested discourse of parapsychology. The Society for Psychical Research was founded in Britain in 1882 for the scientific study of parapsychological phenomena, with its American counterpart established three years later, yet within scholarly circles such data is at best peripheral. While it is not unexpected that those more materialist-minded critics who doubt the legitimacy of NDE testimony also have no interest in the findings of paranormal explorations, there are some notable exceptions. The physicist-turned-philosopher C.D. Broad was both President of the Society for Psychical Research in 1935 and 1958 and Professor of Moral Philosophy at Cambridge from 1933 to 1953. In Broad's words:

> It has always seemed to me most strange and most deplorable that the vast majority of philosophers and psychologists should utterly ignore the strong *prima facie* case that exists for the occurrence of many supernormal phenomena which, if genuine, must profoundly affect our theories of the human mind, its cognitive powers, and its relation to the human body.
>
> *(in Lorimer 1984: 151)*

Indeed, for Broad, philosophers cannot even properly deal with questions of mind–body dualism unless they are prepared to take psychical data seriously, including that of telepathy, clairvoyance, precognition and mediumistic communications, to the point that 'apart from these phenomena there is nothing whatever to support the dualist view that a man's mind or personality can operate independently of the body' (Lorimer 1984: 151). For John Beloff, also, who was responsible for pioneering the academic study of parapsychology in Britain (see Braude 2006: <www.guardian.co.uk/science/2006/jul/04/obituaries.guardianobituaries>), paranormal events 'are, in fact, the only *prima facie* empirical evidence we have for postulating a mind-matter interaction' (in Lorimer 1984: 157). Beloff was based in Edinburgh, where he supervised several doctoral theses in the area of parapsychology and was instrumental in establishing the Koestler Parapsychology Unit within Edinburgh University's Department of Psychology which continues to this day to research the possible existence of psychic activity and belief in the paranormal (see <www.koestler-parapsychology.psy.ed.ac.uk>). Although, as Stephen Braude wrote in his obituary of Beloff in 2006, 'he never overtly encountered the paranormal first-hand' and 'never succeeded in obtaining evidence for psychic functioning in his own experiments, he saw no choice but to accept at least some of the evidence for ESP, PK [psychokinesis], and survival of death' (Braude 2006: <www.guardian.co.uk/science/2006/jul/04/obituaries.guardianobituaries>). Beloff did not have any particular theological axe to grind and openly acknowledged that 'evidence for the paranormal is still, undoubtedly, highly unsatisfactory on many counts' (in Lorimer 1984: 157). Nonetheless, he took the line that empirical data made it 'no longer reasonable to doubt that some paranormal events do sometimes occur' (in Lorimer 1984: 157).

Henry H. Price is another key figure in this area, having been not only President of the Society for Psychical Research from 1939–41 but Wykeham Professor of Logic at Oxford between 1935 and 1959. Rather than a dubious theorist, 'Price was highly respected in both areas of his work, frequently quoted by those who have followed after' (Dilley 1995: xix). Indeed, Frank Dilley identifies Price as 'clearly one of a mere handful of modern western philosophers who have addressed' (Dilley 1995: x) issues of psychical research and parapsychology, and Lorimer attests that his 'importance lies not just in his critique of materialist theories of mind, but also in being a philosopher of the first rank who appreciated the implications of psychical research for philosophy' (Lorimer 1984: 150). Quite simply, for Price, 'philosophers ought to take an interest in Psychical Research', and 'if they do not, they are not doing their job' (Price 1995 [a]: 39). Price's position is thus quite similar in essence to Alan Gauld's claim, in a 1982 book entitled *Mediumship and Survival: A Century of Investigations*, that it is fallacious to take the line, perhaps best epitomised by the eighteenth-century Scottish philosopher David Hume, that 'whenever we encounter supposed evidence for a paranormal event, we are always justified in dismissing that evidence' (Gauld 1982: 10). According to Gauld, 'there can be no law of nature that is so solidly established as to be immune from revision' (Gauld 1982: 10). It was because the 'theoretical side of psychical research has lagged far behind the evidential side' that, in Price's own words, 'the evidence itself is still ignored by so many, and especially by so many highly educated people' (Price 1995 [b]: 61). Price believed that if materialism were true then there would be no scope at all for telepathy to happen – 'But it does happen. So there must be something seriously wrong with the materialistic theory' (in Lorimer 1984: 149). The implications for science and religion are thus far-reaching, and, according to Price, 'we shall have to conclude that psychical research is one of the most important branches of investigation that the human mind has ever undertaken' (in Lorimer 1984: 149). What psychical research therefore does 'is to diminish or perhaps even to remove the chief obstacle which prevents the claims of religious people from being taken seriously', namely, 'the Materialistic conception of human nature' (Price 1995 [c]: 16).

Price's contribution to the present debate is an important one as, for him, if there is to be any personal survival beyond death he proposed that it is our memories that are to play an instrumental role in that process. Whereas in this life, in our normal waking consciousness, we are circumscribed by physical objects, and our sense organs and nervous system all testify to the extent to which we are embodied beings, in the next life we would be entirely dependent on experiences and states of consciousness which, in a manner akin to when we dream in this life, are fashioned by our minds and imagination. As Price put it, 'in the next life mental imagery will play the part which sense-perception plays in this one' (Price 1995 [d]: 266). On this reading, 'The point of life in this present world, we might say, is to provide us with a stock of memories out of which an image world may be constructed when we are dead' (Price 1995 [d]: 266). Its very non-physicality should not deceive us into thinking that such a memory-oriented, mind-dependent world lacks credence. On the contrary, our dreams, for example, may not exist in physical space, but this is not to say that the content of those dreams cannot be 'as vividly felt as any of our waking [experiences], or more so' (Price 1995 [d]: 266), or that they cannot 'force themselves on our attention when we would much rather be without them' (Price 1995 [d]: 267), as in the case of nightmares. Even though, when we are asleep, 'sensory stimuli are cut off, or at any rate are prevented from having their normal effects upon our brain-centres' (Price 1973: 24), this does not prevent us from having experiences. There may be no spatial quality to our dreams as such – they do not exist in any kind of physical or public space, nor do they stand in any 'continuous ascertainable relation to other entities' (Lewis 1973: 148) – but, psychologically, the things I am dreaming about, whether a building, dragon, cat, fire, sunny beach, aeroplane journey, movie star or deceased family member, really do exist, and are no less real to me. The afterlife is, for Price, analogous to our dreams, in that it is comprised of a world of memories and mental images which only appear to be fanciful or, indeed, discontinuous from present existence when judged by what he calls 'the irrelevant standard of the laws of physics' (Price 1995 [d]: 267). If life is simply defined 'in terms of certain very complicated physico-chemical processes, as some people would, then of course life after death is by definition impossible, because there is no longer anything to be alive' (Price 1973: 27). Price's premise is, however, that we could still feel alive provided that we experienced memories, emotions and wishes – 'even if no organic sensations accompanied these experiences, as they do now' (Price 1973: 28).

Though a psychological rather than a material world, Price held that it might '*seem to be physical to those who experience it*' in the respect that the 'image-objects which compose it might appear very like physical objects, as dream objects often do now', even to the point that 'we might find it difficult at first to realize that we were dead' (Price 1995 [d]: 267). This is very much the way in which Chris Nielson in *What Dreams May Come* first apprehends the afterlife. In the novel by Richard Matheson on which the film is based, Nielson communicates from the afterlife that 'what transpires in the mind is just as real as any flesh and blood occurrence' and that '[w]hat had only been imagination in life now became tangible, each fantasy a full reality' (Matheson 2008: 30). In language redolent of Price, Matheson's Chris Nielson discovers Heaven to be 'a state of mind' in which, to quote from the novel,

> what you think *does* become your world ... since death is a refocusing of consciousness from physical reality to mental ... Does a man's existence change in any way when he removes his overcoat? Neither does it change when death removes the overcoat of his body. He's still the same person ... Death is merely continuation at another level.
>
> *(Matheson 2008: 61)*

There are certainly empirical grounds for subscribing to such a position, as when parapsychological data, such as from mediumship, indicates that 'the newly dead have no notion of the fact that they are dead, and may acquire this knowledge only slowly as they are assisted by the discarnate souls around them' (Botting 1991: 123–24). Such an empirical ballast to Price's theory is provided by Heather Botting, whose Master's thesis, entitled 'Intimations of Immortality: An Analysis of the Basis of Belief in an Afterlife', was published by the University of Calgary in 1991. Looking at reported communications from soldiers who were killed in battle, Botting has found testimony which has shown that 'A soldier shot in battle at the bottom of a hill may charge up the hill with his comrades only to realise after the fact that he has left his physical body lying on the ground behind him' (Botting 1991: 134). Citing in particular from a source published in 1922, we learn that, after waking from a deep sleep, a deceased soldier got to his feet and, looking down, saw his body lying among many others on the ground. The testimony continues:

> Soon I found myself among thousands in a similar mental state: none knew just what had happened. I did not know then, as I know now, that I always possessed a Spirit Body and that the Physical Body was only the garment it wore in earth-life.
>
> *(Botting 1991: 135)*

In a number of afterlife-themed films, also, we find accounts which mirror this kind of evidence. When, for example, in *What Dreams May Come* Chris Nielson realises he is dead, the all-encompassing loss and displacement he feels at being separated from his wife and soul-mate, Annie, is very similar in form to the sorrow that the aforementioned soldier felt when learning, through mediumistic communication, that his bereaved wife was not coping at all well with his sudden departure: 'Her great grief, when she learned what had happened, bound me to her condition. We sorrowed together. I could not progress ... out of the dream-like "Hades" into "Paradise" ... or find happiness, until time had healed her sorrow' (Botting 1991: 135). In the film, Annie's grief becomes so intense that she decides to take her own life, precipitating a post-mortem odyssey on the part of Chris to rescue her from damnation. While the source that Botting cites contains no such Orpheus-like salvation motif, what they both have in common is the predilection identified by Price to ground the next life in a world in which the memories, thoughts, emotions and desires we had on earth are transposed to a purely mind-dependent realm where there is 'no reason why we should not be "as much alive", or at any rate *feel* as much alive ... as we do now in this present material world, which we perceive by means of our sense-organs and nervous systems' (Price 1973: 26). Indeed, it might very much be 'every bit as detailed, as vivid and as complex as the present perceptible world which we experience now' (Price 1995 [d]: 267).

One such manifestation of Price's mind-dependent world is in the aforementioned *Jacob's Ladder*, in which one possible reading of the film is that the protagonist, Jacob Singer, died in combat in Vietnam but does not realise this, so continuous and convincing are the set of experiences he is having in his post-mortem state vis-à-vis his pre-mortem memories of life in New York. When Price thus writes that a mind-dependent world 'would be dependent on the *memories* and *desires* of the persons who experienced it', which would in turn 'determine what sort of images they had' – such that, to use the analogy of painting, 'memory would provide the pigments, and desire would paint the picture' (Price 1973: 38) – it is possible to see how Singer's inability to progress in his post-death environment can be accounted for by his unhealthy attachment to the memories surrounding the death of his young son from before the time he was sent to Vietnam. There is an analogy also with *Vanilla Sky* in the respect that Aames is incapable of distinguishing between what happened on earth prior to his decision to enrol as a member of Life Extension Corporation, which has rendered him comatose for the last 150 years of earth time, and his present mind-dependent dreamscape in which the guilt he feels at having been responsible for the death of one or other of his former girlfriends has infected every facet of his world. We know that his mind-dependent existence is qualitatively different in essence from his life on earth because there is no longer any spatial relation between his physical body (which is lying in a state of suspended animation) and the entities and persons about which he is dreaming or imagining. To this we could compare Hick's point, written in the context of Price's theory, that 'other "people" are only appearances that are not animated by independent centres of consciousness' (Hick 1976: 265–66), and that, in such a solipsistic mental world, the experient would not 'be interacting with realities external to his own mind' (Hick 1976: 268). Rather, the laws that operate in Aames' present environment are governed not by physics but by something more akin to Jungian or Freudian psychology (see Hick 1976: 268). Instead of perception there is imaging (cf. Price 1973: 33), and, rather than an actual movement in space, Aames' different experiences arise from changes in consciousness (see Deacy & Ortiz 2008: 194).

Accordingly, it is not difficult to construe traces in Aames' mind-dependent realm of what Price meant when he referred to the way in which desires which we may have repressed in this life might come to play an important part in the next one in determining the kind of images we will have after we die (see Price 1973: 37). No matter how 'real' or 'solid' the next life may seem to be to Aames, what happens to him in the film could also be said to tally with Hick's reading of Price that the mind-dependent world

> may however differ from our present world in the kinds of way [sic] in which the sequence and arrangement of events in our dreams is liable to differ from that of waking life, by exhibiting on occasion discontinuities and all sorts of sudden elisions and transformations.
>
> *(Hick 1976: 265)*

In Aames' case, the traumatic and guilt-ridden mind-dependent world that he inhabits throughout the film finds similar expression in Price's model. The more he tries to repress the memories of his hedonistic, irresponsible playboy past the greater is his paranoia and suicidal impulses. Similarly, as Price saw it, through a wish-fulfilment world, it does not thereby follow that the next world would necessarily be an agreeable place – indeed, it might be too bad, rather than too good, to be true (see Price 1973: 42). For Price, the 'world you would experience after death would depend upon the kind of person you are', so that the desires we are presently repressing 'will manifest themselves by appropriate images, and these images might be exceedingly horrifying' (Price 1973: 42) – worse, even, than the worst nightmare 'because the dreamer cannot wake up from it' (Price 1973: 43). The fact that Aames elects at the end (albeit unsuccessfully inasmuch as he seems to wake up, suggesting that the cycle is simply going to continue) to commit suicide, by jumping off the roof of a tall building, goes some way towards showing just how redemptively barren his life has been, and continues to be. Aside from the theistic question of whether, at the end of the day, we are 'dependent on the will of a Divine Creator' (Price 1973: 43), and so should thus see an external deity as being ultimately responsible for the quality of the post-mortem world that we inhabit, Price was markedly of the view that, in terms of his theory, 'everyone would experience an image-purgatory which exactly suits him', and that each 'man's purgatory would be just the automatic consequence of his own desires' (Price 1973: 43). It would therefore have a fundamentally objective dimension in the sense that it would be the out-growth of our character, represented to us in the form of dream-like images, and we would be confronted with such a world whether we liked it or not (see Price 1973: 45). Hywel Lewis similarly wrote in 1973 that 'The next world, if there is one, will be what it will be irrespective of our own desires', and that 'We have no reason to suppose that we shall fashion it, any more than we make our present world' (Lewis 1973: 155).

Of course, none of this proves that survival after death is inevitable. Price, indeed, saw the evidence as inconclusive, and was keen only on making the concept of another world intelligible (see Lorimer 1984: 150). As he put it, the aim was to show that 'there is nothing self-contradictory or logically absurd in the hypothesis that memories, desires and images can exist in the absence of a physical brain' (Price 1973: 39). Aldwinckle is similarly aware of the dangers involved in taking too dogmatic a line here: 'We have to admit that we do not know for certain whether the "self" can exist without a body of any kind', on the grounds that this 'would involve scientific and philosophical knowledge which modesty compels us to admit we do not at present have' (Aldwinckle 1972: 98–99). There is also the consideration, of course, that no matter how persuasive talk of a mind-dependent world may be, Penelhum is right that it is very difficult for us to imagine what it would be like not to have a body (see Penelhum 2000: 45). We are, after all, embodied beings, and it is significant to this end that neither Price's philosophy nor those films which could be interpreted as bearing witness to some form of a mind-dependent world are exactly devoid of a corporeal dimension. The next life may be mind-dependent, but material and bodily char-acteristics are still being ascribed to the souls of those that die. It is not therefore surprising that Penelhum should feel more inclined to 'defend the doctrine of resur-rection in its starkest form, than to try to mix it in with the belief in disembodied spirits' (Penelhum 2000: 46). Even Paul Badham, who is a keen advocate on the whole of Price's mind-dependent theory, acknowledges that there are potential dif-ficulties with it. For, unless there is new and fresh input after we die, and we do not simply find ourselves – like David Aames and, to a lesser extent, in that at the end of *Jacob's Ladder* the protagonist does seem to progress to a new stage of post-mortem existence, Jacob Singer – re-visiting past traumas from our time on earth, 'a mind-dependent world might eventually come to seem futile and empty' (Badham 1976: 120). For John Hick, likewise, 'All that a wish-fulfilment world would seem able to do in the way of character-formation would be to refine and purify the structure of desires and dispositions that had already been developed on earth' (Hick 1976: 274). Only if its possibilities were 'open-ended' and there were shown to be 'vast depths of reality totally beyond our present range of experience' (Hick 1976: 275) does Hick find a mind-dependent world to have any saliency or value.

Another potential difficulty with Price's model is that the analogy with dreaming, though innovative, breaks down in one crucial respect. When we are awake, in present existence, we know when we are drawing on memories. But this is not the case when we are asleep and dreaming (see Tart 1990: 148). In Tart's words, 'The conventional view of dreaming is that we construct all the objects in our dream world from memory images, yet dreaming is experienced as *perceiving*, not as *remembering*' (Tart 1990: 148). To give an example, when we are dreaming we may not be recollecting an event that took place in our actual past, but we may actually believe that we have become some other person, even someone who, as my earlier examples of Napolean Bonaparte and Adolf Hitler might suggest, we have never even known, whose values we do not share, and who do not even speak the same language as ourselves. As Tart puts it:

> Our sense of identity, our emotions, and our evaluation processes can also operate quite differently while we are dreaming. Sometimes in dreams we seem

to be having experiences that belong to another person – someone with different emotional, evaluative, and intellectual reactions to events. Things that make sense by dream standards may be completely absurd or incoherent by waking-state standards.

(Tart 1990: 148)

On this basis, a mind-dependent world that is akin to the landscape of our dreams has the penchant to be unstable and unpredictable when considered from the point of view of our current, earthbound waking consciousness, which depends for its stability on a number of body-based processes (see Tart 1990: 151). Unless, therefore, what Tart refers to as 'something very analogous to an external world and a body is provided in the after-death state' (Tart 1990: 151), it is unclear whether that which survives can meaningfully be said to be 'me'.

The jury is out, therefore, as to whether Price's model should be taken seriously within either theological or cinematic accounts of the content and form of the afterlife. What works in its favour, however, is the inclusive nature of its attempted delineation of what the afterlife will look like, in the respect that, as with so many afterlife-themed films, including *What Dreams May Come* and *Vanilla Sky*, there is no attempt to conform to any pre-established theological or religious doctrinal position or to allow a particular religious agenda to sneak unnoticed through the back door. Price's theory of a mind-dependent world is not dependent upon a theistic world-view, even though it is not incompatible with belief in a divine Creator, as when Hick writes, in relation to Price's model, that 'we might perhaps sooner or later be prompted by these purgatorial experiences to desire something better, to hunger and thirst after righteousness, and thus to gravitate by the power of our own desiring ... to enter into what christian [sic] tradition has called the vision of God' (Hick 1976: 266–67). In this respect, there is a clear compatibility between Hick's reading of Price and Matthew's Gospel where, in the Sermon on the Mount, Jesus teaches his followers that 'Blessed are those who hunger and thirst after righteousness, for they shall be satisfied' (Matthew 5:6). At the same time, Price's theory could be said to be particularly conducive to a Hindu or Buddhist worldview, as when Hick presents the alternative scenario that, rather than 'gravitate by the power of our own desiring to other and higher worlds', we might, in Eastern terms, find that 'eventually desire becomes satisfied and dies and that our individual personal life fades with it, absorbed into a supra-personal state of nirvana' (Hick 1976: 267). The fact that the 'contemporary preoccupation with evidences for conscious life outside of the body and even beyond death', such as through séances, telepathy, mediumistic communications and other psychic phenomena, may 'also be found, in many cases, to be held by atheists' further demonstrates that, in Anderson's words, '[b]elief in God is not now necessary to support belief in life after death as a personal and conscious existence of the same person' (Anderson 1986: 107). We can add to this the consideration that many spiritualists have opted to adopt more neutral terms such as 'otherworld', 'afterlife' and 'summerland' to refer to the concept of 'heaven' (see McDannell & Lang 1990: 295) – a concept which is, perhaps, rather too laden with Christian connotations. 'summerland', together with 'Homeland' and 'Harvest', is explicitly used, moreover, by Matheson in his novel *What Dreams May Come* (see e.g. Matheson 2008: 60, 83). We can thus begin to see just how Price's theory has the capacity to resonate with a wide constituency of opinion, both religious and non-religious in nature, in addition to being congruent with several cinematic treatments of the afterlife.

4

TOWARDS A CINEMATIC REALISED ESCHATOLOGY

The afterlife as now

As the discussion to date has established, even when films are not explicitly focused on questions pertaining to resurrection, immortality or eternal life, it does not thereby follow that they have no eschatological scaffolding. On the contrary, even those films that are ostensibly about the afterlife are firmly centred on present, this-worldly dynamics. A case in point is *Dragonfly* (Tom Shadyac, 2002), in which a non-believing, rationalist Chicago Emergency Room doctor, Joe Darrow (Kevin Costner), receives other-worldly communications from his wife, Emily (Susanna Thompson), who died, while heavily pregnant, following a coach crash in Venezuela where she was on a Red Cross mission to help the native Yanomami tribal community. Pivotal though NDE testimony is in *Dragonfly*, as when Emily's former paediatric oncology patients return from their brushes with death to pass on messages she has given them, and despite introducing a supporting character, a Catholic nun, Sister Madeline (Linda Hunt), who has conducted research into NDEs among intensive care patients at Chicago Memorial Hospital, the film's denouement is strictly terrestrial in form. We see this when, in the film's climax, Joe undertakes a perilous mission into the Venezuelan jungle to claim the daughter he did not even know existed. Significantly, the language used at one point in the film is redolent of H.H. Price's concept of a mind-dependent world. The scene in question takes place when Costner's character meets with Sister Madeline in a Catholic church, where he is instructed that 'if we can create this world with what we imagine, why not the next?' As the film unfolds, however, it is apparent that any notion of continuing existence beyond physical death is only important insofar as it sheds light on our present lives in the here and now. To an extent, of course, this is inevitable. The only way in which we can articulate the form that life after death will take is by using the vocabulary and imagery with which we are familiar in our present experience. As Penelhum puts it, 'references to the Next World cannot be intelligible for us unless it is possible to use the language of our world of things and persons to describe it' (Penelhum 1970: 46). No matter how advanced or sophisticated our understanding of a future life may be, we are always going to be circumscribed by our human categories and ways of thinking. As we shall see in more detail in Chapter 5, when it comes to the way we conceive of 'heaven', our vocabulary necessarily has its limitations, such that as Jeffery Burton Russell attests 'we have no way of discussing heaven except in the only speech we know, human language' (Russell 1997: 6). Since '[h]eaven itself cannot be described' (Russell 1997: 3), it is not really surprising that filmmakers as well as theologians should have resorted to employing this-worldly and present-oriented visions and metaphors to refer to what will happen after we die.

However, there is invariably going to be a fine line between using earthly language to refer to something that is quintessentially future in scope[1] and according ultimate value and worth to those human constructions themselves. No matter how substantially eschatological visions 'represent a transformation of this' present dimension of existence 'or a Utopian resolution of inherent problems', the very fact that such visions tend to be 'rooted in present reality' (Chester 2004: 246) makes it inevitable that the afterlife may end up coming to be seen for some people as a mere extension of human hopes, fears and aspirations. In traditional terms, Paul Badham may be completely right when he maintains that 'the language of resurrection and immortality has no clear meaning or agreed usage outside the context of belief in life after death, and that language of eternal life although referring in part to present experience nevertheless ... always conveys a further connotation of future destiny' (Badham & Badham 1984: 36). But, theologians cannot ignore the fact that, both in modern theology and in popular culture, there have been some very notable instances in which the line of demarcation between the present and the future has proven to be a very permeable one indeed. Such excursions will be outlined in this chapter, with a view to enquiring into whether eschatological language is being evacuated and excised of its authentic meaning if any future *telos* or goal is substituted for a purely terrestrial frame of reference.

To this end, Aldwinckle may well speak for many when he affirms that the

> transformation of institutions and social life in this world, important as this is as an essential part of the Christian hope, cannot be a substitute for the hope of the Christian for a real personal and corporate existence in Christ after death and when history has reached its divinely appointed End.
>
> *(Aldwinckle 1972: 167)*

Likewise, Polkinghorne and Welker might be correct when they attest that too much 'here and now' eschatology runs the risk of reducing the 'complexity of eschatological symbols to ciphers of inner self-consciousness' (Polkinghorne & Welker 2000: 3). However, with particular reference to the branch of theology known as realised eschatology, this chapter will explore whether there need be quite such a disjuncture between present and future expressions of eschatological language and, moreover, as to whether realised forms of eschatology have necessarily played such a subsidiary and lesser role during the course of Christian history vis-à-vis their more traditional counterparts. Might not those films which lay such a clear emphasis upon this-worldly fulfilments actually prove to be compatible with key tenets of much contemporary Christian theology, in which eternal life is believed to refer exclusively to the quality of experience within the present dimensions of space and time, without the postulate of an other-worldly hope or a life after death?

The origins of realised eschatology

Rather than a deviant or aberrant variety of eschatological expression, there are Christians today who construe eternal life as pertaining to a different quality of life in the here and now as opposed to something that solely delineates personal post-mortem survival (see Vardy 1995: 13). The origins of such a position can be traced back to the New Testament period itself, where, for St Paul, McGrath makes the astute point that although 'it is natural to think of heaven as a future entity, Paul's thinking appears to embrace both a future reality and a spiritual sphere or realm that coexists with the material world of space and time' (McGrath 2003: 164). In 1 Corinthians 1:18, for example, there is a discernibly present-oriented flavour to Paul's teaching that 'the word of the cross is folly to those who are perishing, but to us who are being saved it is the power of God'. Paul may not exactly affirm *this* world – there is never any doubt that he deemed death to be superior to what this life had to offer (see Walsh 2005: 84) – but in his letter to the Philippians Paul is nevertheless torn between his desire 'to depart and be with Christ' (Philippians 1:23) and remaining 'in the flesh' (Philippians 1:22, 24) in order to fulfil his obligations to the Christians at Philippi. While acknowledging that the former 'is far better' (Philippians 1:23), Paul concedes that he is 'hard pressed between the two' (Philippians 1:23) and that the latter, far from unworthy of his time and effort, 'means fruitful labour for me' (Philippians 1:22). This tension between the 'now' and the 'not yet', in which it could even be said that believers are 'in some way sharing in the life of heaven in the present', has led McGrath to conclude that it is 'very difficult to sustain the simple idea of heaven as something that will not come into being until the future, or that cannot be experienced in the present' (McGrath 2003: 165).

For Jesus, also, there are numerous references in the Gospels to how the Kingdom of God has a fundamentally present orientation, as when he instructs the Pharisees in Luke 17:20–21 that 'The Kingdom of God is not coming with signs to be observed' for it is 'in the midst of you'.[2] Despite the future, thorough-going eschatology ascribed to Jesus around the turn of the twentieth century by Albert Schweitzer and Johannes Weiss, according to which Jesus was an apocalyptic preacher and that everything that Jesus said and did was informed and imbued by such an apocalyptic mindset – even to the point that Jesus was 'portrayed as an alien figure, belonging to the bizarre world of Jewish apocalyptic, and having a fanatical and frenzied expectation of an imminent end' (Chester 2004: 249) – a number of New Testament scholars have painted a contrary picture. The theologian and New Testament specialist C.H. Dodd, for example, believed that, as Allison puts it, 'on the historical or mundane plane the kingdom had already arrived, or was already, so to speak, accessible' (Allison 1999: 269).

Accordingly, for Dodd, the 'supernatural order of life which the apocalyptists had predicted in terms of pure fantasy is now described as an actual fact of experience' (Dodd 1944: 65). His position was that by not engaging in 'the restless and impatient straining' after signs of the Second Coming, which 'turned faith to fantasy and enthusiasm into fanaticism', one is able to come to 'a fuller realization of all the depths and heights of the supernatural life here and now' (Dodd 1944: 150). Dodd even went as far as to say that 'it is surely clear that, for the New Testament writers in general, the *eschaton* has entered history; the hidden rule of God has been revealed; the Age to Come has come' (Dodd 1944: 85), such that 'He who believes *has* life eternal' (Dodd 1944: 86). Instead of the world coming to an end as such, Dodd held that, though life continues in a material and physical sense, and that on 'the empirical plane we still live the earthly life', the New Testament writers were nevertheless 'clear that history is henceforward qualitatively different from what it was before Christ's coming' (Dodd 1944: 88). In his words:

> no conception of Christianity as a religion is fully true to the New Testament which does not recognize that the 'Christian Era,' as we call it, marks an abrupt break in the relation in which the people of God, and, indeed, the whole human race, stands to the historical order.
>
> *(Dodd 1944: 88)*

Similarly, in terms of the demythologisation programme propounded by Rudolf Bultmann, arguably the greatest New Testament scholar of the twentieth century, 'There is nothing specifically Christian in the mythical view of the world as such. It is simply the cosmology of a pre-scientific age' (Bultmann 1972 [a]: 3). In an era in which we 'use electric light and the wireless' and 'avail ourselves of modern medical and surgical discoveries', Bultmann took the line that it is 'impossible' at the same time to 'believe in the New Testament world' (Bultmann 1972 [a]: 5) of miracles, angels, demons and spirits. Quite simply, 'Man's knowledge and mastery of the world have advanced to such an extent through science and technology that it is no longer possible for anyone seriously to hold the New Testament view of the world' (Bultmann 1972 [a]: 4). This is very much redolent of Dodd's claim that at the centre of the New Testament 'lies this alien, eschatological Gospel, completely out of touch … with our ways of thought' (Dodd 1944: 76). By his appropriation of Heideggerean existentialism, Bultmann took the line that the real and authentic focus of New Testament eschatology was directed not to the future but to the present, such that, in Henderson's words,

> when the Resurrection is preached to the man of to-day, it summons him here and now to be crucified with Christ by renouncing all claim to find security in the visible and the this-worldly and thereby to rise with Christ – again here and now – to what is his own real existence.
>
> *(Henderson 1963: 20)*

In the case of the Fourth Gospel, for example, Morgan interprets Bultmann's position as being that 'All the key Johannine concepts are shown to refer to human existence, understood in relation to God's eschatological self-revelation in Jesus' (Morgan 1998: 75). To give an example, when in the Prologue to John's Gospel we learn that 'The true light that enlightens every man was coming into the world' (John 1:9), Bultmann saw this not in spatial terms, in the sense of a supernatural redeemer-figure physically descending from the heavens down to the earth. Rather, he interpreted it in the sense of 'the state of having one's existence illumined, an illumination in and by which a man understands himself, achieves a self-understanding which opens up his "way" to him, guides all his conduct, and gives him clarity and assurance' (Bultmann 1976: 18). As opposed to seeing the Resurrection as either a past event (in terms of what happened on Calvary two thousand years ago) or as a future promise (in which believers can expect to be resurrected following Christ's Second Coming in glory on the clouds of heaven [see Mark 13:26]), Bultmann's focus was on 'the ever-present word of God' (Bultmann 1972 [b]: 193). In place of the imminent expectation of the end of the world and the establishment of the Kingdom of God, what is significant about Bultmann's method is the way in which everything points to 'the decisive eschatological event that has *already* taken place on the cross' (Chester 2004: 250). As he put it, 'Christ meets us in the word of preaching as one crucified and risen ... The faith of Easter is just this – faith in the word of preaching' (Bultmann 1972 [a]: 41).

The individual's existential hour of decision thus lies at the heart of New Testament eschatology in a manner not incongruent with Robert Jewett's reading of the trajectory of Phil Connors (Bill Murray) in the comedy film *Groundhog Day* (Harold Ramis, 1993). In line with the teaching adduced in Galatians 6:9 that 'let us not grow weary in doing good, for in its own time we shall reap a harvest if we do not give up', Jewett thinks that the 'arrogant, bitter, and cynical' (Jewett 1999: 89) protagonist of Ramis' film, who eventually 'gives up on the cycle of manipulation ... and begins to help other people' (Jewett 1999: 98) for the first time, throws light on the two Greek words for 'time' which can be found in the New Testament. These two words are *chronos*, which refers to chronological, linear time, and *kairos*, which refers to 'eschatologically fulfilled time', or 'time for decision' (Jewett 1999: 90). This links in with our discussion of Bultmann in that, for both St Paul and Phil Connors, 'the present moment of decision is fraught with significance' (Jewett 1999: 91). Jewett himself is more partial than I am to the idea that Paul's teaching was strictly future in scope. In his words, 'By placing their faith in Christ, [people] grasp the significance of the present routine because it leads to a future called "eternal life"' (Jewett 1999: 91). However, when he writes that 'In Paul's view, the way people respond to life in the present shapes the kind of future they will have' (Jewett 1999: 91), this corresponds both to the type of existentialist, realised eschatology held by Bultmann as well as how, for Phil Connors, to live according to the spirit is 'to find fulfillment in the midst of daily routines' (Jewett 1999: 92). Rather than wait until a future Judgement, the present moment has inherent value – according to 2 Corinthians 6:2, 'Behold, now is the acceptable time; behold, now is the day of salvation'. Admittedly, for Paul, it is difficult to separate this idea from the prospect of a future Judgement, as when in his first letter to the Corinthians Paul wrote:

> Therefore do not pronounce judgment before the time, before the Lord comes, who will bring to light the things now hidden in darkness and will disclose the purposes of the heart. Then every man will receive his commendation from God.
>
> *(1 Corinthians 4:5)*

In his first letter to the Thessalonians, also, Paul instructs his readers in decidedly future-oriented, apocalyptic language that 'the day of the Lord will come like a thief in the night', whereupon 'sudden destruction will come … and there will be no escape' (1 Thessalonians 5:2–3). Jewett also points out that even in Galatians 6:8, where Paul writes that 'he who sows to his own flesh will from the flesh reap corruption', '[m]ost commentators feel that "corruption" is used here in the sense of an eschatological judgment of "eternal damnation"' (Jewett 1999: 96), and, to paraphrase Ronald Fung, as physical death and disintegration from which there is no rising to eternal life (in Jewett 1999: 96). That said, Jewett does concede that in such passages as Romans 1:22 and 8:20–21, 'corruption is a present experience of futility', as well as, with reference to 1 Corinthians 5:5, 'alienation from the saved community'. He refers also to 1 Corinthians 10:11 which, in quite overt realised language, Paul indicates that the moment of decision lies in the here and now, as when he writes that it is upon the present generation that 'the end of the ages has come'.

To an extent, it is not surprising that the language of eschatology can be seen to have shifted in the New Testament from the future and towards the present. At the time of the Fall of Jerusalem in 70 CE and other occasions when members of the Christian community were being persecuted and morale was at a low ebb, it follows that expectations of an imminent *parousia*, or Second Coming of Christ, would have intensified. As Robert Strachan put it in his commentary on the Fourth Gospel, first published in 1917, 'the earliest Church had lived in hourly expectation of His coming, as their records showed' (Strachan 1920: 17). But, Christ's triumphant return did not materialise: 'Believers were dying, and He did not come' (Strachan 1920: 17). In view of the passage of time, Jane Smith is right when she argues that 'new theories had to be developed to account for the state of the soul in what came to be seen as a waiting period before the messianic age' (Smith 1989: 91). We thus have the situation today in which questions of eschatology can no longer credibly be construed in terms of *where* or *when* the Son of Man or the Kingdom of God is to appear in the future, as was the case for the first generation of Christians when the imminence of the Second Coming was all too real. For the Montanists of the second century, for instance, the 'heavenly city' of Jerusalem was due to appear visibly in the sky, before descending to the city of Pepuza at which location Christ's one thousand year reign would be established. In the words of the prophetess Priscilla, 'Christ came to me in the likeness of a woman, clad in a bright robe … and revealed that this place [Pepuza] is holy, and that here Jerusalem comes down from heaven' (in Stevenson 1992: 107). Today, in marked contrast, these are not spatial or geographical questions, but are more fittingly seen in terms of one's present behaviour and experience. When Jerry Walls thus writes that for many people today salvation is 'less and less conceived as a matter of eternal life, and more and more as a matter of personal fulfillment in this life', there is a biblical and theological antecedent to such a way of thinking, even if, as Walls continues, 'salvation comes to sound increasingly like a means of dealing with psychological problems, gaining in positive self-image, developing a better out-look on life' and 'liberation from oppression' (Walls 1992: 7).

Banal though such language may be, eschatological talk today is so far removed from its original future-oriented frame of reference that it is not altogether startling or wide of the mark when theologians and philosophers go so far as to suggest that belief in the survival of death need not even be deemed a necessary pre-requisite of belief in immortality. For D.Z. Phillips, for example, a Wittgensteinian philosopher based from 1965 until his death in 2006 at the University of Wales, Swansea, language pertaining to the soul, to immortality or to eternity referred not to a life beyond this one but could be better understood as an ethical matter of what we value here and now:

> Questions about the immortality of the soul are seen not to be questions con-
> cerning the extent of a man's life, and in particular concerning whether that life
> can extend beyond the grave, but questions concerning the kind of life a man
> is living.

> *(Phillips 1970: 49)*

That there has been a genuinely seismic shift in the way eschatology has been articulated in the modern world can also be seen with reference to Paul Tillich. In Aldwinckle's words, Tillich 'seems to be denying in a categorical way any idea of the preservation of the individuality of personal existence after death', to the point that immortality 'is not a natural quality of the human soul' (Aldwinckle 1972: 89). Rather, it is not the individual soul that is immortal but 'the spirit or the essence of being: not the essence of the *human* being but the essence of all being' (McDannell & Lang 1990: 351). As Tillich saw it, the language used in describing eternal life is necessarily symbolic and is not to be confused with the thing itself: 'Symbols such as life after death, immortality, reincarnation, heaven' are 'dangerously inadequate' (in McDannell & Lang 1990: 328).

There are also reports of clergy in the nineteenth and twentieth centuries fearing that if too great a discordance was set up between this present dimension of existence and talk of a future life after death then such a future hope would have only limited value. In the words of Presbyterian theologian William Adams Brown, for instance,

> How empty and shallow the heaven to which we have often been asked to
> look forward, a heaven of untroubled bliss, with nothing to achieve and
> nothing to anticipate … a heaven in which there is nothing to do but to enjoy,
> year after year, and aeon after aeon, through a monotonous eternity.

> *(in Moorhead 1999: 91)*

Brown's concerns are effectively a mirror-image of the problems raised by Badham in the previous chapter concerning the efficacy of a mind-dependent world which simply took the form of allowing individuals who had died to re-live and re-visit their past lives on earth. As Badham puts it, 'Even the best of old comrades would ultimately tire of exchanging memories of the past or weaving new theories about what might have been' (Badham 1976: 120). However, whereas for Badham, any future life that had no such fresh input would end up being 'futile and empty' (Badham 1976: 120), Brown's position was that what would really be futile and empty is a future life that was discontinuous from the present. For Brown, in contrast to Badham, 'There is but one life here and hereafter, and the change we call death is but opening the door from one room to another in the Father's house' (in Moorhead 1999: 91). The most profitable talk, therefore, of an afterlife is that which posits, albeit paradoxically, a future life that is 'not different from our hope for the life here' (in Moorhead 1999: 91). Within Roman Catholic circles, also, Karl Rahner has written that the environment of which a departed spirit is conscious and in relation to which it lives is still *this*-worldly, as there is no other sphere of operation than this physical universe. The departed remain, quite simply, earth-bound (see Hick 1976: 231).

In Judaism, too, outside of the Orthodox tradition Eliezer Segal points out that discussions of the afterlife are 'almost entirely absent' from religious discourse 'which has focused on the absolute commitment to this world as the setting for the encounter with the divine, the covenant between God and Israel, and the obligation to serve humanity' (Segal 2000: 27). According to Franz Rosenzweig, for example, eternity should be seen as a religious dimension of *life* rather than an afterlife state (see Segal 2000: 27). Following the Holocaust, theologians such as Emil Fackenheim, Elie Wiesel and Richard Rubenstein have been discernibly reluctant to appeal to a post-mortem, supernatural retribution beyond death. Although Fackenheim was fixated on the concept of survival, it was survival in this world rather than in an afterlife state that was of supreme significance to him. Fackenheim's thinking was that, in the present, it was incumbent upon all Jews

> to survive as Jew, lest the Jewish people perish … They are forbidden to des-pair of man and his world, and to escape into either cynicism or otherworld-liness, lest they co-operate in delivering the world over to the forces of Auschwitz.
>
> *(in Cohn-Sherbok 1996: 45)*

Survival for Fackenheim was thus more about ensuring that Hitler is not handed a posthumous victory (see Levenson 2000: 282), such as by the creation of the state of Israel – which, while no compensation for the losses sustained during the Holocaust, is at least a sign that Jewish life after the Holocaust is possible (see Levenson 2000: 282) – than about resurrection, immortality or eternal life as such. In Fackenheim's words, 'Faced with the radical threat of extinction, [Jews] were stubbornly denying it, committing themselves, if to nothing more, to the survival of themselves and their children as Jews' (in Cohn-Sherbok 1996: 43). As Cohn-Sherbok thus puts it, 'After Auschwitz Jewish life is more sacred than Jewish death' (Cohn-Sherbok 1996: 46).

Although Richard Rubenstein came to a different conclusion than Fackenheim, in the respect that, for him, the Holocaust had discredited traditional Jewish theology, his position was no less focused on this-worldly dynamics. For Rubenstein, it was impossible to sustain a belief in a supernatural deity after what happened at Auschwitz (see Cohn-Sherbok 1996: 80). Accordingly, when, in the 1960s, Rubenstein, together with the American Protestant theologians William Hamilton and Thomas Altizer, was associated with the so-called 'Death of God' movement, the point of reference was not so much that God had died (though Hamilton and Altizer did actually proclaim that God was dead[3]) but that this was a cultural and anthropological, as opposed to a theistic, event. Indeed, it was bound up not with what was happening to God but solely with respect to human experience. Hence, for Rubenstein, it was preferable to say 'we live in the time of the death of God' than that 'God is dead' (see Miller & Grenz 1998: 81).

Such thinking ties in well also with the New Testament scholar and former Bishop of Woolwich, John A.T. Robinson. In 1963 Robinson's *Honest to God* was published. This was a short paperback which comprised a very readable, lay-oriented and, for a Church of England bishop, controversial distillation of the thinking of contemporary trends in German theology (in particular, Bultmann, Tillich and Bonhoeffer). In it, Robinson dismantled the idea that God existed in the heavens and interacted with the world from above. For him, the presupposed platforms upon which the Church had always sought to rest the Gospel were no longer in place, in a modern climate where belief in God and life after death were out-of-date and anachronistic to many people. Robinson's emphasis was very much on this world rather than the next, and, like Bultmann, he queried 'how far Christianity is committed to a mythological, or supra-naturalist, picture of the universe' (Robinson 1963: 33). In his words, 'Is it necessary for the Biblical faith to be expressed in terms of this world-view, which in its way is as primitive philosophically as the Genesis stories are primitive scientifically?' (Robinson 1963: 33). Robinson, like Rubenstein, was of the view that theological statements are, ultimately, 'affirmations about human existence' (Robinson 1963: 52), though Robinson did not seek to excise the transcendent altogether. Rather, in language reminiscent of Bonhoeffer, he maintained that 'Statements about God are acknowledgements of the transcendent, unconditional element in all our relationships, and supremely in our relationships with other persons' (Robinson 1963: 52). In lieu of the traditional theistic idea that God was above the world, Robinson's position was that, in Tillichian terms, God exists as the 'Ground of our Being' (Robinson 1963: 45ff.) and was deep within the human person, such that one has to look within – rather than up to the heavens – in order to encounter God. Accordingly, for Robinson, 'The man who acknowledges the transcendence of God is the man who *in* the conditioned relationships of life recognizes the unconditional and responds to it in unconditional personal relationship' (Robinson 1963: 55). Although Robinson preferred to use the language of 'inaugurated' rather than 'realised' eschatology, his understanding that, in the person and ministry of Jesus Christ the goal of history has already become present in history and that the rule of God has begun, is very similar in essence to the language of Bultmann, Dodd and other exponents of realised eschatology.

Finding realised eschatology in film

This sense of appropriating future, supernatural language in the context of present existence – perhaps best typified by Robinson's claim that it would 'be wiser to concentrate on personal immortality in a noneschatological context' (Robinson 1968: 53) – finds a significant corollary, also, in a number of recent films where the transcendent is interpreted through the lens of this-worldly phenomena. There are obvious differences, in that, for exponents of realised eschatology, the absence of a future hope does not thereby entail the abandonment of theological values or virtues. Conversely, as we shall see, in a number of contemporary films a non-theistic, naturalistic and even nihilistic framework is often normative. Such a position would have been an anathema to Robinson, who made it clear in *Honest to God* that the Christian Gospel does not 'stand or fall' (Robinson 1963: 41) by its identification with theism or transcendence. There may be no future life, but this did not mean, for Robinson, that Christianity had no foundation. Seeing God as deep within the human person, and grounded in unconditional love, Robinson thought that 'at no point is the naturalistic view … shallower or more discredited than in its estimate of what is wrong with the world and of what is required to put it right' (Robinson 1963: 79). Rather than the antithesis of the secular, Robinson believed, in tandem with Bonhoeffer, that 'the "secular" is not a (godless) section of life but the world (God's world, for which Christ died) cut off and alienated from its true depth' (Robinson 1963: 87). To this end, I suspect that Robinson would not have found much redeeming worth in films of the western genre where often analogous language to that found in Christianity is employed. As Peter French puts it, the westerner 'typically ascends to a state of grace by his vengeful death-risking and death-dealing acts' (French 1997: 86), and the 'achievement of or ascension to a state of grace in such moments is, perhaps, the only viable explanation for the ability of the hero to survive the barrage of bullets' (French 1997: 86–87). But, crucially, there is no corresponding emphasis on unconditional love or, as Bonhoeffer saw it, the importance of being a person for other persons. In Bonhoeffer's words:

> To feel that one counts for something with other people is one of the joys of life. What matters is not how many friends we have, but how deeply we are attached to them. After all, personal relationships count for more than anything else.
> *(Bonhoeffer 1963: 128–29)*

In marked contrast, the western hero is a pathological loner and outsider who, like John Wayne's wandering, taciturn Confederate war veteran Ethan Edwards in *The Searchers* (John Ford, 1956), is forever excluded from home. This motif is best encapsulated in that film's final image in which we see Ethan, after his five-year odyssey to track down and kill both the Comanche Indian who kidnapped his niece and (though he does not in the end go through it) the niece herself now that she has been defiled – or, in Ethan's own words, the 'leavin's of Comanche bucks' – unable to set foot in the doorway of the family home from which he is now permanently detached, both physically and psychologically. As one reviewer puts it: 'He can find nowhere where he can be at peace and accepted' (Fox & McDonagh 2003: 671). None of this squares with Bonhoeffer's emphasis on the non-negotiable importance of deep, personal relationships: ' ... people are more important in life than anything else ... what is the best book or picture or house, or any property to me, compared with my wife, my parents, or my friend?' (Bonhoeffer 1963: 129).

That there would appear to be something supernatural or religious-like about westerns is not, of course, in dispute, as when at the end of *Unforgiven* William Munny (Clint Eastwood) slaughters six men gathered in a saloon yet 'never receives a scratch' (French 1997: 87). Likewise, in *Pale Rider* the anonymous Preacher (Clint Eastwood), who even wears a dog collar, appears invincible when we see him returning unscathed from a gunfight with five adversaries, all of whom are violently killed. But, these are superficial parallels, and, though the protagonist in *Pale Rider*, for instance, would appear on a surface level to comprise some form of Christ-figure, not just as a result of his priest-like attire but in his actions, too (namely, when he takes it upon himself to destroy a corrupt federal marshal and his minions in order to ensure that those who are unable to defend themselves are appropriately recompensed and delivered from evil, greed, malice, intimidation and injustice [see Deacy & Ortiz 2008: 143]), it is his lack of a human connection that makes the parallels with the person of Christ less, rather than more, efficacious. It is true that Bonhoeffer's involvement in the Confessing Church, in which he sought to use violent means in order to remove Hitler from power, could be considered analogous to the Preacher's function as liberator. But, there is a crucial difference. In *Pale Rider*, the Preacher belongs to no community and he rides from out of nowhere at the beginning of the film and returns there again at the end, unable, like Wayne's Ethan Edwards, to assimilate into any kind of familial or social community once the job of restorative justice has been accomplished. In Bonhoeffer's case, although he did not live to see the end of the Second World War, it was precisely the desire to be a person for other persons and to form personal attachments with his fellow countrymen that led to his decision to return to his native Germany rather than remain in safe exile in America:

> I have to live through this difficult period in our nation's history with Christians in Germany. I will have no right to participate in the reconstruction of Christian life in Germany after the war if I do not share the tribulations of this time with my people.
>
> *(in Miller & Grenz 1998: 77)*

For Eastwood's Preacher, in contrast, his motives for coming down from afar and entering the small nineteenth-century mining community of Carbon Canyon are far less selfless and other-oriented. As he admits at one point in the film, his raison d'être is one of personal vengeance, as the villain, Stockburn (John Russell), had once shot him and left him for dead. In the Preacher's words, 'It's an old score and it's time to settle it'.

Despite the overt symbolism that the film borrows from the Book of Revelation – in the respect that at the beginning of *Pale Rider* a young girl, Megan Wheeler (Sydney Penny), reads aloud from a passage in Revelation which speaks of 'a pale horse' and its rider whose 'name was Death' who is given 'power over a fourth of the earth, to kill with sword and with famine and with pestilence' (Revelation 6:8) – *Pale Rider* is not altogether coterminous with certain core elements of New Testament teaching. As Jewett points out, in Romans 12:19, St Paul instructs his followers *not* to take vengeance and be a judge in one's own cause: 'Beloved, never avenge yourselves, but leave it to the wrath of God'. The very sort of vengeance that we see on display in Eastwood's film is thus contrary both to Pauline and to Bonhoeffer's theological principles. Whereas in Romans 12:19 Paul teaches that vengeance should be left to the will of God – 'Vengeance is mine, I will repay, says the Lord' – the Preacher has a private vendetta to settle, and any salvific or redemptive dimension that his actions may bring about are purely self-conferred. Significantly, although French uses the language of 'grace', there is no divine referent, here. Rather, in French's words, 'The westerner confers on himself the grace that protects him. He has taught himself to set aside ... his normal human feelings. He hardens his heart, and in doing so, elevates himself above that ordinary run of men who blink' (French 1997: 88). For Bonhoeffer, it is precisely by what he called 'participation in the suffering of God in the life of the world' (Bonhoeffer 1963: 123) rather than any sort of detachment from human affairs that grace was a meaningful category. Whereas 'the westerner achieves success because of his pride, a justifiable confidence in himself', which 'elevates him to a state of grace' (French 1997: 102), Bonhoeffer drew a distinction between 'costly' grace, which entails faith with involvement, in the form of obedient, costly discipleship, and mere 'cheap' grace which entails 'the justification of sin and the world' (Bonhoeffer 1959: 41) and amounted to nothing more than a passive and complacent assent to a doctrine or creedal formula. In a nutshell, the difference between the Preacher's and Bonhoeffer's understanding of grace could not be more discordant. Whereas for Eastwood's Preacher grace cannot be dissociated from his function as a remote, seemingly invulnerable and almost supernatural, transhuman liberator, for Harvey Cox, one of Bonhoeffer's most vociferous defenders, grace's point of reference is not an invincible and transcendent deity but 'the crucified one, recognized, not by his heroic powers but by the nail- and spear-marks' (Cox 1975: 545).

Although Bonhoeffer did not rule out belief in an afterlife, he objected to those trends in religion that were more predilected to concentrate on the future at the expense of the vicissitudes and exigencies of the present. It was thus rather more important to concentrate on *this* world, and to leave the afterlife until it comes, on the grounds that only if God is real in life is there a *telos* in death. In lieu of projecting God's work on the Cross into the future, Cox perfectly sums up Bonhoeffer's position when he wrote that 'Calvary's cross means that God dwells for good and forever with those who are hurt and mocked and broken by the powers that be' (Cox 1975: 545–46), and that 'All theories of God's transcendence and immanence must be constantly corrected by this brutal fact' (Cox 1975: 546). Indeed, as Cox attests, 'A God who is *no longer* living among the poor and absorbing the scoffs and insults of the keepers of law and custom' – for which we could read either Hitler's persecution of the Jews in Germany or the despotic treatment meted out to the citizens of Carbon Canyon by an oppressive federal marshal and his entourage – 'might just as well be dead' (Cox 1975: 545).

While such thinking may appear to be at odds with mainstream Christian thinking, it is significant that many other influential theologians have expressed a similar reluctance to indulge in afterlife speculations. For Friedrich Schleiermacher, the father of Modern Protestant Theology, writing at the turn of the nineteenth century, only a sceptical attitude towards the possibility of life after death was possible. In his words, 'Certainty beyond this life is not given to us' and 'we can form no conception of it, we can form only poetic visions' (in McDannell & Lang 1990: 324–25). Moreover, he thought that conventional concepts of an afterlife 'imply thousands of unanswered questions, and thus lose much of their consolatory force' (McDannell & Lang 1990: 325). As McDannell and Lang put it, 'The problem of life after death, for him, was insignificant because it was remote from the inner life and immediate religious feelings', such that 'Christians should not bother themselves with speculations about the other world, but instead concentrate on the world they occupied now' (McDannell & Lang 1990: 333). For Karl Barth, also, despite his neo-orthodox credentials, belief in the resurrection of the body and in a life after death was not a corollary of his strongly Christological theological principles. Paul Badham has recently indicated that for many years he assumed that Barth was an advocate of a future hope, until he came to see, upon reading McDannell and Lang's *Heaven: A History*, and from his own correspondence with Lang, that Barth took the line that, in Christ, we are already in heaven and thus have no future life to look forward to as such.[4] Indeed, we have just the one life which begins at birth and ends in death, and, in Barth's words, there can be 'no question of the continuation into an indefinite future of a somewhat altered life' (in McDannell & Lang 1999: 342). The most we could expect is to live a truncated life in which there would be no new experiences or relationships that could 'mar our relationship with the divine', and in which – in language that is redolent of one of the criticisms adduced with respect to Price's model of a mind-dependent world – we would 'be able to talk only about the past, about earthly existence' (McDannell & Lang 1990: 350). So, even though Barth is able to use the language of eternal life, it is worth stressing that, for him, this does not amount to any sort of continuous personal existence post-death.

In films, also, it is not, perhaps, surprising to this end that when, as was discussed in Chapter 1, Clive Marsh presents a case study of three films in his chapter on eschatology and 'The end' in *Theology Goes to the Movies*, he notes that none of these pictures 'necessitates any clear, single conviction about life beyond physical death' (Marsh 2007 [a]: 145). At the same time, however, what is significant is that the movies concerned do address the meaning of resurrection and the impact of death upon life in the here and now, in a manner which is congruent with realised trends in theological discourse. In addition to those films of the western genre already discussed, a realised eschatology can also be discerned in the ending of *Cool Hand Luke*

(Stuart Rosenberg, 1967), which is one of the most commonly cited movies in literature on cinematic Christ-figures. As Carl Skrade wrote in 1970, the protagonist, Lucas Jackson (Paul Newman) – a non-conformist inmate in a Florida prison camp – is 'the filmic Christ-figure par excellence' (Skrade 1970: 21). The scene concerned involves a superimposition of the image of a crossroad, as seen from a heavenly viewpoint, with the image of Luke right in the centre of the cross, in an overt attempt at crucifixion symbolism. As Greg Garrett puts it:

> Luke has been wounded unto death, shot down like a dog, but in his shameful death, he has achieved a sort of victory over blind justice ... It is a victory that leads to immortality and to a cult of believers who tell and retell his story, the good news of this unlikely savior.
>
> *(Garrett 2007: 38–39)*

Garrett is referring, here, to the scene that immediately precedes the image of the crossroads, when we see Luke's fellow prisoners clearly transformed by their encounter with him. Physically incarcerated though they may be, as conveyed by the sight of them shackled and chained on the prison work farm so as to ensure that no-one else escapes, we are led to believe that, in a spiritual sense, they are free. They are, after all, inspired by Luke's indomitable spirit to rise above their captivity and incarceration, to the point of being brought to the verge of confronting themselves as authentic human individuals, and for seeing in their disenfranchised lives some reason for being (see Deacy 2005: 93). This is arguably similar to Jewett's attestation that when St Paul uses the term 'redemption' in his epistle to the Romans there is no supposition that those who have been redeemed are thereby set free from affiliation in any physical or material sense. In Romans 8:24–25, it would appear, rather, from what Paul writes – 'Now hope that is seen is not hope. For who hopes for what he sees? But if we hope for what we do not see, we wait for it with patience' – that there is a situation of ongoing vulnerability for those who have been redeemed. This is because the 'slaves and former slaves who made up the bulk of the Roman Chur-ches could not entirely overcome exploitation by their masters and patrons' (Jewett 1999: 164). In other words, slaves are still slaves, even though, in a non-material sense, something emancipating has taken place. Jewett's thesis, indeed, is that redemption is not about escaping from terrestrial dispare including imprisonment, but, rather, prevailing over the current hopelessness courtesy of the love and grace of God that is administered to his redeemed people (Jewett 1999: 165).

Such language is, of course, very much in keeping with that of realised eschatology, and can be seen to pervade a range of other films and film genres, also. In the case of the horror film *Stigmata* (Rupert Wainwright, 1999), for example, although the controversy that the film generated upon its release at the beginning of the millennium was largely on account of the 'missing' fifth Gospel and supposed Vatican conspiracy, what is no less insightful is the way in which what Richard Walsh refers to as 'the horror of possession and death' has taken a back seat to 'an affirmation of this life in the stereotypical Hollywood form of the romance' (Walsh 2005: 101). What Walsh is referring to, here, is the way in which a film whose ostensible subject matter is stigmata, crucifixion and death – it is signposted throughout the film that Frankie Paige (Patricia Arquette), the Pittsburgh hairdresser who receives the five stigmata wounds of Christ, will surely die from her afflictions, on the grounds that no previous recipient has survived all of the concomitant bleedings, whippings and lashings – ends with a relatively prosaic romance between the protagonist and the Catholic priest who offers her protection and counsel. In Walsh's words, '*Stigmata* offers romance–love–sex as an attractive option to stigmata and death', with a quite unexceptional ending in which Frankie is nourished back to health in a garden environment in which 'traditional religious figures have become mere statues in the background' (Walsh 2005: 101).

Although such an unambiguously pedestrian focus on the here and now in a film which had hitherto sought to delineate a rich supernatural concoction of demonic possession and exorcism is far from unrepresentative of mainstream Hollywood cinema, it is notable that in American independent cinema, also, realised forms of eschatology tend to predominate. A case in point is *The Big Lebowski* (Joel Coen, 1998), a film remarkable in modern cinema not least due to its audacious presentation of a laidback dopehead protagonist, The Dude (Jeff Bridges), 'who spends his time smoking weed and bowling with his friends' (Falsani 2009: 109). In the film, The Dude becomes involved in a case of kidnapping, extortion, double-crossing and mistaken identity when all he wants is for someone to compensate him for the rug in his apartment having been urinated upon by a trio of 'marmot-wielding nihilists' (Falsani 2009: 116). Surreal and flippant though the film may be, what is significant is that in the decade or so since it was first released an entire religious movement has developed around it known as Dudeism, or the official Church of the Latter-Day Dude, the central philosophical teaching of which is a sort of secularised version of the Old Testament book of Ecclesiastes:

> Life is short and complicated, and nobody knows what to do about it. So don't do anything about it. Just take it easy, man. Stop worrying so much whether you'll make it into the finals. Kick back with some friends and some oat soda and whether you roll strikes or gutters, do your best to be true to yourself and others.
>
> *(in Falsani 2009: 118)*

In her recently published book *The Dude Abides: The Gospel According to the Coen Brothers*, Cathleen Falsani, religion columnist for the *Chicago Sun-Times*, even writes that she is herself 'a duly ordained Dudeist priest' – the Church ordains Dudeist priests over the internet – and is 'capable of lawfully presiding at weddings in most states' (Falsani 2009: 118).

This is glaringly tongue-in-cheek, as the cinema advertisement in the UK at the beginning of 2010 for Volkswagen – which features a member of the Church of the Latter-Day Dude essentially promoting a Volkswagen car as the perfect recreational vehicle for laidback dropouts everywhere – hilariously suggests. Yet, there is a discernibly realised eschatological undertone to this philosophy and the Coen

Brothers film (their 'most blatantly spiritual' [Falsani 2009: 119], according to Falsani) which inspired it. Indeed, reference is even made by Falsani to 'the here and now of the Dude-iverse' (Falsani 2009: 118), and it is significant in this regard that the final words that The Dude utters, and which prompts the film's 'spiritually soaked soliloquy' (Falsani 2009: 119), is 'The Dude abides'. This is quite a fitting self-designation in the respect that, as Walsh puts it, the film's protagonist simply accepts 'death as he does the rest of life. He does not expect to conquer, to escape, or to find some larger meaning. He is far too inept and lazy. He simply "takes it easy" at his neighborhood bowling alley' (Walsh 2005: 102). Such an affirmation of this life, with the concomitant tendency to concentrate on human, rather than divine, forgiveness, is quite in keeping both with *The Big Lebowski* and Walsh's own theological position, in which he thinks, contrary to his own reading of St Paul, that 'it is hardly trite to reduce death to ethical lessons about this present life' (Walsh 2005: 82). Walsh's concern is that St Paul, despite being 'fascinated by death', is unable to 'affirm *this* world' (Walsh 2005: 83), to the point that only by 'decentering Paul' may we be enabled 'to go on living and working out our salvation' (Walsh 2005: 180). According to Walsh, 'For Paul, the cross undoes the world's wisdom and power, because the crucified, rejected Christ is God's wisdom and power' (Walsh 2005: 83). This is betokened by Paul's references in his first letter to the Corinthians to God having 'made foolish the wisdom of the world' (1 Corinthians 1:20) and to the fact that 'the foolishness of God is wiser than men, and the weakness of God is stronger than men' (1 Corinthians 1:25). Walsh's own position, though, is that '[a]mid life's admitted pain, we would be better off laughing and dancing than expecting transcendent help' (Walsh 2005: 181), in a manner that is congruent with *Lebowski*'s Ecclesiastes-like eschatology. Indeed, when Qoheleth, the author of what is by far the most sceptical and theistically uncommitted book to appear in the canon of the Hebrew Bible, wrote that

> the fate of the sons of men and the fate of beasts is the same; as one dies, so dies the other. They all have the same breath, and man has no advantage over the beasts; for all is vanity. All go to one place; all are from the dust, and all turn to dust again
>
> *(Ecclesiastes 3:19–20)*

as well as that 'it is an unhappy business that God has given to the sons of men to be busy with' (Ecclesiastes 1:13–14), it is clear that this is very much in keeping with Walsh's affirmation, in realised eschatological language, of 'this life and human responsibility rather than fantasies about dues ex machinas' (Walsh 2005: 181). In other words, for Walsh, it is much more theologically efficacious when humans take responsibility for their own lives instead of expecting any sort of divine deliverance, even to the point that the specific language of 'resurrection' can be better understood in 'quite material and this-worldly' (Walsh 2005: 192) terms. As Walsh writes with respect to the overtly theological film *The Apostle* (Robert Duvall, 1997), which was on release in the UK at the same time as *The Big Lebowski* (June 1998), in which

Robert Duvall plays a Pentecostal preacher who tries to atone for committing a murder by building a new church, the word 'resurrection', when applied to this film, entails not so much escaping the world or condemning the world apocalyptically as about the attempt to 'make a way within the ongoing world' (Walsh 2005: 192).

That said, underlying both Ecclesiastes and *The Big Lebowski* is the far more upbeat recognition that there *is* a positive certainty in life. According to Ecclesiastes 2:24, for instance, 'There is nothing better for a man than that he should eat and drink, and find enjoyment in his toil'. If, in other words, one accepts the reality of one's own death and the absurdity and meaninglessness of human existence without the illusions which the fear of death so easily tends to create (see Blenkinsopp 1983: 65), then the mind can be set free from what amounts to 'a major source of crippling activity' (Blenkinsopp 1983: 66) and it is possible to start living life as a gift. As I have outlined elsewhere, we can subsequently learn to live authentically within the prescribed limitations of our existence, and can come to enjoy our successes, transitory though they may be, even though we know we cannot depend on them (see Deacy 2001: 62). There are, then, compensations to be found in human existence. Indeed, a withdrawal from life could be construed as a deprivation of the one gift that humankind possesses, such that 'if a man lives many years, let him rejoice in them all', even though 'the days of darkness will be many' (Ecclesiastes 11:8). Death, in short, may be the least thing under our control, but to accept the reality of this situation, as opposed to escaping from life's very capriciousness and unpredictability, can be liberating.

This is not so far removed from the world of *The Big Lebowski* where The Dude is presented as 'a kindly soul' and 'a passionate pacifist who loves his friends, judges not, and mostly minds his own business', yet who, at the same time, 'has a firm moral center. He knows what's right and what's wrong and isn't afraid to stand up for the cause of love and peace' (Falsani 2009: 112). In Falsani's words, 'The Dude always tries to do the right – or righteous – thing' and he is 'unfailingly kind' (Falsani 2009: 115). Moreover, Falsani even draws a link between the voice-over that appears at the end of the film, in which we are told that The Dude is 'takin' her easy for all us sinners' and 'the kind of grace Jesus … talks about in the Gospels' (Falsani 2009: 120). While, as the earlier discussion of grace in the context of westerns has shown, the word 'grace' has very different connotations in Christian theology, where it refers to unconditional love – and in Bonhoeffer's terms, the importance of being a person for other persons – to what can be found in a film such as *Pale Rider* where it is something self-conferred and has no necessary 'other'-referent, in the case of *The Big Lebowski* a much closer conflation between the two distinct uses may be discerned. The Dude's raison d'être may lack a Christological or theistic referent – his attitude to life may be more akin to Zen Buddhism than to Christian theology. But there is an analogy to the Bonhoefferian understanding of costly grace at work in Falsani's claim that 'The kind of grace that The Dude, in his inimitable way, exudes in every one of his relationships' entails an 'unexpected kindness' and the granting of 'unmerited goodwill' (Falsani 2009: 120). Bonhoeffer may not have gone quite so far as The Dude in his tendency 'to endure without yielding, to accept without objection' (Falsani 2009: 120) – his involvement in the Confessing Church was an overt case of not yielding to corrupt governance – but the present, this-worldly, person-oriented *telos* of the Coens' ingenious celluloid creation at least provides a fruitful starting-point for dialogue with the tenets of realised eschatology.

While to more conservative thinkers such realised, this-worldly expressions of eschatology may be no more than diversionary and facetious, it is notable that outside of Christianity such language is, if anything, even more mainstream. As Peter Clarke has written, for example, it is rare for New Religious Movements to mention death itself, let alone what lies beyond it. With the exception of the Unification Church and the Worldwide Church of God 'there are few developed eschatologies and little about death *per se* and the future beyond the grave' (Clarke 1995: 131). Charles Hallisey also makes the point with regard to Pure Land Buddhism that one becomes a Buddha not after death but in *this* world; there is, simply, no need to wait in antici-pation for the moment of death (Hallisey 2000: 27). A similar pattern is also found in the Buddhist idea of *Nirvana*, which, if not annihilation as such, amounts to the transcending of suffering and rebirth – that is, an end to the cycle of karma. Although, in Hallisey's words, 'life in this world is in radical opposition to nirvana', he thinks that 'the experience of nirvana is, at the same time, possible while still living in this world' (Hallisey 2000: 27). It comprises, for example, a quenching or blowing-out of the three-fold ingredients of greed, hatred and delusion, such that *Nirvana* in this life denotes a transformed state of personality where greed, hatred, delusion and negative mental states and emotions no longer exist. In his chapter entitled 'If I Should Die before I am Awakened: Buddhist Reflections on Death', Malcolm David Eckel also refers to this shift of focus from the point of death to the process of life as having deep roots in Japanese Buddhism and notes that it 'carries with it a shift in the understanding of the Pure Land itself' (Eckel 2001: 80). Indeed, Eckel cites a source from a Buddhist priest in 1385 who wrote that 'the Pure Land is the ultimate and absolute reality, and that is everywhere, so that we may be identified with it right here where we are' (in Eckel 2001: 81). Finally, with respect to Chinese religion, Geddes MacGregor makes the instructive point that there are no supernatural concepts, such as divine judgement or the working out of karmic law, at all (see MacGregor 1992: 105), such that Confucianism 'has been strikingly geared to the this-worldly' (MacGregor 1992: 4). Likewise, although Taoism has been open to speculative ideas including that pertaining to personal immortality, MacGregor argues that it too has been directed largely towards this-worldly concerns (MacGregor 1992: 4).

Criticisms of realised eschatology

Of course, the debate is far from over. As Hick puts it, it is a moot point as to whether it is 'a responsible use of language to speak of eternal life, immortality, the life to come, heaven and hell, and then to add that this language carries no implications whatever regarding the continuation or otherwise of human personality beyond the grave' (Hick 1973: 147). Hick's concern, here, is that theological language may be being evacuated of all meaning if the future eschatological dimension is lost. Polkinghorne and Welker, in their edited collection of essays which looks at eschatology and the end through the lenses of science, theology, ethics and biblical hermeneutics, are, similarly, sharply critical of what they see as 'the existential eschatology of the *here and now* characteristic of much earlier twentieth-century theology' (Polkinghorne & Welker 2000: 3). For Terence Penelhum, moreover, it is essential for the Christian to believe in an afterlife as opposed to thinking that ideas relating to salvation can be applied to the transformation of our personalities in the here and now, since 'if there were no hereafter' then 'all the Christian language about salvation, eternal life, cleansing, and the rest would be utopian and false' (Penelhum 2000: 41). In Penelhum's view, 'the afterlife is a necessity, not just a doctrinal bonus' (Penelhum 2000: 41). Russell Aldwinckle takes the similar line that even though 'we might speak in a meaningful way about eternal life as a quality of life in the present', there is, nonetheless, 'a proper distinction to be made between qualitative eternal life now and the future existence of persons after death' (Aldwinckle 1972: 84).

Aldwinckle is not being wide of the mark, here. For, if Christ's resurrection and redemption have already been realised in the present, there is the not insignificant consideration that evidence for such a transformation is somewhat lacking. As he puts it, 'Even though Jesus has lived, died and risen again, we do not yet see all things subject unto Him', and the 'triumph of God's redeeming love is not yet unambiguously evident' (Aldwinckle 1972: 126). This, indeed, is one of the obvious criticisms of the existentialist thinking of Bultmann and others who appear to be 'dissolving the substance of the Christian Gospel … into some sort of self-understanding subjectivism' (Miller & Grenz 1998: 51). There is something so inner-orientated about existentialist realised eschatology, with its lack of interest in community or any social relations, that it becomes difficult to ascertain, at least in any empirical sense, whether the *eschaton* has taken place. There is no yardstick as such for gauging whether salvation has been realised and whether its effects are permanent. Only at the end of time is Aldwinckle confident that 'we can be absolutely certain of the ultimate victory' (Aldwinckle 1972: 126). How, otherwise, can one say, with confidence, that, in Christian terms, death has been defeated? In Aldwinckle's words, 'Is Jesus really alive with God now or is He alive only in the hearts and minds of believers? There is obviously a great difference' (Aldwinckle 1972: 127). It is thus not enough, for Aldwinckle, 'to say that the Parousia only expresses symbolically the implications of our present experience of God' (Aldwinckle 1972: 128).

Even if one extends the parameters of realised eschatology to refer to the transformation not (only) of the individual in his or her privatised, individualistic, existential state but to the transformation of our social and political agencies and structures, then, even here, we encounter a difficulty. Without denying that this is 'an essential part of the Christian hope' (Aldwinckle 1972: 167), Aldwinckle is unwavering in his belief that, in theodicy terms, no this-worldly eschatology can comprise 'the fulfilment of the divine purpose unless the earthly kingdom is everlasting' and all those who have died throughout history 'have a chance to share in it' (Aldwinckle 1972: 167). Despite the tension that was outlined at the beginning of this chapter concerning the way St Paul's teachings on eschatology are formulated in his epistles, Aldwinckle and other more traditional thinkers would be more inclined to agree with the apostle when he wrote in his first letter to the Corinthians: 'If for this life only we have hoped in Christ, we are of all men most to be pitied' (1 Corinthians 15:19). As Vardy attests, 'Christianity is built upon the claim that Jesus rose from the dead on Easter Sunday as an individual' (Vardy 1995: 14). If this claim is false then 'although Christianity may have some advice to offer on how life should be lived' in the here and now, the implication is that Christianity itself 'is essentially false' (Vardy 1995: 14), so inextricably connected is the future hope with the very kernel of Christian teaching.

In response, I would be inclined to take the line that a commingling of realised and future elements has always existed at the heart of Christianity, as the various interpretations of Paul's own thinking have suggested, not least by McGrath. Jeffrey Burton Russell encapsulates this juxtaposition when he writes that, for the early Christians:

> Heaven comes down and transforms the earth rather than hovering above the earth, waiting for the saved to arrive. Heaven is also now because Christ's saving action is eternal and extends to past, present, and future. The just who lived before Christ, particularly the faithful Jews, are saved by Christ equally with those who live after him.
>
> *(Russell 1997: 41–42)*

Accordingly, it makes sense to say that the kingdom 'is both now and also not yet' (Russell 1997: 41–42). In other words, it is simultaneously both already realised and also still to come in the future. Dale C. Allison, Jr. makes a similar claim with respect to the Old Testament Book of Daniel which, he thinks, understands the kingdom as both a present and a future phenomenon. For him, although Daniel 2:44 is unmistakably future in scope ('And in the days of those kings the God of heaven will set up a kingdom which shall never be destroyed … It shall break in pieces all these kingdoms and bring them to an end, and it shall stand for ever'), Daniel 4:34, in which Nebuchadnezzar praises God whose 'dominion is an everlasting dominion, and his kingdom endures from generation to generation', has an overtly present, and realised, dimension to it (see Allison 1999: 274). The eschatological transformation is thus a gradual process on this reading, which has already begun and which will reach its consummation in the future without there being an explicit line of demarcation between the two. It need not be a simple either/or process, therefore, whereby one has to conform to either a realised or a future eschatological model. As Allison writes with regard to the ancient Jewish Book of Jubilees, 'The one time will (simply) become the other' (Allison 1999: 275).

With specific reference to Christianity, Jesus could thus be seen in terms of such a reading to be holding to an 'inaugurated' eschatology in which he saw himself as standing in the middle of the unfolding eschatological drama (see Allison 1999: 275). As Andrew Chester puts it, throughout the New Testament 'the final events are not only about to happen; they are already set in motion. Jesus sees the kingdom as already beginning to arrive in what God is doing through his activity, above all his healing and exorcising ministry' (Chester 2004: 244). This 'tension between present and future, the "now" and the "not yet"' not surprisingly, therefore, 'pervades almost the whole New Testament' (Chester 2004: 244). Even though the full effects of the kingdom are not going to be manifest until the future, Kathryn Tanner argues that eternal life is not otherworldly as such as one does not only enter it after death. Rather, eternal life infiltrates 'the present world of suffering and oppression, to bring life, understood as a new pattern or structure of relationships marked by life-giving vitality and renewed purpose' (Tanner 2000: 231). The transcendent is not therefore something that will simply come into being in the future, such that all we can do in the meantime is, as it were, to 'make do'. The dichotomy is not simply between the present and the future, or the 'now' and the 'not yet'. The disjunction is more properly to be understood in the sense of, on the one side, living a pattern of existence marked by futility, hopelessness, injustice and exclusion, which for her comprises 'the realm of death', and, on the other, 'the new paradigm of existence empowered by life in God as a force working in the present' (Tanner 2000: 234). It would not be wide of the mark, then, to talk about not 'a transcendent future' but 'a transcendent present', which takes the form of living life in the here and now with reference to 'God as the source of goods that the world one lives in fails to match' (Tanner 2000: 234). To this end, Tanner's work owes much to the writings of the twentieth-century theologians of hope Moltmann and Pannenberg, whose work was discussed in Chapter 1.

Such a commingling of realised and future elements can also be located in contemporary film. In the case of *Babette's Feast* (Gabriel Axel, 1987), in which a French refugee in 1870s Denmark lays on a lavish banquet for her employers, two elderly Lutheran sisters, Marsh draws a link between Holy Communion and ultimate meaning when he writes that 'Holy Communion is an eschatological act: it looks forward to "the end", when all will be well, and all will be fed' (Marsh 2007 [a]: 121). At the same time, however, the culinary feast concerned could also be said to anticipate that end now, in the sense that the messianic banquet has not only entered the present realm but 'serves as a prompt to those who participate to play their part in making that "kingdom" come' (Marsh 2007 [a]: 121). It is not simply the case, therefore, that the 'end' has come and has been realised in the present, such that salvation might be deemed to have arrived, or been inaugurated, already. Instead, the banquet has the type of quality that Tanner is talking about, namely, the sense of eternal life infiltrating the present realm with a view to changing the way in which the present is henceforth able to operate. Just as Tanner refers to living life in the here and now with reference to God's, rather than human, goals and standards, such that a new structure of human relationships, marked by life-giving vitality and a renewed purpose for being, can be enacted, it is significant that, in *Babette's Feast*, 'the function of the meal is to rejuvenate the community in its own work of caring for the poor in its locality, which its members can now do more joyfully than before' (Marsh 2007 [a]: 121). Indeed, although the meal is at first seen as an embarrassment to the puritan and austere community on the Jutland coast, its impact 'is such that the community rediscovers both a sense of joy and its lost communal dimension' (Marsh 1997 [b]: 209). As Marsh wrote in 1997, 'The film records the shift from the community's initial resolve to think nothing of the food … to a new found enjoyment of each other, via a process of healing and reconciliation of the wounds of scarred relationships between them' (Marsh 1997 [b]: 209). Living with respect to the Kingdom of God which is still to come thus becomes a present and practical option, in which, as in Bonhoeffer's case, being a person for other persons is something that can, and must, happen now rather than something that is merely left to the distant, and rather less pressing from today's standards, future.

5

HEAVEN AND THE NEW JERUSALEM AS A PLACE ON EARTH

Case studies of *Working Girl* and *The Shawshank Redemption*

Popular belief in heaven

When such realised trends are properly scrutinised, it is ironic that belief in the existence of heaven continues to exert such a strong hold on the popular imagination. Although, in the case of Europe, belief in heaven has declined since the second half of the twentieth century, to the point that fewer Europeans purport to believe in heaven than in the existence of God (Brown 1995: 42), the statistics that have come out of America in recent decades make for startling reading. According to a Gallup poll published at Easter time in 1989, 77 per cent of Americans believe in heaven, while just five years later the figure had risen to 93 per cent, with as many as 69 per cent of these believing that they themselves had either a good or an excellent chance of going there (Walls 2002: 6). With respect to more current data, as of 2004 the figure had dropped only slightly, with 81 per cent of Americans affirming belief in the existence of heaven (Russell 2006: 4). Once one unpacks the data, however, a more nuanced and imprecise picture emerges. According to Christopher Lewis, who undertook a study of popular conceptions of heaven for his chapter 'Beyond the Crematorium – Popular Belief', for most people who believe in an afterlife the actual shape is indefinite: 'there is just *something* beyond' (Lewis 1995: 204), the grounds for which being nothing more sophisticated or dogmatically sound than that it simply feels comforting and reassuring to hold to a vision of the hereafter. When it comes to establishing the specific content, location and layout – the geography – of heaven, McDannell and Lang thus epitomise the paradox afoot here in their claim that 'the desire to discuss the details of heavenly existence remains a low priority' (McDannell & Lang 1990: 307). Jeffrey Burton Russell similarly attests that, whether they affirm or deny belief in the existence of heaven, many people today 'have little idea of what it is they are thinking about' (Russell 2006: 133).

This is not helped by the tendency in many churches today to sidestep this very topic, a situation not surprising when one considers that, within Anglicanism, heaven does not even feature as one of the Church of England's 39 Articles of Faith. The closest we get is the repudiation of Purgatory in article 22 (see Gibson 1902: 537) and the reference in article four to Christ ascending into heaven following his resurrection from the dead (in Gibson 1902: 181).[1] To add to the confusion, according to a BBC poll conducted in 1999, 40 per cent of Anglican clergymen said they did not believe in heaven as a physical place (see Stanford 2002: 301). Even among conservative, traditionalist theologians more generally, MacGregor makes the point that the notion of heaven as a place 'is widely regarded … as a superstition to be discarded' (MacGregor 1992: 166). As Douglas Davies wrote in his recent study *The Theology of Death*, published in 2008, 'mainstream British churchgoers are hardly ever likely to hear a sermon on heaven: still less one on hell', despite the fact that the existence of heaven 'furnishes the frame for a great deal of Christian worship and the doctrine of God' (Davies 2008: 77). Within Roman Catholicism, also, it is significant that, prior to 1999, Pope John Paul II did not seek on any occasion, in the entire two decades of his pontificate up to that point, to mention the concept of heaven during his public ministry. When he did eventually refer to heaven he did so in the most opaque of terms, declaring that the 'heaven in which we will find ourselves is neither an abstraction nor a physical place among the clouds' (in Stanford 2002: 299).

This raises broader questions concerning theology's very ability to delineate the afterlife. As our earlier discussion of *What Dreams May Come* (Vincent Ward, 1998) highlighted, there are good grounds for being critical of Hollywood's forays into eschatology. For, what we characteristically see is a hotchpotch assortment of realised and future, transcendent and immanent elements, in which teachings pertaining to reincarnation tend to sit alongside literal renderings of hell as objective punishments for those who breach universal moral injunctions. But, one thing for which the filmmakers cannot be criticised is the lack of authenticity or realism pertaining to their artistic imaginations. As Russell puts it, 'Heaven is not a place in space and time like Japan or the Roman Empire' (Russell 2006: 2). Rather, it is experienced as something 'ineffable' and 'beyond words' (Russell 1997: 6) which, if it is to be discussed at all, must be through the use of human language and concepts. Writing in 1970, Terence Penelhum took much the same line, in his claim that 'references to the Next World cannot be intelligible for us unless it is possible to use the language of our world of things and persons to describe it' (Penelhum 1970: 46). In other words, the only way in which we can articulate the form that life after death will take is by using the vocabulary and imagery with which we are familiar in our present experience. No matter how qualitatively or ontologically different heaven may be from our present existence on earth, Chester is right that such visions, even when they represent a transformation of this life 'or a Utopian resolution of inherent problems', are nonetheless 'rooted in present reality' (Chester 2004: 246).

In such a light, it is not difficult to see why, for Paul Tillich, heaven was necessarily a symbol rather than a description of a material place. Writing in the third volume of his *Systematic Theology*, Tillich attested that both heaven and hell 'are symbols and not descriptions of localities' (Tillich 1963: 418), and 'metaphors for the polar ultimates in the experience of the divine' (Tillich 1963: 418–19). Further, for McGrath the concept of heaven 'is an excellent example of a Christian idea that is fundamentally imaginative in provenance, and that demands an imaginative mode of encounter with the reality that it mediates' (McGrath 2003: 2). Even if there is an afterlife, on such a reading, there is a limit to how far we can conceptualise or image it, not least because our intellect is finite whereas the reality to which it points belongs, at least in traditional terms, to the realm of the infinite. When one talks, therefore, of the experience of heaven – what it will look, feel, sound or even smell like – it is metaphorical or anthropomorphic rather than literal language that is being conveyed. The most we can therefore say is that the modern heaven comprises 'a symbolic, imaginative representation of the unknowable' (McDannell & Lang 1990: 308) in a world where our finite minds are unable to fully grasp that which transcends present experience. There will of course always be intellectual questions that theologians and philosophers of religion need to raise about the intellectual credibility of heaven as a concept. For example, is residence in heaven for everyone or is it only for an elite? Does heaven exist in time or in eternity? Is it static or dynamic (see Russell 1997: 187)? Is it corporeal or soul-based? Or, as the previous chapter has highlighted, does it exist now, or in the future, or in some sort of combination of the two? But, aside from these questions, what may not be so readily understood is that filmmakers' often crude and, as we shall see, characteristically this-worldly and earth-bound depictions of heaven have tended to resonate more strongly in western culture over recent decades than anything that theologians or philosophers have managed to engender. By the same token, Russell makes the instructive point that popular novels, such as the 'Left Behind' series, with their Dispensationalist millenarian teachings based on Revelation, 'may have had more influence on current beliefs about heaven than any contemporary historian, critic, or theologian' (Russell 2006: 149) has been able to put forward. Quite simply, if theologians are unable or unwilling to determine the specific contours of heaven, it may not be too surprising if artists, poets, authors and filmmakers have sought to fill the vacuum. As Stanford puts it, 'If Christianity has given up talking about heaven, others are still using the bank of imagery it built up to good effect' (Stanford 2002: 332). This is precisely what happened in the nineteenth century, for example, when between 1830 and 1875 over 50 books on heaven were published in the United States alone, one of which, Elizabeth Stuart Phelps' novel *The Gates Ajar* (1869), was the second most popular book of the period, second only to Harriet Beecher Stowe's *Uncle Tom's Cabin* (see Walls 2002: 6).

With this in mind, it is my aim in this chapter to focus on a case study of two films which seem to have caught the popular imagination in much the same way, *Working Girl* (Mike Nichols, 1988) and *The Shawshank Redemption* (Frank Darabont, 1994). While neither of these films is explicitly about eschatology or, for that matter, Christian theology, they have, in different ways, managed to encapsulate something significant about the way in which heaven has been imaged in a secularised modern American milieu. Building on the syllogism identified by Russell that 'In popular thought, if heaven exists, it has to be somewhere, and if it is not locatable anywhere in the universe, then it cannot exist' (Russell 2006: 32), this chapter will show that not only is heaven popularly construed as a place but it is a place that exists in physical, spatio-temporal form *within* this universe. It is, in other words, a place on earth, as opposed to having a purely metaphysical (or metaphorical) and celestial frame of reference. Moreover, as this chapter will show, both films draw on quintessentially theological motifs yet rework them in a way which says something important about the blurring of the conceptual boundaries that has long taken place between different varieties of eschatological language, and in a way that invites, and necessitates, scholarly engagement. Indeed, there have been many instances throughout history of eschatological terminology having been desacralised and reappropriated from the sacred to the secular domain. A case in point is when James Moorhead cites an 1859 entry in the nineteenth-century Cincinatti-based Methodist periodical *The Ladies' Repository* according to which the invention of the telegraph 'is to be the means of extending civilization, republicanism and Christianity over the earth … Then shall come to pass the millennium' (in Moorhead 1999: 76). My aim is to show how *Working Girl* and *Shawshank* are no less than contemporary manifestations (albeit, as we shall see, imperfect ones) of the terrestrial heaven.

Background to the two case studies: The materialisation of heaven

It might seem incongruous that two films which are set in a distinctly twentieth-century American environment should be chosen as case studies of cinematic explorations of heaven. But, it is worth noting that, even in films where heaven is more explicitly delineated, as in Michael Powell and Emeric Pressburger's wartime propaganda fantasy *A Matter of Life and Death* (1946), heaven is far from a uniform or objective construct. Indeed, Powell and Pressburger's fable of an RAF pilot, Peter Carter (David Niven), who improbably survives serious injury after his plane is shot down by enemy fire and he bales out of his aircraft without a parachute, only for a celestial emissary, Heavenly Conductor Number 71 (Marius Goring), to belatedly come down to earth to collect him, is far from clear as to whether the monochrome heaven on display is not simply 'a delusional construct' (Ruffles 2004: 133). It would seem to this end that the heavenly experience has 'merely' been triggered by the anaesthetic Carter is given while on the operating table where he is being treated for brain damage. As with *What Dreams May Come*, there is a strong underlying suggestion during the film, which was produced at the behest of the Ministry of Information who wanted to make a picture that reinforced relations between Britain and America following the countries' collaboration in the Second World War, that an entire environment has been created by the subjective imagination. There is thus something flimsy and insubstantial about many overt cinematic treatments of the afterlife, a situation not helped when one considers that, in theological discourse, also, heaven has multiple frames of reference. As Russell attests:

> Heaven is the City of God, Zion, Jerusalem glorified and transcended, a city with walls, gates … and streets of gold … In the city is the court and throne of

God, about whom the blessed ... sing and dance in celestial harmony. Heaven is also a lush garden with pure air, trees, fruit, flowers ... , or meadows and pastures with rivers. Heaven is an *agape*, banquet, celebration, holy communion, of all the blessed ...

(Russell 2006: 12)

This concept of heaven as a banquet or communal meal fits in well with the discussion at the end of the previous chapter concerning *Babette's Feast* (Gabriel Axel, 1987). More pertinently, such ideas of heaven as being a New Jerusalem and an Edenic paradise[2] – the epitome and quintessence of all that is urban and pastoral, respectively – have a particular resonance with respect to the metropolitan setting of *Working Girl* and the open and unspoiled natural habitat that is realised at the end of *The Shawshank Redemption*. But, there is, simply, no objective or fixed notion of heaven on which even theologians themselves have been able to agree. This position is underscored by Russell's attestation that heaven is both the original earthly paradise (albeit on an earth transformed and sanctified) *and* the Kingdom of God within us *and* the paradise at the end of the world (Russell 1997: 13). The fact that pre-Biblical and Biblical accounts also seem especially vague on the subject further suggests that no particular cinematic realisation has credence over any of the others. Detailed and finely realised though Powell and Pressburger's hierarchical and bureaucratic heaven is in *A Matter of Life and Death*, in which a heavenly tribunal is set up to decide whether Carter can remain on earth following the Heavenly Conductor's celestial blunder, this does not make it any more authentic or real. No Biblical literature, not even in the New Testament, supplies the sort of particular detail that we find in *A Matter of Life and Death* with its exquisite production design from Alfred Junge consisting of a colossal staircase which reaches into the sky at the top of which lies an extravagant amphi-theatre filled with heaven's infinite population, whom we see peering down over the edges at the Technicolored earth beneath. Rather than the New Testament, the closest precursor to Powell and Pressburger's spectacle is the fourteenth-century poetry of Dante's *Divine Comedy*. Even here, though, as with John Milton's *Paradise Lost* in the seventeenth century, we know rather more about the Devil and Hell than we do about the celestial abode. For the New Testament writers, indeed, Jesus' resurrection does not so much prove that heaven exists, and that believers can expect to go there, as that Jesus' mission has been vindicated (see Wilson 1995: 190). The particular topography of heaven thus takes a back seat.

The Old Testament is even more ambiguous, with its emphasis upon this present life as the highest of all goods, God being a god not of the dead but of the living. According to Psalm 104:29 ('when thou takest away their breath, they die and return to their dust'), it is clear that God's breath animates and sustains all that lives, but that when God withdraws it the creature is reduced to nothingness (see Anderson 1986: 39). We see a similar thread in Psalm 103 where we learn that

As for man, his days are like grass;
he flourishes like a flower of the field;

for the wind passes over it, and it is gone,
and its place knows it no more

(Ps. 103:15–16)

For the early Jews, therefore, the afterlife was not a viable area of discourse. At best, it was obtainable only to an heroic elite, such as Elijah and Enoch, who had already enjoyed all the benefits and pleasures that earth had to offer. For everyone else, it was a truncated and impoverished – even mutilated – existence where, in the gloomy, hopeless underworld of Sheol (a vast subterranean cavern or pit, effectively a synonym for death itself), individuals would no more than exist as atrophied, vapid and feeble shadows of their former selves and there would be no opportunity for development or even escape. As Hick puts it: 'to go down to sheol was to pass for ever out of the land of the living and out of the on-going life of the nation … The dead were not in active communion with God' (Hick 1976: 59). If there was to be any kind of immortality, it was in the sense that the nation, the corporate body of Israel, was to persist rather than that individuals themselves were bound for heaven (or hell). In Wheeler Robinson's words, 'The Israelite felt that he went on living in his children to a degree that really made their life his own' (in Hick 1976: 66–67). Likewise, for Segal, 'For better or for worse, it was believed that immortality would be achieved through the continuity of future generations rather than in a supernatural afterlife' (Segal 2000: 14).

Pertinent though it may therefore be to concentrate on Dantean-inspired supernatural odysseys such as *What Dreams May Come* when examining celluloid representations of heaven, there is no outright biblical support for such endeavours. *Working Girl* and *The Shawshank Redemption* may seem, at face value, to be an atypical choice of films for featuring in a case study into celluloid heaven. But their this-worldly dynamics are no less terrestrial-based than what we find in the Old Testament where it is apparent that Jews placed the kingdom of God *on earth* rather than in any celestial order of existence. Indeed, it was not until the Book of Daniel, a fairly late book in the Hebrew canon, dating from around 165 BCE during the persecutions of the Hellenistic monarch Antiochus IV Epiphanes[3] when, as with the sixth-century Babylonian Exile, the chain of national life was broken that expectations for a future dimension of existence following death came to be consolidated. In Daniel 12:2, for instance, we find the earliest reference to individual resurrection in the teaching that 'many of those who sleep in the dust of the earth shall awake, some to everlasting life, and some to shame and everlasting contempt'. Yet, even here, heaven itself does not feature as a concept. It was enough that, as the reference to resurrection in 2 Maccabees 12:43–45 (albeit a text outside of the canon of the Hebrew Bible) suggests, resurrection itself was a quite controversial idea, and one which was not widely accepted by Jews until the erosion of Sadduceean Judaism following the destruction of the Second Temple in 70 CE. In terms of the state into which one would be resurrected, there is, then, no clear picture on display. In the New Testament, also, no single view of heaven – which is mentioned some 240 times, most notably in Philippians 3:20 (where Paul writes that 'our commonwealth is in heaven, and from it we await a

Saviour') – can be seen to exist. This may not be surprising in view of the anticipation, as outlined in the previous chapter, concerning the imminent Second Coming at which, in Russell's words, 'Christ would unite Jew and Gentile, circumcised and uncircumcised, in the realized Kingdom of God or Kingdom of Heaven' (Russell 1997: 41). The need for a celestial paradise as such was somewhat peripheral in such a realised and this-worldly context.

Despite Badham's assertion that it was the 'absolute assurance of the reality of heaven which made the first followers of Christ so ready to suffer and die as martyrs to their faith' (Badham & Badham 1984: ix), Delumeau makes the more subtle point that there is a certain vagueness in the minds of the faithful in the early Church concerning the journey of the elect in the post-mortem world. As Delumeau puts it, there was some confusion over whether there would be 'a sleep preceding the resurrection or a relaxed and pleasant stay in the green pastures where the just sang and danced as they waited for the gates of heaven to be opened' (Delumeau 2000: 35). In other words, rather than proceed straight to heaven, some sources suggest that there would be an intermediate, purgatorial period where the soul would wait until the final Resurrection and Judgement at the Last Day (see Chester 2004: 248). It may have been the case for St Paul that the question of the status of the person between death and resurrection was not one that needed to be considered (see Anderson 1986: 117). But, in the Middle Ages the idea developed that, before being admitted to heaven, an interim earthly paradise was required for those souls that required further purification prior to enjoying beatitude (see Russell 1997: 107). In Dante's *Purgatorio*, furthermore, reference is made to the earthly paradise, consisting of 'everlasting shade', 'flowery branches', 'red and yellow flowers' and 'sweet sounds' (Dante 1977: 290),[4] which lies atop the mountain of purgatory, a seven-storied structure which one must ascend. Dante was not simply allowing his creative imagination to run wild. This idea of the terrestrial paradise of Eden situated at the peak of a mountain was also shared in Christian history by such figures as Lactantius in the third century, John of Damascus and the Venerable Bede in the eighth century, and Peter Lombard in the twelfth century. The grounds for their thinking were that paradise needed to be situated somewhere high enough where the waters of the Flood could not reach. While there is an unmistakable assumption that a celestial paradise would follow (once the pilgrim had been cleansed in the river Lethe, after which his sins would be erased, and the memory of his virtues restored in Eunoë), the line of demarcation between the celestial and the terrestrial does seem to be a very permeable one indeed.

This emphasis on the terrestrial extends back also to the Greco-Roman world, where heaven was conceived either in rural and countrified terms or as an island paradise. Accordingly, poets from the time of Homer in the ninth century BCE described a verdant and fecund environment, untainted by mortality, redolent in singing, partying, endless leisure and a perpetual supply of refreshments (see Russell 1997: 21). As Russell puts it:

> Vergil's garden is an idealization of the Italian countryside, its plains grown
> golden with grain, its vineyards hung with ripe and juicy grapes, its oaks

dripping honey, its sheep obligingly changing the color of their fleece … so that we may vary our clothing. Wolves and lambs lie together, leopards and kids, vipers and infants. Earth and trees and cattle yield their fruits of wine, honey, milk, and grain.

(Russell 1997: 21)

Within early Christianity, also, this picture of heaven as a garden was very much in vogue, at least in the eastern part of the Roman Empire. There were, of course, those in the west, in the Alexandrian tradition, who thought that the account in Genesis 3 of the Garden of Eden was to be understood in a figurative manner. For Philo of Alexandria, indeed, 'To think that it here meant that God planted vines, or olive trees, or apple trees, or pomegranates, and any trees of such kinds, is mere incurable folly' (in Delumeau 2000: 15). However, they were outnumbered by those for whom paradise constituted the fulfilment of material, earthly pleasures. According to Hippolytus in the early third century, contrary to those persons who claim that 'paradise is in heaven and is not a created thing', his position was that 'when one sees with one's eyes the rivers that flow from it and that can still be seen today, one must conclude that paradise is not heavenly but part of creation' (in Delumeau 2000: 16). For Theodore of Mopsuestia, also – one of the most important early Christian thinkers on the question of Christology, in view of his Antiochene defence of the two natures of the person of Christ against the Alexandrian repudiation of the human – the Edenic paradise amounted to 'a special region' and the 'most estimable part of the world' which 'the rising sun illumines first' (in Delumeau 2000: 17). Similarly, for Irenaeus in the second century, the prediction in Revelation 20 of the thousand year reign of Christ that the righteous can expect to enjoy following the great war in heaven provided the template for his teaching that the next life would be a continuation and a fulfilment of this present one. Holding to three periods in history which follow on from one another – the present era, characterised by persecution, the Kingdom of the Messiah and, finally, the Kingdom of God the Father – Irenaeus believed that, following death, the just would dwell in a glorified material world in which suffering, persecution, infertility, old age and death would be no more (see e.g. McDannell & Lang 1990: 52). Heaven would thus be a place on earth, in which material delights would be paramount, wine would be in abundance and work would be superfluous (see e.g. Lerner 1999: 328). Although his third phase suggested something more celestial, Irenaeus was not particularly detailed here, indicating that it was sufficient that the faithful shall see God (see Stanford 2002: 90).

This 'geographicalisation' of heaven as an earthly paradise could also be linked to the quest for paradisal islands that took place from the fourteenth through to the nineteenth centuries.[5] Delumeau cites an anonymous English writer from 1554 who said of Brazil that 'All who have gone there agree that the best and greenest fields and countrysides in the entire world are to be found there', not to mention gold, silver, spices and fruits which are 'so abundant' that 'until now it has not been possible even to imagine that they [sic] could be as many elsewhere as here' (in Delumeau 2000: 111). Not surprisingly, he drew the conclusion that 'it is now thought that the earthly paradise can only be located on the equinoctial line close to it, for the only perfect spot on earth has its spot there' (in Delumeau 2000: 111). A similar claim was made in a letter to Portugal in 1560 by Rui Pereira, according to whom 'If there is a paradise on earth, I would say it exists presently in Brazil … Anyone who wants to live in the earthly paradise has no choice but to live in Brazil' (in Delumeau 2000: 111). What is significant about this testimony is the idea that not merely were certain geographical regions of the earth believed to be so unspoiled and paradisiacal that they corresponded, in a symbolic manner, to Eden, as when George Alsop described Maryland as a new earthly paradise whose trees, plants, fruits and flowers were 'hieroglyphs of our original, adamic situation' (in Delumeau 2000: 115). Rather, such countries and islands were thought to have *preserved* some of the properties and characteristics that the progenitors of the human race had been able to enjoy before they were seized by sin. In the Tillichian sense that symbols, unlike mere signs, participate in the power of that which they symbolise, so the quest for paradisiacal land was not simply about seeing the earthly paradise as an approximation of, or analogous to, its supposed celestial counterpart. Instead, the two were coterminous and inextricably linked in more than a mere sign-pointing way. This idea is reinforced by Delumeau's assertion that, at the end of the seventeenth century, 'the most widely accepted view was that the earthly paradise had indeed existed as a "historical reality," but that it had been erased from the surface of the planet' (Delumeau 2000: 154) – presumably by the Noachian Flood recounted in Genesis 6–9.

Paradisiacal islands were, in other words, an actual physical remnant of the Garden of Eden, an idea which, since nineteenth-century biblical criticism, has long been consigned to the realm of the mythical and the pre-scientific. As Bultmann put it in *Jesus Christ and Mythology*, 'Are we to read the Bible only as an historical document in order to reconstruct an epoch of past history for which the Bible serves as a "source"? Or is it more than a source?' (Bultmann 1958: 51). Since Bultmann saw it as his mission to clear 'away the false stumbling blocks created by modern man by the fact that his world-view is determined by science' (Bultmann 1972 [b]: 183), it could be argued that any suggestion that Eden ought to be seen in physical, geographical terms as the site of our primordial, prelapsarian condition should be construed as a throwback to an anachronistic and antiquated cosmology. Quite simply, in James Barr's words, 'the culture of Biblical man is mythological throughout, while that of modern man is more scientific in character and lacks this mythological element' (Barr 1973: 49–50). But, this idea of heaven as an actual space on earth has had its defenders, and, albeit paradoxically, is the reason why I have decided to focus in this chapter on *Working Girl* and *The Shawshank Redemption*, as the concept of heaven as an earthly paradise is, arguably, integral to the edifice of both pictures. Despite the ostensibly secular context within which they are set, I want to argue that a re-sacralised, terrestrial eschatological reality underlies their respective treatises on fulfilling the American Dream (*Working Girl*) and attaining redemption both in, and beyond, institutionalisation in a corrupt and dehumanising prison environment (*Shawshank*).

Where these two films do, however, depart from traditional Christian expressions of heaven is in their indissolubly secular framework, where any overt Christological or theistic scaffolding (beyond the purely literal 'use' of the Bible in the case of *Shawshank*) is conspicuous by its absence. This failure of either of these films to develop any sort of theistic frame of reference is not an incidental problem. Although he later changed his mind on whether heaven would have any social or family dimension, for the early Augustine heaven was understood in theocentric terms as a world dominated by the spirit and where an all-encompassing contemplation of God could be situated. No dimension of human fellowship was required, with eternal joy consisting simply of reflection upon the Beatific Vision. This idea of heaven is, of course, wholly different from Irenaeus' material, and literal, portrait. But, for both the early Augustine (his later teachings of a social heaven, as discussed in Chapter 1, were more in keeping with those of Irenaeus) and Irenaeus heaven was inseparable from God. The name given to Irenaeus' millennial reign was, after all, the Kingdom of the Messiah, and it was not a realm in which everyone could expect to partake: it was for the righteous only (see McDannell & Lang 1990: 51).

The anthropocentric side of Irenaeus' model may eventually have become the standard for much Christian teaching on heaven, not least in the nineteenth century. However, it is hard to see Nichols' and Darabont's films as bearing witness even to this model of heaven as an ideal kingdom or realm where the soul is able to progress intellectually and spiritually, no longer frustrated by carnal or physical distractions, and where families, social institutions and ethical modes of living are, by virtue of having been given heavenly endorsement, sublime and the perfect outworking of Jesus' teachings in, say, the Sermon on the Mount (see Matthew 5–7). There may be constructive and edifying social relationships at work between the characters in each of these films. But it would be a challenge, to say the least, to find anything in either *Working Girl* or *The Shawshank Redemption* that corresponded to John Lachs' description of heaven as a 'friendly and social place, where the good fortune of all is the condition of the delight of anyone' (Lachs 2001: 132), and as a place, indeed, 'without friction, anxiety, destructive competition, conflicting interests, and debilitating hatreds' (Lachs 2001: 135). If the absence of these is a necessary pre-requisite of life in heaven, then neither film comes close to the threshold of what is required. The characters in both pictures are caught up in problems of corporate and individual sin and guilt, where inequality and discrimination (as particularly evinced in gender terms in *Working Girl*) and corruption and murder (a defining characteristic of the prison environment of *Shawshank*) epitomise the landscape that their protagonists, Tess McGill (Melanie Griffith) and Andy Dufresne (Tim Robbins), inhabit. There are, simply, no human relationships devoid of conflict and struggle in these pictures. It is not therefore clear, at least at first glance, how these films might be found to even approximate a vision of heaven on earth.

It may have been the case for the Anglican Charles Kingsley, author of *The Water Babies* (1863), in the nineteenth century, that the focus of heavenly bliss was less on God than on everlasting sexual embrace with one's marriage partner, in the respect that, in the words of Kingsley's biographer, Kingsley saw heaven as consisting of 'one perpetual copulation in a literal, physical sense' (Chitty 1974: 17). Indeed, writing to his wife Kingsley anticipated that 'Those thrilling writhings are but dim shadows of a union which shall be perfect' (in Chitty 1974: 17). But, even on this score there is little in *Working Girl* or *Shawshank* that would support anything approximating what Kingsley had in mind. Rather, Tess McGill's long-term partner, Mick Dugan (Alec Baldwin) – dismissed by Rita Kempley in *The Washington Post* as 'a philandering, icy blue-eyed hunk who reads Motor Trend in bed' (Kempley 1988: <www.washi ngtonpost.com/wp-srv/style/longterm/movies/videos/workinggirlrkempley_a0c9d9. htm>) – cheats on her with their mutual friend Doreen DiMucci (Elizabeth Whit-craft), and the price that Tess pays for putting her career first is self-imposed exile from her former environment of strong working-class friends whose more limited aspirations of marrying young and having children she has outgrown. For Andy Dufresne, meanwhile, the only female relationship indicated in *Shawshank* is the one for which he is sentenced to life in prison – the murder of his adulterous wife, glimpsed briefly during the opening credits sequence.[6]

Aside from the absence of a God-referent in these films, therefore, what is apparent is that even the anthropocentric dimension of heaven, so prevalent in Victorian literature and theology, cannot easily be reconciled with the broken and dysfunctional portrait of human relationships to which Nichols and Darabont are pointing. As Stanford puts it, 'Throughout the nineteenth century, especially in high-thinking, plain-living, church-going circles, heaven became an extension of people's lives on earth', thereby dovetailing 'neatly with the dominant Victorian ideal of the family' (Stanford 2002: 252). In Phelps' *The Gates Ajar*, for instance, heaven consisted of a reunion of family members, with pianos and sing-songs very much in abundance. Indeed, as one of the characters puts it: 'if you will be a good girl, and go to heaven, I think you will have a piano there, and play just as much as you care to' (Phelps 1869: 146). While, elsewhere in the novel we read that, in heaven, conversations will take much the same form that they do now except that 'there will be no troubles nor sins, no anxieties nor cares, to talk about; no ugly shades of cross words or little quarrels to be made up' (Phelps 1869: 81). It is also conjectured that 'the artist will paint his pictures, the poet sing his happy songs, the orator and author will not find their talents hidden in the eternal darkness of a grave' (Phelps 1869: 162). Essentially, it was this life but without the suffering.

Heaven was so like this world, moreover, that its inhabitants would continue the 'occupations begun on earth' and also occupy themselves 'with a round of museums, universities and concerts' (Moorhead 1999: 91) – comfortable middle-class pursuits, in other words. In her sequel *Beyond the Gates* (1883), Phelps even documented the 'width and shining cleanliness of the streets, the beauty and glittering material of the houses, the frequent presence of libraries, museums, public gardens … and places of shelter for travelers' (Phelps 1883: 118). Yet, the glorified urban vision of her novel, even when allowing for the different historical context, does not translate well to that of the late-twentieth-century New York documented in *Working Girl*, where the city is portrayed as a vicious, competitive, avaricious, cut-throat capitalist jungle where it is the values of Wall Street rather than those of Matthew 5:3 ('Blessed are the poor in spirit, for theirs is the kingdom of heaven') that hold sway.

Working Girl and the New Jerusalem

Even while allowing for the fact that, in both religious and secular circles, the concept of a terrestrial heaven has a long and established history, it is clear that their respective goals are far from coterminous. In *Working Girl*, the goal or *telos* is construed largely in material and financial terms as an escape from the drudgery of working-class life, with its attendant limited career opportunities. In Scott's words, 'The goal is success', even if, as he acknowledges, there is more to Tess' trajectory in the film than just 'a matter of financial rewards' (Scott 1994: 137) alone, in the sense that, as she escapes from her life in the working-class ghetto, Tess also represents the fulfilment of the American Dream (see Scott 1994: 138). Even if the language is deemed sufficiently malleable to warrant the labelling of Tess' ambition in eschatological terms – as when Scott writes that the 'upward mobility' celebrated in the film 'has its own eschatology' (Scott 1994: 137) – there is nothing in this personal improvement eschatology that matches up to what the Christian tradition has to say on the subject, where the language employed is often much more social in orientation. In terms, for instance, of the 'kingdom-building' eschatology of the Christian Social Gospel movement, only by accomplishing God's will in this world – in effect, to create a heaven on earth by means of the Christian imperative to work for social justice – can the categories of eschatology be meaningfully employed. According to the nineteenth-century American economist and founder of the Christian Social Union, Richard T. Ely, 'Christianity is primarily concerned with this world, and it is the mission of Christianity to bring to pass here a kingdom of righteousness and to rescue from the evil one and redeem all our social relations' (in Moorhead 1999: 95). For Walter Rauschenbusch, too, the pivotal figure in the Social Gospel movement, the ultimate aim of social improvement was to mark the beginning of the 'great day of the Lord for which the ages waited' (Rauschenbusch 1920: 422). Heaven was not, on this interpretation, a place we go to after we die but a social and historical reality which we should be seeking to implement in the here and now, by way of social action and activism. Likewise, for Harvey Cox in the 1960s, writing in his groundbreaking work *The Secular City*, 'God manifests Himself to us in and through secular events' (Cox 1966: 233), even to the point that 'secularization represents an authentic consequence of biblical faith' (Cox 1966: 15). After all, in the Genesis Creation narrative, God has, as Cox sees it, given humans the task of tending to and making use of Creation, and assuming the responsibility assigned to Adam (see Cox 1966: 20). Concomitant, therefore, with living in the secular city is the need to demonstrate a mature and accountable stewardship of the created order and to facilitate through the modern urban landscape 'the fashioning of new patterns of human reciprocity' (Cox 1966: 95).

These are, of course, all admirable aims and pursuits, but *Working Girl* could hardly be construed as a film whose raison d'être is one of building God's reign. Cox may have been urging his fellow Protestants to channel their energies into, as Moorhead puts it, 'the search for pragmatic solutions to the problems of urban civilization' (Moorhead 1999: 102). But this lies quite outside the remit of *Working Girl* which is focused on Tess' rise from what is portrayed as a menial job as a secretary in a large brokerage corporation at the start of the film, where she is systematically and humi-liatingly passed over for promotion (unless she is willing to demean herself by sleeping with her coke-snorting, misogynistic male executives) to having an office of her own, overlooking the Manhattan skyline, at Trask Industries where her enterprise skills and business acumen are finally rewarded at the film's denouement. Curiously, this is delineated, quite blatantly, in the film as the attainment of the New Jerusalem. During the closing credits, we hear Carly Simon singing her Oscar-winning song 'Let the River Run'. Juxtaposed with the visual image of a triumphant Tess being con-gratulated over the telephone by her best friend Cyn (Joan Cusack) on her elevation are the song's lyrics: 'Let the river run, / Let all the dreamers wake the nation. / Come, the New Jerusalem'. This overt correlation between the New Jerusalem and the American Dream is inscrutable at best. Are we to suppose that, to paraphrase one film reviewer, Tess McGill is a pilgrim on a religious journey to the Holy Land of high finance (see Nuckols 2008: <http://illinformedgadfly.com/?p=354>)?[7] Aside from the superficial parallel between the 'rivers' alluded to in the song title and Revelation 22, which speaks of 'the river of the water of life … flowing from the throne of God and of the Lamb through the middle of the street of the city' (Revelation 22: 1–2) of the New Jerusalem, it is hard to discern a convincing parallel. In the Bible, the New Jerusalem, which can be traced back to the writings of Ezekiel in the sixth century BCE (see Russell 1997: 14), stands as the 'eternal city' to which the faithful are journeying and which will be inaugurated on earth upon the Last Judgement. The film, however, has no specific anchorage in biblical salvation history. Indeed, it offers something quite at variance to the image of transformed *social* gath-ering and participation invoked in Revelation 21, whose author records that, in a vision, 'I saw the holy city, new Jerusalem, coming down out of heaven from God' (Revelation 21:2), and from whose throne came a loud voice attesting: 'Behold, the dwelling of God is with men. He will dwell with them, and they shall be his people, and God himself will be with them … and death shall be no more' (Revelation 21:3–4).

As Fiddes puts it, the New Jerusalem is 'the true living-space for human fellowship and culture, and the place in which God dwells in fullness' (Fiddes 2000: 282). There is nothing, however, in *Working Girl* which remotely bears witness to any such divine, societal indwelling or participation. The focus, instead, is on social class, ambition and climbing the corporate ladder in what Richard Combs, writing in the *Monthly Film Bulletin*, refers to as 'a tale of making it in the New Yuppie World' (Combs 1989 [a]: 99). There is something quintessentially present-oriented, personal and individualistic about Tess' self-improvement and attainment of the American Dream which stands in marked contrast to the corporate, social and cosmic phe-nomenon of the New Jerusalem in biblical salvation history. Indeed, the city that Tess inhabits, and whose class divisions she seeks to surmount, is not really akin to the image of the city found in the ancient world which was far more community-oriented. As McGrath puts it, 'Cities were understood to be cohesive corporate entities, rather than aggregates of individuals, defined by a definite set of beliefs and values, which in turn determined those of its members' (McGrath 2003: 7). Whereas the city of Nichols' film is a dysfunctional, urban sprawl where differences between class and gender are acutely realised, the picture of the New Jerusalem that appears in the Hebrew Bible is a far more homogeneous entity, consisting of the community of the faithful. Though an earthly city,[8] it has a future referent, also, in that it exists in a symbiotic relationship with the *heavenly* city (in effect, the heavenly Jerusalem pre-exists its earthly counterpart[9]) that will come into being at the end of the world, after the present order has passed away and the heavenly Jerusalem has come down to earth 'at the moment of the last judgement and the defeat of God's earthly enemies' (Fiddes 2000: 283). Rather than having any intrinsic importance, the earthly city is thus only really significant insofar as it 'points toward the union of the community with Christ in heaven' (Russell 1997: 43) – hardly something one could extrapolate from what is going on in the world of corporate mergers and acquisitions and high finance evinced in *Working Girl*.

On the plus side, however, Price makes the important point that the New Jerusalem does not have to be spatially or geographically related to the site of the 'Old' Jerusalem in Palestine in order to be an intelligible construct (see Price 1995 [d]: 265–66). It is true that Price has in mind the possible existence of the New Jerusalem, as well as of heaven more generally, as existing in a mind-dependent realm post-death, different from, though analogous to, the space we presently inhabit on earth, as when he writes that 'it might just be in a space of its own, different from the space of the physical universe' (Price 1995 [d]: 266). But, it does suggest that, once more supple interpretations of the New Jerusalem are brought fully into play, the analogy between the New Jerusalem of the Old and New Testaments and the New York in *Working Girl* is not quite so discrete after all. Indeed, without losing the importance of the material and geographical aspect of the edifice of the New Jerusalem which is so essential to its foundation in Scripture, if we see *Working Girl* as a secularisation of the eschatological quest for purity, perfection and renewal that is evidenced in the Old and New Testaments then a different picture emerges. The film's interpretation of the New Jerusalem may lack any concrete image of the biblical idea of 'the presence and providence of God within its sturdy walls' (McGrath 2003: 6). Nor does it comprise 'a pointer to the fulfillment of messianic expectations' (McGrath 2003: 6) along the lines of Zechariah 8:3 which attests 'Thus says the Lord: I will return to Zion, and will dwell in the midst of Jerusalem, and Jerusalem shall be called the faithful city'. Yet, there is a more practical eschatological expression on display in the Bible to which the film bears at least partial witness.

In Isaiah 27:13, Jerusalem is not just the place where the righteous 'will come and worship the Lord' in praise and glory. Rather, there is an inter-human dimension at work in the respect that Jerusalem is also branded as the site of homecoming and security for the lost and exiled (see Miller 2000: 163). Instead of referring only to the Jews, the expectation is that it is in Jerusalem, atop Mount Zion,[10] that *all* the peoples of the world will gather – 'On this mountain the Lord of hosts will make for all peoples a feast … And he will destroy on this mountain the covering that is cast over all peoples, the veil that is spread over all nations' (Isaiah 25:6–7). Both Jew and Gentile, religious and secular, are accommodated within this new society. As Miller puts it, 'the banquet is not exclusive and in-house; it is a feast "for all peoples"'

(Miller 2000: 162). Former divisions are transcended in this new societal structure, where, as Fiddes puts it, the 'city's gates are open to all, bringing in "the kingdoms and nations of the earth"' (Fiddes 2000: 286). Likewise, for McGrath, the city, being 'filled with eternal light', has the capacity to draw 'people from afar to the safety and rest that it offers' (McGrath 2003: 9). The fact that the city's 12 gates[11] are identified as being permanently open[12] only reinforces the point: 'Whereas the classic fortified city of ancient times was designed to exclude outsiders, the architecture of the New Jerusalem seems designed to welcome them within its boundaries' (McGrath 2003: 12).

It would be counterintuitive to interpret the Book of Isaiah as bearing witness to the promise of an egalitarian society, where discrimination on grounds of gender or social class would be outlawed. This is not least in view of the unequivocally theocentric predilection of the literature which is more adept at stressing God's victory over the forces of evil ('On that day the Lord will punish the host of heaven, in heaven, and the kings of the earth, on the earth' [Isaiah 24:21]) and dispensing divine justice ('For by fire will the Lord execute judgment, and by his sword, upon all flesh; and those slain by the Lord shall be many' [Isaiah 66:16]) than documenting the finer details of what life post-judgement, following 'the enthronement of the deity in the holy abode of God' (Miller 2000: 163), will be like for the remnant. But, an ideal society – albeit one categorised in unremittingly theocentric language – does comprise an important *telos* of those texts which speak of the New Jerusalem, not least in the Book of Revelation. For John Hick, indeed, the New Jerusalem is understood in Revelation to be an ideal society where the social and interpersonal character of human existence is brought to perfection (see Hick 1976: 203). In Zechariah, also, we learn that, upon the establishment of the New Jerusalem, 'Old men and old women shall again sit in the streets of Jerusalem, each with staff in hand for every age. And the streets of the city shall be full of boys and girls playing in its streets' (Zechariah 8:4–5). Hick's talk of the New Jerusalem as a city where 'there is no need of temples because God is present with his people in the person of Christ, the Lamb'[13] and where life is understood in hallowed terms 'as a community wholly responsive to God' (Hick 1976: 203) may be somewhat at odds with the secular disposition of *Working Girl*. But Nichols' film, though ostensibly lacking a social and inter-communal dimension, does, crucially, point towards the establishment of an ideal society, freed from the stigmas and constraints of the past. Indeed, Nichols himself has suggested that Tess' realisation of her goals at the end of the film is not the zenith of all that she, and we, should be working towards.

While the film concludes in such a way as to suggest that Tess' personal success comprises the fulfilment of the American Dream, as the words pertaining to the New Jerusalem are juxtaposed with the view of the New York Harbor and the Statue of Liberty that is afforded to Tess from her new office window, Nichols has qualified this triumph in interviews given at the time of the film's release. In *Sight and Sound*, for instance, Nichols appeared to be signalling that, while within the dynamics of the plot Tess represents the epitome of success, the American Dream is, in truth, only half-fulfilled. In Nichols' words:

The Wall Street firms are going to the colleges to drag the A students into them at $50,000 a year. And they're burned out in four years. That to me was the significance of the last shot, of Tess in her own office at last but surrounded in this building by dozens of identical offices … Perfectly legitimate, absolutely necessary to be won, but small, modest.

(in Combs 1989 [b]: 78)

Real equality and purity is thus incompatible, in Nichols' understanding, with a world where money alone ultimately talks, and it is fitting to this end that Nichols intimates that Tess' ultimate dream is egalitarian: 'And that absolute equalness – if it's not measure for measure it won't work – is my dream' (in Combs 1989 [b]: 78). Tess could be construed as unmistakably resourceful and cunning, as when she takes advantage of her boss' absence following a skiing injury in order to capitalise on a business deal and even takes on a false identity in order to wheedle her way into the wedding of the daughter of a business mogul, Oren Trask (Philip Bosco), whom she wants to impress. Yet, her drive to prosper against all odds does not involve resorting to the unscrupulous tactics perpetrated earlier in the film by the men who offer Tess promotion in return for sexual favours or her disingenuous female boss in the mergers and acquisitions division at Wall Street firm Petty Marsh, Katharine Parker (Sigourney Weaver). Parker, indeed, turns out to be worse than her male counterparts after she shamelessly steals Tess' idea for a merger proposal with Trask Industries. In Nichols' words, 'I suspect … that Tess is so deeply democratic and gentle that she wouldn't stay in that world at all' (in Combs 1989 [b]: 78).

It is not quite true, therefore, to construe the New Jerusalem as a city that we cannot really 'picture except in fairy-tale terms' (Hick 1976: 189). If *Working Girl* were a straightforward rags-to-riches story, Hick's critique might have had a certain applicability, here. After all, Tess' elevation from poverty to success is somewhat redolent of Vivian Ward's (Julia Roberts) journey in *Pretty Woman* (Garry Marshall, 1990) from being a (literal, in this case) working girl, who is refused service in a clothing store on account of her inappropriate apparel, to becoming the princess in the castle rescued by the white knight, in the shape of business tycoon Edward Lewis (Richard Gere). In *Pretty Woman*, Gere's character even literally climbs the ladder (fire escape) leading to her tower (block) in order to love and protect her forever. Tess similarly requires the fairy tale white knight (in her case an investment broker, Jack Trainer [Harrison Ford]) in order to attain the happy ending that she seeks. Indeed, the film has even been categorised as 'a modern day corporate Cinderella story for females' (Schwartz 2008: <http://homepages.sover.net/~ozus/workinggirl. htm>) and 'a delectable reworking of the ultimate girl's myth, a corporate Cinderella story with shades of a self-made Pygmalion'[14] (Kempley 1988: <www.washingtonpost. com/wp-srv/style/longterm/movies/videos/workinggirlrkempley_a0c9d9.htm>) in which Tess is 'Cinderella in a Business Suit' (Maslin 1988: <http://movies.nytimes. com/movie/review?res=940DE5DD153AF932A15751C1A96E948260>), Jack Trainer is 'a white collar Prince Charming' (Frederic & Mary Ann Brussat, date unknown: <www.spiritualityandpractice.com/films/films.php?id=2750>) and 'Harrison Ford and Sigourney Weaver are handsome arbitrageur and evil stepmentor to Griffith's struggling Tess McGill' (Kempley 1988: <www.washingtonpost.com/wp-srv/style/longterm/movies/videos/workinggirlrkempley_a0c9d9.htm>). The fairy tale dimension is flagged up from the moment we first set eyes on Tess during the opening credits sequence when she marks her 30th birthday by blowing out three candles on a cupcake while making a wish, accompanied by the sound of Carly Simon singing 'Let all the dreamers wake the nation'. From the limited horizons of her home in the 'forgotten borough' of Staten Island, from which she yearns to escape, Tess' dreams are directed towards the 'steel-and-glass towers across Upper New York Bay', as represented by the camera's 'vertiginous whirl around the head of the Statue of Liberty, then a dip into the water before a pan up to the skyscrapers of the financial district' (Nuckols 2008: <http://illinformedgadfly.com/?p=354>). As another reviewer puts it:

> Our downtrodden heroine gazes wistfully upon the Statue of Liberty from the deck of the Staten Island ferry on her way to work each morning, longing to turn the monumental platitudes of opportunity, free choice, and the American Dream into realities.
>
> *(Goldsmith 2006: <www.notcoming.com/reviews/workinggirl>)*

But, the ambiguity of the film's ending casts doubt on the fairytale predilection of this film. Tess may have climbed the corporate ladder of success, but the ending is far more ambiguous than that of the more formulaic closure brought to *Pretty Woman* where realism takes a back seat to escapism and fantasy. Indeed, as Roger Ebert says about the ending of Marshall's film:

> There could … be, I suppose, an entirely different movie made from the same material – a more realistic film, in which the cold economic realities of the lives of both characters would make it unlikely they could stay together. And, for that matter, a final scene involving a limousine, a fire escape and some flowers is awkward and feels tacked on.[15]
>
> *(Ebert 1990: http://rogerebert.suntimes.com/apps/pbcs.dll/article?AID=/19900323/*
> *REVIEWS/3230305/1023)*

The conclusion of *Working Girl* is thus somewhat more sophisticated in the way in which it subverts the Hollywood predilection for happy endings. The helicopter shot of the somewhat impersonal Manhattan skyline which concludes Nichols' picture does not picture Tess on the top floor as an executive of her own business empire. She may have her own office, and for that matter a secretary of her own, but she is nevertheless a mere functionary, and instead of the princess at the top of the tower Tess' office is drab (consisting of little more than a desk, a lamplight, a telephone and a computer), anonymous and indistinguishable from all the others. As one reviewer puts it: 'She is rewarded with an office and an "assistant" at the end of the film, though both are noticeably shabbier than in her former, falsified position' (Goldsmith

2006: <www.notcoming.com/reviews/workinggirl>). We do not even know which floor she is on, for as the camera starts to pan out from her window it is super-imposed with a more distant shot of the building in which she works. Having broken away from her roots in Staten Island, with its vibrant and pulsating community of family and friends, Tess is now cast adrift in a cut-and-thrust world which even the film's director doubts is right for her. To this end, I would disagree with the reviewer who wrote that the film's final shot 'mirrors the first but replaces yearning with satisfaction' (Nuckols 2008: <http://illinformedgadfly.com/?p=354>). The film may superficially be portraying Tess as a pilgrim on the road to the New Jerusalem of modern-day Manhattan multinational-corporation capitalism. But when it comes to assessing whether the success she dreamed about at the start of the picture has been accomplished, we are left wanting. Rather than a march forward towards the New Jerusalem, Tess' trajectory is actually a backwards one, prompting one internet reviewer to interpret the end of *Working Girl* 'as the completion of her transformation from working girl to career woman to little schoolgirl' (Goldsmith 2006: <www. notcoming.com/reviews/workinggirl>).[16] If anything, therefore, the New Jerusalem of the Book of Revelation is more 'make believe' and fairytale-oriented than this particular Hollywood confection. For, against the film's lack of closure (and lack of belonging on the part of Tess) is the biblical picture of the New Jerusalem 'paved with gold and decked with jewels and precious stones, dazzling its inhabitants and intensifying the sense of longing to enter through its gates on the part of those still on earth' (McGrath 2003: 11).

The New Jerusalem that Tess supposedly reaches at the film's denouement, in marked contrast, is hardly one characterised by the glitter of gold and jewels. The anticipated 'happy ending', so typical of Hollywood in the 1980s, is, albeit subtly, undermined by the final shot. Indeed, in a decade that was obsessed with 'restating therapeutic, triumphal narratives that tended to exploit clearly established perimeters between good and evil' (Stern, Jefford & DeBona 1999: 288), the 1980s was a time when Hollywood was obsessed with positive role models who, after the malaise and disaffection of the 1970s post-Vietnam and Watergate, could only be victorious in the face of adversity, in the mould of John Rambo and Rocky Balboa. The same national pride that we see on display in *Rocky IV* (Sylvester Stallone, 1985), in which America, in the form of Stallone's Rocky, is somewhat predictably triumphant over the Soviet Union, represented by the merciless and barbaric Captain Ivan Drago (Dolph Lundgren), is, arguably, not on display at all in *Working Girl* (and not simply because the film lacks *Rocky*'s overt Cold War, 'good' vs. 'evil' ideological underpinning). In its place we see a critique, not the fulfilment, of the American Dream. *Working Girl* may explicitly draw the correlation, but the New Jerusalem of the Old and New Testaments is, somewhat ironically, closer in spirit to the revisionist milieu of *Rambo* than it is to Nichols' picture. When, writing in the same year that *Working Girl* was made, Auster and Quart described John Rambo as 'the ultimate fighting machine, with whom no amount of police, national guardsmen, helicopters' or 'antitank weapons … can cope' (Auster & Quart 1988: 93), and, also writing in the same year, Robert Kolker posited that *Rambo: First Blood, Part Two* (George Pan Cosmatos,

1985) brings 'events back to a better place than when they started or were originally left unfinished' (Kolker 1988: 263), the parallel with the Biblical New Jerusalem is not completely wide of the mark. For, as McGrath puts it:

> [The New Jerusalem's] security is beyond question. It is perched on the peak of a hill that no invading army could hope to ascend. Its walls are so thick that they could not be breached by any known siege engine, and so high that no human could hope to scale them.
>
> (McGrath 2003: 11)

This is, quite simply, a picture to which Hick's fairy story designation lends a particularly vivid imaginative potency, not least when McGrath adds, with reference to the assertion in Revelation 21:12 that in post at the 12 gates of the city of the New Jerusalem are 'twelve angels', that 'the New Jerusalem is defended against invasion by supernatural forces' (McGrath 2003: 11). There is an otherness about the Biblical New Jerusalem to which *Working Girl's* somewhat cautious, even cynical, embrace of the American Dream hardly accords. Augustine in the fifth century may have spoken with some optimism of the pleasure involved in the fact that our human weaknesses would be transcended and overcome in the New Jerusalem (see McGrath 2003: 16). But, in *Working Girl* Tess' accomplishments are partial and provisional (and most certainly temporal) at best. If Tess is a fairy-tale heroine, this should be qualified by Kempley's observation that 'Happily-ever-aftering is hard as hell' in a modern context where 'The divorce rate being what it is, Prince Charming just isn't the answer anymore. Today's Cinderella first sets her sights on a career ... Girls in glass slippers want car phones, briefcases, seats on the stock exchange' (Kempley 1988: <www. washingtonpost.com/wp-srv/style/longterm/movies/videos/workinggirlrkempley_ a0c9d9.htm>). In such a revisionist milieu, it is somewhat fitting that, after Tess has explained how she came up with her idea for the merger with Trask Industries, her (truthful as it happens) version of events is derided by Katharine Parker, in an over-blown exchange with Oren Trask, the CEO of Trask Industries, as fanciful: 'Oren, we really don't have any more time for fairy tales'.[17] If the film does possess a fairy-tale dimension, it is a subtly demythologised one, stripped of any pretence that Tess' wish-fulfilment has come true.

Despite departing, however, in many ways from the Biblical New Jerusalem, *Working Girl's* eschatology is no less a geographical construct, and the product of a particular time and place – specifically late 1980s Reagan-era Manhattan – than its scriptural counterpart. The New Jerusalem that Tess seeks may not lie atop a mountain, have 12 gates, be fortified by angels or consist of the dwelling place of the saints. Nor, indeed, could its identification with the world of cut-throat capitalism be further removed from Augustine's understanding that the New Jerusalem would be characterised by rest (see McGrath 2003: 16). But it is an expressly concrete entity nonetheless. As with *The Shawshank Redemption*, to which the discussion will now turn, the film ends with an aerial shot of water and the drama in both pictures is played out against the backdrop of a very precise physical location – Manhattan in the case of *Working Girl* and Zihuatanejo on the Mexican coast in *Shawshank*. The Statue of Liberty obviously represents the emancipation and freedom that Tess craves, but throughout Nichols' drama we are also privy to carefully executed shots which position Tess looking out over the New York Harbour with the Statue within the same frame. This 'concretisation' of eschatological expectations is also central to *Shawshank*, to the point indeed that the 'redemption' evoked in the film's title has an ultimately very physical referent, despite the vast array of symbolic and spiritual theological frameworks concerning redemption within which the film is ostensibly situated.

The Shawshank Redemption and the concretisation of 'redemption'

Aside from a few brief pages in Bernard Brandon Scott's *Hollywood Dreams and Biblical Stories*, published in 1994, *Working Girl* has received little if any (even cursory) treatment by theologians. In marked contrast, Frank Darabont's prison escape drama *The Shawshank Redemption* has been the explicit subject of a considerable body of work in the theology and film field since its rather unpromising theatrical release in America in September 1994.[18] Indeed, for a film whose production budget was $25 million but which only barely managed to make a profit, with gross box office takings of $28,341,469,[19] even allowing for a theatrical re-release following its seven Oscar nominations, including one for Best Picture, the following February, the degree of investment in *Shawshank* by theologians has been, on one level, quite disproportionate. The highest ranking that *Shawshank* achieved in the US box office charts was number 8, in the second weekend of October 1994, when it lagged far behind the Sylvester Stallone action thriller *The Specialist* (Luis Llosa, 1994), which was at number 1 with $14,317,765.[20] *Shawshank*'s gross that weekend, by contrast, was a paltry $1,968,808.[21] The film performed much better, however, on video cassette, becoming one of the top renting films of 1995 (see Kermode 2003: 12). For the past decade it has consistently featured at the top, or at least in the top two, of the *Internet Movie Database* Top 250 films of all time, voted for by 'ordinary' filmgoers rather than film critics or industry professionals. As of July 2010 more than half a million votes have been cast on the IMDb for *Shawshank*, more than 100,000 more votes than its nearest rival, *The Godfather* (Francis Ford Coppola, 1972).[22] The IMDb also gives it a rating of 9.1 out of 10.

Since then, it has been an intensive repository of research by a number of theologians, most notably Clive Marsh whose *Cinema and Sentiment* accords the film extensive treatment. In a *Journal of Religion and Film* article in 1998 Marsh also highlighted some of the ways in which the film's use of the word 'redemption' can actually be a barrier to the practice of good theology, on the grounds that just because redemption is a theologically efficacious word it does not follow that 'a "religious" reading of the film – in a general sense – must result' (Marsh 1998: <www.unomaha.edu/jrf/marshrel.htm>). That the film should have received so much attention is on one level unsurprising in view of the fact that, in Marsh's words, this is a 'hugely popular film, in the title of which is a term (redemption) that invites theological exploration, yet the precise meaning of which is left relatively ill explored in the film itself' (Marsh 2004: 47). Without wishing to re-visit every aspect of an already over-crowded field of theological-film analysis, *Shawshank* is worth further attention here precisely because it seems to bear witness to the idea of heaven – or, even, on a different though no less untenable reading, hell[23] – as a physical and geographical location on earth.

In contrast to *Working Girl*, however, whose delineation of the New Jerusalem is explicitly rooted in a particular time and place, the 'redemption' proffered in Darabont's film is a far more heterogeneous concept. As Kermode sees it:

> ... although the film may seem on one level to suggest a primarily religious 'redemption', it is also ... an exemplary escape fantasy which allows for a whole range of 'exits' from the horrors of confinement or repression; playing with models of revolutionary transformation ... and celebrating the consummate escape machine of cinema itself.
>
> *(Kermode 2003: 12)*

Indeed, there are scenes in the film which suggest that the most authentic form of escape is, albeit ironically for a film which culminates in a prison escape, one where the mind or imagination is set free, despite the body's physical incarceration, by the creative or magical power of music, film or (in view of Andy's Ivy-League back-ground and his keenness to inculcate his fellow prisoners with the power of learning) education. A case in point is the scene in which the protagonist, Andy Dufresne, has finally succeeded in obtaining funds from the State Senate to build a more extensive library for the inmates at Shawshank. In addition to books Andy receives a supply of gramophone records, one of which, an aria from Mozart's *Marriage of Figaro*, he proceeds to play at the highest decibels over the Warden's public address system for everyone in the prison yard to hear. The voice-over of Red (Morgan Freeman) encapsulates the spiritual possibility afforded by this scene:

> I have no idea to this day what those two Italian ladies were singing about. Truth is, I don't want to know. Some things are best left unsaid. I'd like to think they were singing about something so beautiful it can't be expressed in words ... It was like some beautiful bird flapped into our drab little cage and made those walls dissolve away, and for the briefest of moments every last man in Shawshank felt free.

There is a great personal cost to Andy as a result of this episode. Due to this 'stunt', as the Warden calls it, Andy is sentenced to two weeks in solitary confinement, a form of punishment designed to make him conform even further to what is a particularly brutal and corrupt institutional regime. Yet, when he returns from the darkness and isolation of 'the hole' his spiritual strength is, we are led to suppose, even stronger than it was before. His body may have been subject to abuse and deprivation, but on a psychological or mythological level he has triumphed over evil in the underworld and been 'reborn'. Ferrell sums up Andy's trajectory very well in this regard when he writes that if Andy 'can accept the pain and degradation of being buried behind prison bars as a test, if he passes (survives), he will be rewarded by entering paradise, freedom' (Ferrell 2000: 71). After all, as Andy explains to his fellow incredulous inmates, he had 'Mr Mozart to keep me company' and 'there's something inside that they can't get to, can't touch … Hope'.

As with the aforementioned *Jacob's Ladder*, also starring Tim Robbins in the lead role, there is something purgatorial about Andy's plight in this film. For, like Jacob Singer, he seems to lie betwixt two dimensions of existence, one physical, anguished and transitory, the other luminescent and the quintessence of hope. The fact that the ending of *Jacob's Ladder* presents a literal white light into the auspices of which the protagonist literally ascends is not exactly discrete from Andy's trajectory in *Shawshank*. In Kermode's words, 'This sense of being a man at one remove from the material world is central to the character of Andy Dufresne' (Kermode 2003: 29), an idea reinforced by Red's voice-over which refers to Andy in quite Docetic terms as a man who seemed to wear 'an invisible coat that would shield him from this place'. Indeed, there are clear suggestions in this film that Andy seems almost to transcend the material nature of his existence. Kermode even offers as one reading of the film the idea that 'Dufresne is only partly of this earth, a displaced angel traipsing through the dirt of the world, untarnished by its imperfection' (Kermode 2003: 30). This may be taking things a little too far – after all, Andy, unlike the Gnostic understanding of the Messiah, as typified in the second century by Basileides (see Stevenson 1992: 76–78), is not a divine saviour-figure who merely *pretends* to be human. The suffering Andy undergoes in prison, the most vicious of which is depicted in the scenes showing Andy fending off repeated attempts by 'The Sisters' (or 'bull queers') to gang-rape him, are hardly coterminous with Basileides' teaching that the Messiah, being divine in essence, could not have demeaned himself to undergo the ignominy of death by crucifixion. Andy is brutally tortured and in need of hospitalisation, and as Red puts it: 'I wish I could tell you that Andy fought the good fight and The Sisters let him be … but prison is no fairy-tale world'. But, and this is the crucial point, what is not in doubt is that Andy is able to deal with affliction in a more stoical and resilient fashion than everyone else.

It is all the more remarkable, then, that, after painting a picture of redemption and hope in such symbolical terms, with a protagonist who seems to be far more spiritually-attuned than anyone else, the filmmakers should have opted for an ending whose exclusive focus is on the physical, the material and the concrete. This is the scene where Red follows instructions that have been left for him by Andy, concealed under a volcanic rock in a Buxton hayfield, to enable them to be re-united in the small fishing village of Zihuatanejo on the Pacific coast. Kermode rightly feels that this final scene – which was not in Darabont's original screenplay, nor in the Stephen King novella from 1982, *Rita Hayworth and Shawshank Redemption*, which inspired the movie, but was a later addition – has 'no earthly business being in *The Shawshank Redemption*' (Kermode 2003: 85). Up until this point, Zihuatanejo has been a metaphor for the hope that Andy embodies. When the name is first introduced, it is a place where, as Andy confides to Red, he escapes at night in his dreams. He is drawn to the fact that it lies on the shores of the Pacific, and he informs Red: 'You know what the Mexicans say about the Pacific? They say it has no memory. That's where I want to live the rest of my life – a warm place with no memory'. Rather than a geographical location *per se*, it denotes a utopian environment, somewhat in keeping with the sort of secular literature that came to prominence in the sixteenth century. This is epitomised by Thomas More's *Utopia* from 1516 with its vision of an imaginary island called Utopia where human desires would be fulfilled and which would amount to 'a place of well-being and harmony between individual, society and nature' (Fiddes 2000: 223).

Just as More's vision of Utopia 'served as a kind of refuge' (Delumeau 2000: 120) from the empirical world of everyday reality, where there was such a disjuncture between the real world and the world of one's dreams and aspirations, so for Andy Dufresne Zihuatanejo is a place characterised by the absence of memory. As Kermode puts it, this is a place where 'the tribulations of his former life will cease to exist; a vision of paradise by another name' (Kermode 2003: 68). Even the language is very similar, in that Dufresne's talk of Zihuatanejo being a place with no memory ties in with Fiddes' claim (written within the context of the 'Death of God' theology of Thomas Altizer) that 'in [Aldous] Huxley's vision of Utopia, the "here and now" of the present moment is identified with a total moment which is the absence of time' (Fiddes 2000: 247). For Thomas More, the imaginary island has physical and spatial properties. Indeed, we read that his dreamland consists of 'fifty-four city-states, all spacious and magnificent, identical in language, traditions, customs, laws' (More 1965: 113), whose farmers 'breed a vast quantity of poultry' (More 1965: 115), whose 'streets are well laid out both for traffic and for protection against the winds' and whose gardens are 'so well kept and flourishing that I never saw anything more fruitful and more tasteful anywhere' (More 1965: 121). But, it could not be found on a map. It is the idea that is far more important. There is no need or desire which cannot be sated in Utopia. This is consonant with the way in which Zihuatanejo represents the idea of freedom from corruption and institutionalisation and functions as a metaphor for a place where all boundaries, which, like Shawshank prison, stifle human flourishing, have been abolished.

What Darabont has done, however, is to reduce this metaphor to what is effectively a banal pretty picture on a seaside postcard. In the last scene, we witness Red's arrival, by public transport, at the town of Zihuatanejo where we see him strolling along the beach, his face beaming with joy, and warmly embracing Andy, who is busy building boats. The clear suggestion is that the concretisation of redemption in this way constitutes the fulfilment that Andy and Red have been seeking up to this point. As Marsh succinctly puts it: 'It is sunny there. This is heaven: heaven on earth' (Marsh 2004: 50). There is undoubtedly something quite satisfying on one level about this ending, in the respect that after decades of abuse we are privy to the sight of Andy and Red enjoying a new life in what is, for all intents and purposes, a new world order. As I have written previously, it is as dichotomous from their former life on earth as heaven is from earth in traditional Christian interpretation (see Deacy &

Ortiz 2008: 198). But, it also belies all that has gone before. Indeed, there is something precisely a-historical about the utopia that Zihuatanejo represents which is diminished by the decision taken to circumscribe it to a particular geographical representation. Significantly, in the original screenplay the film was due to end on the bus that Red is taking to the Mexican border, from which he will continue on his journey to Zihuatanejo, with Red's voice-over referring to

> ... the excitement only a free man can feel. A free man at the start of a long journey whose conclusion is uncertain. I hope I can make it across the border. I hope to see my friend and shake his hand. I hope the Pacific is as blue as it has been in my dreams. I hope.

The decision to give the hope that Red speaks of so poignantly a concrete, material expression emanated from concerns expressed by the film's producers that audiences are more likely to want a happy ending where the two main characters are reunited. Admittedly, this decision was corroborated by the subsequent positively received test screenings, after which some audience members even spoke about the new ending as being their favourite scene in the whole film (see Kermode 2003: 87). Darabont, too, has attested that, despite some initial reservations, after shooting the final scene there was no way he was going to be persuaded to take it out for 'I'd started falling in love with it' (in Kermode 2003: 87). For Morgan Freeman, also, the ending that the filmmakers eventually settled on was a necessary one, on the grounds that the film's 'final moment of reconnection was very powerful, and I think it gave it a better sense of closure' (in Kermode 2003: 87). Tim Robbins likewise attests that 'personally I think you *need* that ending' (in Kermode 2003: 87). Yet, when Robbins also says that there is something universal about the film's appeal wherein on 'a metaphysical level, people feel enslaved by their environments, their jobs, their relationships, by whatever it is in the course of their lives that puts the wall or the bars around them' (in Kermode 2003: 69), this ironically makes the originally conceived ending, which concluded with the *journey*, far more efficacious. This is because if, as Robbins is here saying, we each have our own Zihuatanejo, then it follows that not everyone's idea of Zihuatanejo, or utopia, will take the form of a Mexican beach. The fact that the ending was actually filmed not in Zihuatanejo but on St Croix in the Virgin Islands only reinforces the point that it is the *idea* of Zihuatanejo which is more important than the place itself.

A similar tension between the idea of paradise and the experience thereof can be seen to lie in *Shirley Valentine* (Lewis Gilbert, 1989), a superficially frothy comedy[24] about a bored, middle-aged Liverpudlian housewife, Shirley Valentine (Pauline Collins), who escapes to a Greek island on a two-week holiday and decides to stay there. This is another film which has generated some interest among theologians, most notably Clive Marsh, though in the context of a discussion of pneumatology, and the Christian understanding of the Holy Spirit, rather than eschatology (see Marsh 1997 [a]: 193–205). As with *Shawshank*, there is much that *Shirley Valentine* has to say about the earthly paradise. Shirley's fellow British holidaymakers are disappointed at what they find when they arrive on the Greek island of Mykonos. Dougie (George Costigan) exclaims, 'Travel agent said we'd like it here. I'm a bit dubious myself', and he replies to Sydney's (Ken Sharrock) shock, upon alighting from the rickety bus that has just transported them from the ferry, at the apparent lack of amenities compared to previous holidays in Majorca – 'Where's the disco? Where's the bar?' – with the none-too-intelligent observation that there's 'more life in a crematorium'. For Shirley, on the other hand, the island could not be more perfect: 'It was like I'd come to the far side of paradise. And I loved it'. As time unfolds, however, Shirley comes to reappraise whether, having 'led such a little life … when inside me there was so much more, and it's all gone unused, and now it never will be', her dream has been realised. She informs the owner of a Greek taverna, Costas (Tom Conti), with whom she is about to embark on a brief fling, that 'I've got this soft little dream about sitting at a table by the edge of the sea' – a dream she is then enabled to realise as Costas sets her a table and chair on the beach overlooking the beautiful, red sunset, to the accompaniment of the film's upbeat (and Oscar nominated) musical score. In voice-over, Shirley then offers the following wry rumination:

> Funny, isn't it? When you've pictured something, when you've imagined how something's going to be, it never turns out like that, does it? I mean, for weeks I've pictured myself sitting here. Sitting here, drinking wine by the sea. And I knew exactly how I was going to feel. Now I'm here, it doesn't feel a bit like that. I don't feel at all lovely and serene, I feel … pretty daft actually. And awfully, awfully old.

Costas then replicates her disappointment by discerning that dreams 'are never in the place you expect them to be'. Although Shirley opts to remain in Greece, it is not because the place itself is paradisiacal. Rather, it is because her time away from her drab, suburban alienated existence in England has prompted her to confront and reappraise what she has been doing for the last two decades of her life, and, in her inner voyage of existential self-discovery, she is able to come to the conclusion that 'I've fallen in love with the idea of living'. For someone who had earlier lamented the fact that, as human beings, 'we get all these feelings and dreams and hopes', yet 'we don't ever use them', Shirley has undoubtedly undergone a transformative, even, to cite some of the language used by reviewers, a redemptive[25] experience. This is betokened by Rita Kempley's review of the film in the *Washington Post*, in which she refers to *Shirley Valentine* as 'a tale of a phoenix risen from the frying pan' that 'reaffirms that most hopeful of notions: It's never too late to start over again' (Kempley 1989 (b): <www. washingtonpost.com/wp-srv/style/longterm/movies/videos/shirleyvalentinerkempley_ a0c997.htm>). Yet, the physical attainment of (what she thought was the epitome of) Paradise, in Mykonos – the functional equivalent of Zihuatanejo – is nothing more than a means to an end. Her spiritual journey is facilitated by her geographical journey to the terrestrial Paradise, but Mykonos is not the end in itself.

To this end, *Shirley Valentine* betrays a more sophisticated awareness of the limitations of heaven, or paradise, as 'place', than *Shawshank*, where, we are led to believe,

Andy's utopia is supposed to represent a new life in a world freed from the institutions and structures that defined his past. Darabont himself attests that it is marked by a place where 'the horizon is limitless' and where the characters have travelled 'from darkness to light, from coldness to warmth ... , from physical and spiritual imprisonment to total freedom' (Kermode 2003: 87). But, we can contrast *Shawshank*'s ending to *Shirley Valentine*'s decided lack of closure, as Shirley and her estranged husband, Joe (Bernard Hill), do not find reconciliation and have no clear future together against what is a very similar backdrop of (an albeit setting) sun, beach and water where she invites him to join her for a drink. Moreover, in keeping with Foucault who doubts that an alternative world, or utopia, can ever break free from the power structures and manipulative relations of present society, *Shawshank*'s ending paradoxically generates new political, economic and social power structures and institutions which militate against the establishment of an earthly Eden. Foucault refers, for instance, to 'the vast space separating the garden of God and the cities which men, driven from paradise, have built with their own hands' (Foucault 1967: 63). Evidence of this disjuncture between the 'real' utopia and the human representation of it can be seen in the decision to show Andy building boats for a living on the Zihuatanejo beach. Attractive though such an enterprise may be, Marsh makes the pertinent point that the 'boat business in Mexico will have to deal with questions of investment, cash flow crises, taxation, paperwork and employment legislation' (Marsh 2004: 53–54). In transplanting the dream that sustained him at night in his prison cell to an actual socio-political-cultural location, in other words, questions are raised which the film, in its overarching mission to supply an unapologetically upbeat ending, is unable to satisfactorily address. No geographical territory exists in a vacuum, which makes the filmmakers' decision to correlate Paradise with Mexico a particularly incongruous one. Zihuatanejo may be a transcendent utopia for Andy, at least in his dreams, but Mexico is also a country often associated with violent crime and drug-trafficking (particularly in relation to the ongoing Mexican Drug War), and, in April 2009, was the origin of the worldwide outbreak of swine flu. The association between a Mexican beach and the fulfilment of one's hopes may not therefore be explicit for all audience members. The further consideration that the only humans we see at the end of the film, despite the Mexican setting, are Americans, only serves to reinforce Jewett's observation that the 'escapist vision of an idyllic life there, without any Mexicans in sight or any awareness of their story of institutionalised bondage, seems to be a sad example of ethnocentric American imagination' (Jewett 1999: 175–76).[26]

The ambiguous ending of *Working Girl* in marked contrast is quite mature in the way that it eludes the cheap and transitory thrills of the Hollywood happy ending with its purported, but unsustainable, suggestion that adversity has been overcome. At the end of that film, we can see the disparity between the words that invoke the New Jerusalem and the image of Tess looking out from a nondescript office block, still waiting for her dream (whether it is construed as the New Jerusalem or as a utopian realm does not ultimately make any difference) to be fulfilled. *Shawshank*'s somewhat ham-fisted climax may be closer in essence to the material and geographical dimension of Virgil's garden and Irenaeus' Kingdom of the Messiah than to the more symbolic, subjective and existential approach to eschatology that is redolent of Bultmann and other exponents of realised eschatology. But this only serves to highlight the paucity of any eschatological rendering which delimits the afterlife to the fulfilment of earthly delights. Appealing though it may be to filmmakers to attempt to bring paradise down to earth, this only reinforces Russell's argument, as broached at the beginning of this chapter, that it is not heaven itself but only the human articulation of heaven that is being established: 'Heaven itself cannot be described, but the human concept of heaven can be' (Russell 1997: 3).

Pictorially, and cinematically, artists and filmmakers are afforded much scope to indulge their creative imaginations. With the development of CGI (and increasingly the use of 3-D), filmmakers have opportunities open to them that were unavailable just a decade or so ago when Vincent Ward was in the process of creating what was at the time a groundbreaking and visually rich evocation of heaven in *What Dreams May Come*. But, theologically, the ending of *Shawshank* is impoverished, as the type of material and concrete representation that is so intrinsic to Darabont's picture bears little resemblance to how, in the Bible, for example, a sacred place comprises a concrete site that mediates the divine Other and allows God access into profane reality (see Ostwalt 2003: 79).[27] McGrath also encapsulates the divergence when he writes that to 'speak of paradise is not to hanker after a return to a specific physical place, but to yearn for the restoration of a specific spiritual state' (McGrath 2003: 42). The *telos* of Zihuatanejo, in contrast, is the idea that, as Kermode puts it, 'a beach and a boat are the greatest rewards imaginable' (Kermode 2003: 86).

In this sense, Zihuatanejo bears witness to something of a postmodern worldview, in terms of Ostwalt's model, insofar as it is not God or heaven that is the object of reference but (profane) 'place' itself. Indeed, Zihuatanejo has been reified in *Shawshank* to the embodiment of 'otherness' and utopian perfection (cf. Ostwalt 2003: 79) in much the same way that Ostwalt discusses the 'utopian idealism' (Ostwalt 2003: 86) of Graceland or the North Carolina community of Love Valley in the United States which do not mediate otherness but function *as* otherness. Love Valley, indeed – a self-styled constructed 'community built on utopian idealism' (Ostwalt 2003: 86), specifically rural agrarianism and urban myth – has, for more than half a century, enabled anyone who wishes to escape from the vicissitudes of modern living to undergo a process of spiritual and ethical renewal in what amounts in essence to 'a holy community that would in time lead to the regeneration of the larger society' (Ostwalt 2003: 83). Yet, rather than a beach in Mexico, or anywhere else for that matter, heaven within a Christian context has a very different frame of reference. As Russell attests:

> For Christians, heaven is where Christ is. Going to heaven, or, better, being in heaven is being in the presence of Christ, whether one encounters him, sees him, merges with him, or in a sense becomes him. One is in heaven insofar as one is 'in' Christ.
>
> *(Russell 1997: 4)*

Whereas *Shawshank* concludes with a secular utopian image of two former prison inmates having effectively absconded to Mexico, and able to enjoy in the present a degree of freedom hitherto denied them, the Christian hope has a much wider, and potentially cosmic, frame of reference. As Janet Soskice puts it: 'Christian hope looks forward to God's time, the kingdom, when all will be well and when every tear will be dried, when all the suffering of the world through its ragged and jagged history will be made whole' (Soskice 2000: 78). Even for those who subscribe to more realised expressions of eschatology, and who thus lack the implied future referent, belief in heaven does not simply equate to the fulfilment of individual hopes and dreams in the way that anchors *Working Girl* and *Shawshank*. As was discussed at the end of the previous chapter, the goal for exponents of both realised and future eschatologies is the living of life with reference to clearly demarcated theistic, rather than merely human and transitory, goals and standards, in which it is the pattern or *telos* of existence that ultimately matters. As Russell attests, 'Heaven is the state of being in which all are united in love with one another and with God', the antithesis of which condition 'is isolation and retreat' (Russell 1997: 5). This corporate understanding of heaven as 'the community of those whom God loves and who love God' (Russell 1997: 5) is strikingly absent from the trajectory of Andy Dufresne.

But, this is not to say that any 'redemption' that operates in *The Shawshank Redemption* is thereby deficient because it fails to meet the purported 'higher' standards of Christian theology. There is no reason why the film cannot work on its own terms as an analogue of the Christian eschatological drama. It may work, for example, along the lines of Michael Grosso's argument that when this-worldly terms are employed to refer to the celestial abode this can, paradoxically, have the effect of reinforcing rather than undermining the hope for a future life. Obviously, *Shawshank*'s presentation of Zihuatanejo may fall short on account of its lack of a transcendent referent. But what Grosso appears to be saying is that there is a symbiotic relationship between the earthly and the heavenly paradise in the respect that the closer one gets to transforming earth into a paradisiacal order the closer we will be towards materialising the afterlife and moving toward 'overcoming the dualism of heaven and earth, eternity and time, divine and human' (Grosso 1990: 254). Moreover, as Grosso sees it, it is 'in the liberation and transformation of earthly existence that the "afterlife"' (Grosso 1990: 253) is, even, *proven*, and that the 'best way to "prove" life after death is to bring paradise down to earth' (Grosso 1990: 253). The grounds for this are that, in his, 'Every life saved, liberated, enhanced adds to the building of the new earth and the new heaven' (Grosso 1990: 253). Although the filmmakers themselves may not overtly be using the Christian concept of heaven as a template for wanting to transform the present in the light of a Christian *telos*, Grosso's position is helpful in showing where a Christian eschatological reading of *Shawshank* may be initiated. For, Christian viewers may find that the film's ending, though not theological *per se*, kick-starts, and fleshes out, a theologically informed reading of the film in much the same way that, as I have outlined before, a film such as *Cape Fear* (Martin Scorsese, 1991) can provide a possible entry-point to theologically efficacious questions about truth-telling, confessing one's sins or atoning for the transgressions of the past without necessarily preaching to an audience about how they should live their lives (see Deacy 2008 [a]: 20). We do not have to have spent time in, or escaped from, a prison ourselves – let alone committed murder – in order to be able to relate to what is happening on screen in *The Shawshank Redemption*. The film has scope beyond the specific constituency of people or communities being realised on screen. We can see this, for instance, in Marsh's assertion that Red's regret for the crime he committed decades earlier 'will find an echo in any deep experience of regret summoned up in the viewer' and will prove useful theologically 'when the film's reception is located within a wider cognitive framework in which key concepts such as redemption, salvation, liberation and atonement are given substance' (Marsh 2004: 55).

Just because the delineation of the earthly paradise of Zihuatanejo may be unfulfilling does not thereby mean it has no theological utility. On the contrary, it is only when this present life is taken seriously that any theological and eschatological enquiry is meaningful. A good analogy would be the emphasis in liberation theology on the value of human activity in *this* world (with the political liberation signified by Exodus the most fitting paradigm) and on the idea that human action, the world and all of its history, comprises the necessary and authentic point of departure for all reflection. After all, as John Hick was quoted as saying in this book's introduction, we can no more speculate about death than we can refrain from speculating about life – 'the one is inseparable from the other' (Hick 1976: 21). Instead of closing down dialogue with Christian theology, the end of *Shawshank* thus enables the theologian to ask questions about how all of our terrestrial goals, whether construed in social, individual, political, cultural, historical, ecological, economic or material form, need to be taken seriously rather than diminished because of any purported absence of ultimacy. David Brown similarly talks about how heaven only makes sense when it is built upon the identity we have acquired in *this* life, to the point that death should shape our present lives (Brown 1995: 47–48).

In other words, a new way of seeing eschatology is called for, one which, as in Brown's case, involves construing heaven as being alongside and all about us, rather than simply being 'above' us (Brown 1995: 52). To this end, *Shawshank* can go some way towards contributing to the resulting conversation. Rather than let the conversation thus come to an end because, as for Kermode, correlating heaven with a beach and a boat is too shallow and inadequate when set against the traditional Christian picture of heaven, Marsh is right that 'given that "a beach and a boat" *is* presented and the film is thus offering images of salvation/redemption which are not solely other-worldly, then to fail to develop the "this-worldly" salvation sells the viewer short' (Marsh 2004: 53). Indeed, Marsh continues, the materiality of the ending actually 'turns in the film's favour, and becomes a challenge to readings of salvation which are simply too narrowly spiritual' (Marsh 2004: 56). After all, if people are using the language of 'being saved' in a this-worldly context then, no matter how much such language or such hopes may appear to fall short in light of the transcendent or metaphysical End, the fact remains that 'this salvation must matter to them here and now, or it may not be worth as much as Christianity claims' (Marsh 2004: 56). If, in short, 'the film's views of salvation can challenge Christianity to look at the images of heaven that it has presented' then the film has actually served a positive purpose, particularly when its unapologetically material and this-worldly ending has the net result of 'confronting Christianity with a weakness in the contemporary viability of its own symbol system' (Marsh 2004: 56).

All of this is, of course, a far cry from any attempt to Christianise a non-Christian picture into being an outworking of the Christian drama of redemption, salvation and future hope. Such approaches, though counterproductive, are all too reminiscent of recent attempts within some theology and film circles to baptise 'secular' film characters as so-called Christ-figures.[28] Instead of looking for points of artificial convergence, it is more intellectually satisfying when, as in line with Lynch's revised correlational model, both film and theology can be seen to undergo a change with respect to the way in which they both address questions of salvation, redemption and heaven. *Shawshank*'s range of interpretations is undoubtedly enhanced when the film is examined through the lens of Christian theology in the respect that theologians are able to help fine tune and contextualise that to which the 'Redemption' of the film's title might be referring. By the same token, the film's failure to delineate an adequate vision of heaven on earth in the final reel has the capacity to enable theologians to revisit the paucity of those attempts throughout history to delimit heaven by concretising or materialising it.

We can already see traces of the way in which *The Shawshank Redemption* has impacted on scholarly endeavours in the area of redemption, as when, in *Cinema and Sentiment*, Clive Marsh argued, following a detailed discussion of Darabont's film three chapters earlier, that an 'appropriate concrete next step for the theology/religion-film debate must … be to gather empirical data … about how films work' (Marsh 2004: 131). Having looked at such data, as when in the summer of 2004 Marsh was involved in a research project that sought to gain a sense of who was watching films, and for what purposes, in British cinemas (see Marsh 2007 [b]: 146), Marsh is better equipped to comment on the implications afforded by escapist movies such as *Shawshank* for the theologian. Instead of dismissing the film as an ultimately uncreative and theologically deficient repository of eschatological material, Marsh understands very well that theologians have much to learn from what a film like *Shawshank* says about contemporary sensibilities. It may be a legitimate cause of concern to the theologian that 'Entertainment is taking the place of religion as a cultural site where the task of meaning making is undertaken' (Marsh 2007 [b]: 150) and that 'Escapism is a dominant motif in [audience members'] declared purpose in cinemagoing' (Marsh 2007 [b]: 149). But this does not warrant the sidelining of a film like *Shawshank* simply because its theological or eschatological utility is found wanting. As Marsh seems to be suggesting elsewhere, the students who are going to university today to study theology are doing so because what has ignited their enthusiasm for tackling issues pertaining to salvation, liberation and atonement is their having seen, and reflected upon, *The Shawshank Redemption* rather than more conventional routes into the topics such as through theology books and journals (Marsh 2007 [a]: 4). If this is the case then it only serves to confirm just how mutually (and simultaneously) reciprocal and challenging the study of films has the capacity to be in the context of eschatology.

6

PUNISHMENT OR REHABILITATION?

Competing perspectives on hell in theology and film

Hell in the modern world

Building on the discussion in the previous chapter, another rich subject of theological analysis pertains to the area of construing hell either as a tangible and physical location or as a metaphor of present human experience. At first sight, this would appear to be a somewhat retrograde step in view of the focus to date on the inability of filmmakers to do adequate justice to the rich nuances of what the Christian tradition has to say on the topic of heaven. For, although attempts to construe heaven in geographical terms as an earthly paradise have plenty of historical antecedents, not least from the Antiochene tradition of the early Church with its tendency to play up the material at the expense of the spiritual, this is not the way in which most theologians have, over the centuries, interpreted the doctrine. Indeed, as Turner puts it, 'The concept of Heaven is instinctively understood as a metaphor, an inadequate attempt to convey the bliss or ecstasy of the soul dwelling in God's grace, rather than a real address with pearly gates, harps and halos' (Turner 1995: 3). With notable exceptions – Swedenborg in the eighteenth century and the discussion in the last chapter concerning the anthropocentric predilection of the Victorian picture of heaven being among the more obvious ones – the tendency in the case of heaven has been to focus not on the specific details of its landscape and topography. Rather, as in the case of the early Augustine, the focus has been upon the idea of heaven in theocentric terms where it is the spirit, rather than the flesh, that is dominant, and where (mystical) communion with God, who is the *telos* of all our striving, takes centre stage. This is very much typified by the timeless, spaceless, immutable and incorporeal concept of the Beatific Vision. When it comes to hell, however, a much more flamboyant and anthropocentric (often even corporeal) dimension can be evidenced throughout works of literature and theology over the centuries, and upon which filmmakers have unapologetically seized. Rather than a speculative and abstract hope, the landscape of hell has, more often than not, had very clearly demarcated (albeit often expressed metaphorically) contours, to the point, indeed, that Turner sees hell as 'the largest shared construction project in imaginative history' and whose 'chief architects have been creative giants' (Turner 1995: 3). Although Turner has in mind the likes of Homer, Virgil, Plato, Augustine, Dante, Milton and Blake, my aim in this chapter is to explore the extent to which modern filmmakers are no less responsible for constructing a highly imaginative and influential cultural repository of images of hell.

That filmmakers should have found the opportunity to delineate hell on celluloid more appealing and satisfying than the opportunities afforded by imaging heaven should come as no surprise. Dante's *Inferno*, for example, has tended to attract more interest than his *Paradiso* (see Stanford 2002: 12), just as Milton's *Paradise Lost* has, in Stanford's words, 'been vastly influential in shaping modern thinking on the Devil and his hellish lair, but those sections of the text which describe heaven are overlooked' (Stanford 2002: 12). Stanford also cites the Irish playwright George Bernard Shaw for whom 'Heaven, as conventionally conceived, is a place so inane, so dull, so useless, so miserable, that nobody has ever ventured to describe a whole day in heaven, though plenty of people have described a day at the seaside' (in Stanford 2002: 13). This is not technically accurate, of course, as the earlier discussion relating to the Victorian penchant for anthropomorphising heaven, as evidenced in the novels of Elizabeth Stuart Phelps, has shown. But, there is more than a grain of truth at the heart of Shaw's flippant observation. For all the excitement that has been generated by the final scene of *The Shawshank Redemption* (Frank Darabont, 1994), on account of, as we have seen, its purportedly sublime vision of heaven on earth, an arguably more fecund approach to Darabont's prison escape drama would be to focus on the degree to which its corrupt and dehumanising institutional environment more readily evokes a sense of hell realised on earth.[1] This is especially germane when one bears in mind that the concept of hell has tended to remain potent for reasons other than the fact that it is deemed to correspond, or not, to specific religious or theological doctrinal formulations. The theological idea of hell as a place of eternal torment has, if anything, been evacuated from contemporary discourse, even to the point that, as Walls shrewdly notes, hell ultimately 'poses no threat since its only basis is fantasy and imagination' (Walls 1992: 2). He attests also that '[g]enuine concern about hell seems to be lost in our past, along with powdered wigs and witch trials' (Walls 1992: 2). Even among theologians themselves, Walls refers to a 1981 survey in which it was found that 50 per cent of those who teach in theology faculties reject the idea of hell as an actual place of everlasting suffering (Walls 1992: 3).

So, what are the reasons behind hell's enduring, and quite colourful, legacy? From the outset, it is clear that we find ourselves in a strangely paradoxical situation whereby hell plays a discernibly stronger role in popular culture than it does within the very theological milieu from which it originated. The most that Christian denominations do today, with the exception of Catholic traditionalists and Protestant fundamentalists (see Turner 1995: 238), is pay lip service to belief in an eternal hell. There is no mention of hell in either the Apostles' or the Nicene Creeds, such that, as Walls observes, it could be interpreted as 'a peripheral matter which is isolated from the main body of Christian teaching and could be lopped off without changing much of anything' (Walls 1992: 6). Even in evangelical churches in Britain and America in which belief in hell has been more widely subscribed to, Lindsey Hall makes the instructive point that published articles on the subject have significantly decreased over the last century or so (Hall 2003: 1). Pope Leo XIII may have issued a papal bull in 1879 affirming the existence of an eternal Hell (see Turner 1995: 238) and the English Methodist Catechism for children may well define hell as a dark and bottomless pit, full of fire and brimstone, where the torments will last forever (see MacGregor 1992: 171). But, today, Turner writes that 'Hell has become something of an embarrassment, and a bishop who resorts to threats of damnation is quickly roasted in the popular press' (Turner 1995: 238). Likewise, whereas 11,000 Church of England clergymen were to sign a public declaration of belief in an eternal hell back in 1864, Lewis observes that '[v]ery few would sign such a declaration today', in a world where 'damnation is now rarely mentioned' and if hell *is* referred to 'then it has been altered to a kind of purgatory for the therapeutic treatment of persistent offenders' (Lewis 1995: 203). Davies further writes that we live in a psychologically-attuned, and by definition 'secular', age where 'the inner torment and sense of abandonment allows "hell" to resonate with experience without the need for an afterlife underworld', and that 'questions on the heat of hell-fire or what prevents the damned from being consumed by it whilst suffering constantly within its flames are redundant' (Davies 2008: 85).

Inevitably, these are generalisations, and Turner makes the judicious point that, though 'Hell is out of favor now', it nevertheless 'still seems more "real" to most people than Fairyland or Atlantis … or other much imagined places' (Turner 1995: 3). Hall also shrewdly comments that, so integral is the doctrine of hell to Christian tradition, that the burden of proof does not lie 'entirely on those who do believe in its existence' (Hall 2003: 6). In other words, there are still at least some vestiges of the idea of hell which it has not been possible to completely dismantle or move on from due to the inextricable link that exists between the concept of hell and other teachings, such as those relating to sin, alienation, redemption and salvation, at the heart of Christian tradition. Jerry Walls even argues passionately in his 1992 publication *Hell: The Logic of Eternal Damnation* that, as betokened by the publication of a Gallup poll in the US in 1990 which found that 60 per cent of American people still believe in hell, the concept has undergone something of a revival in recent years. Unless there are clear and compelling scriptural and philosophical grounds for abandoning belief in hell, Walls takes the line, indeed, that it is worth preserving: 'The fact remains that the doctrine of eternal hell has in its favor an impressive consensus which outweighs the universalist strand in theology' (Walls 1992: 158) – that is, the belief in the salvation, rather than damnation, of all people.

But, these are minority perspectives, certainly within the academy. For every Jerry Walls there are a dozen Alice Turners according to whom Hell is only a human construct rather than one fashioned by God or the Devil (see Turner 1995: 4), and even one that, as Turner suggests, has 'seemed romantic' (Turner 1995: 3) to some people. That the doctrine of hell has undergone something of a sea change in recent decades, or even centuries, is thus not in doubt. Even in scriptural texts, it is possible to find traces of the shift in the way that hell has been conceived, particularly in those writings where, it is suggested, hell serves as a metaphor for present human experience. Despite the teaching in the Qur'an that Gehenna – effectively the 'fire of hell', which amounts to an underworld realm of seven descending depths of a vast funnel-shaped fire, and which is also depicted as a four-legged beast, each leg of which is composed of 70,000 demons with each demon having 30,000 mouths (see Long 1989: 169) – is a material site of unending punishment and torture (see Tober & Lusby 1989: 154), it also comprises a figurative expression in the Hebrew Bible for a place where one would rather not be (see Turner 1995: 41). In Turner's words, 'The name Gehenna served as a metaphor for an unpleasant place and also as a curse, for death in such a place would have indicated a life far removed from the laws of Yahweh' (Turner 1995: 41). It thus represents a site of alienation and a lack of belonging. The focus in our discussion to date may have been on the problems that are attendant in interpreting the ending of *The Shawshank Redemption* as a manifestation of an earthly heaven. But, the fact that the Hebrew concept of Sheol was even likened to a prison (see Turner 1995: 40) goes some way towards showing just how theologically sustainable it is to read a film such as the prison-set *Shawshank* as a metaphor of hell on earth. Indeed, taking the prison metaphor further, it is significant that Turner points out that Gehenna also refers in the Old Testament to 'a sort of garbage heap or town dump where, in addition to refuse, the bodies of criminals and animals were thrown into fires' (Turner 1995: 40–41).

Origen's hell as a site of rehabilitation

Persuasive though such readings are, however, it is striking that the hell that is delineated so cogently and imaginatively in *Shawshank* should prove to have only a provisional and transient quality when seen within the light of the film as a whole. For, the film culminates, as we have already discussed, in a vision of heaven. Hellish though Shawshank prison unequivocally is, and notwithstanding its explicit purpose as a facility for the brutal administration ('execution' might be a more fitting word) of punishment of those who have violated society's codes and laws – in the words of the corrupt Warden, Samuel Norton (Bob Gunton), 'I believe in two things, discipline and the Bible; here you will receive both' – what defines the film is not the picture of hell but the theme of rehabilitation. For, both Andy and Red leave the prison – by breaking out in the case of the former and after a third, eventually successful, parole hearing in the case of the latter – changed and reformed men. Red atones for the crime of murder he committed when a young man, while Andy, despite joking that 'Everyone's innocent in here', comes to recognise that, while he may not have actually pulled the trigger that led to the death of his wife and her lover, he was responsible, by not being a sufficiently affectionate husband, for bringing about the circumstances which led to her being placed in harm's way. To this end, the dynamics of *Shawshank* are in accordance with the teachings of Origen in the second century. For, according to Origen, hell was not efficacious *per se* as a place of retribution and suffering. Rather, it had a remedial, educative, medicinal and rehabilitative function (see McGinn 1999: 375) whereby all those who were being punished – including, eventually, the Devil himself – would come to repent of their crimes. While postulating the existence of a future life – and to this end many scholars have suggested that Origen was ultimately inclined towards a belief in reincarnation (see Turner 1995: 77; Lorimer 1984: 76) – Origen saw the purpose of suffering as efficacious only for the extent to which it facilitates one's growth towards salvation (see Daley 1991: 49). Hell and redemption are thus conjoined for Origen, in his understanding of a process that is the result of our own free decision either to 'mount upward' in the direction of God and the spirit or to 'sink further' (Russell 1981: 126) away from God and towards sin and evil.

In a manner consonant with the trajectory of the protagonist in Christopher Marlowe's Elizabethan drama *Doctor Faustus*, everyone has, according to Origen's schema, two guardian angels – what Russell calls 'a guardian angel of justice and a corrupting demon of iniquity' (Russell 1981: 135) – who represent the moral struggle taking place within us all between good and bad. On a daily basis, therefore, we are in Origenistic terms engaged in a perpetual struggle with the hell of our own making and we are thus responsible, due to the exercise of free will, for bringing judgement upon ourselves. Punishment is, accordingly, a means to an end, and the fires of hell are only meaningful, on this reckoning, as a metaphor for the disintegration of the soul and the pain or lack of cohesion that we feel from being separated from God and that which is good. According to Origen, the fires of hell are not objective as such. We are not 'plunged into a fire which has been previously kindled by some one else' – but, rather, 'every sinner kindles for himself the flame of his own fire' (Origen 1973: 142),[2] until

> ... the mind or conscience, bringing to memory through divine power all things the signs and forms of which it had impressed upon itself at the moment of sinning, will see exposed before its eyes a kind of history of its evil deeds, of every foul and disgraceful act and all unholy conduct.[3]
>
> *(Origen 1973: 142)*

Crucially, for Origen, such punishment is not everlasting or permanent: 'For when the body is punished the soul is gradually purified ... For all wicked men, and for daemons, too, punishment has an end ... ' (Origen 1973: 146).[4] Indeed, as he saw it, 'when the soul, thus torn and rent asunder, has been tried by the application of fire, it is undoubtedly wrought into a condition of stronger inward connexion and renewal' (Origen 1973: 143).[5]

For Origen, the time scale was different for each individual, such that rather than a process which should 'be understood to happen suddenly', it was one more correctly categorised as happening 'gradually and by degrees' since 'the improvement and correction will be realised slowly and separately in each individual person' (Origen 1973: 251).[6] Such a reading ties in with the way in which, when we initially meet Red at the beginning of *Shawshank*, he is facing the first of three decennial parole hearings, at which he is merely going through the motions of claiming to be rehabilitated ('I can honestly say I'm a changed man. I'm no longer a danger to society. That's the God's honest truth about it'). At the third, however, marking Red's 40 years behind bars for the crime of murder, he has had time to reflect on who he is and what he has done, and we feel we have come to know him well enough to believe that he is speaking candidly when he tells the parole board:

> There's not a day goes by I don't feel regret ... I look back on the way I was then, a young stupid kid who committed that terrible crime. I want to talk to him, I want to try and talk some sense into him, tell him the way things are. But I can't.

For Origen, in like manner, the suffering we experience throughout our lives must have an ultimate *telos* or resolution. Specifically, in theistic terms, Origen had in mind the retrospective as well as prospective idea of the re-establishment of an original unity in creation when we will return to God, the Creator, so that God will be all in all (cf. Russell 1981: 144 and Origen 1973: 254[7]). The word Origen used to this end was *apocatastasis*. Holding to the type of universalism advocated by Hick, according to whom after this life we may encounter a further series of progressive lives in what will necessarily be soul-making environments where the process of transformation into being a child of God can take place (see Hick 1976: 455; Hall 2003: 9), Origen was adamant that such a reformation would take place 'during the lapse of infinite and immeasurable ages' (Origen 1973: 251).[8]

Obviously, in the case of *Shawshank* the film does not proffer the possibility that Andy's or Red's attainment of redemption will take place in another dimension of existence beyond the terrestrial. In this regard, the film thus departs in a fundamental way from Hick's Origenistic argument that 'If salvation in its fullness involves the actual transformation of human character, it is an observable fact that this does not usually take place in the course of our present earthly life', such that there must 'be further time beyond death in which the process of perfecting can continue' (Hick 1976: 455). Indeed, there is also a non-negotiable God-referent in Hick's theodicy, which also underlies Lindsey Hall's argument that the rationale for having a person-making theodicy is that God 'desires the salvation of every person' and that 'the fate of every individual is a matter of some importance to God' (Hall 2003: 12). This is clearly something that *Shawshank* does not possess except in the trivial sense in which the dialogue possesses a 'repetitively religious tone', whereby 'biblical judgements are invoked at every turn, and each profanity tends more toward blasphemy than sexual vulgarity' (Kermode 2003: 14).[9] The most we can therefore say is that the film bears witness to a secularised version of Origen's eschatological programme in which in lieu of his talk of there being many lives in many worlds or the passing of countless ages lies an unconditional emphasis on the individual's eschatological predicament in the present. In terms of such a schema, hell is efficacious only as the precursor to Andy and Red's eventual attainment of redemption which is situated on a Mexican beach.

Even here, however, though a potentially long-drawn-out, and thus future-oriented, process, what is significant to our present discussion is that hell, suffering and punishment were, for Origen, inextricably linked to the arena of present decision-making rather than to the 'next' world *per se*. This is not dissimilar from the eastern concept of *karma*[10] as the direct, and proportionate, consequence of transgressions perpetrated in our lifetime, here on earth. As Chilton puts it, for Origen the 'only time that truly matters is the time until one's death, which determines one's experience in paradise and in the resurrection' (Chilton 2000: 93) – or, of course, for that matter, in hell. Moreover, despite the allegorical nature of Origen's language, which accounts for his reservations concerning hell as being a literal and tangible entity and his disdain for those who, like Irenaeus, anticipated an earthly millennial kingdom or a future beatitude that consisted of material plenty in an earthly Jerusalem (see Collins 1999: 409), there was also a concrete and material basis to Origen's programme which befits the trajectories of Andy and Red in *Shawshank*. It is certainly true that, as we have already discussed, any suffering that Andy undergoes is secondary to the almost Docetic manner in which he is able to transcend the horrors of being locked up in 'The Hole' through the redemptive and purgatorial pleasures afforded through music and the creative imagination. But, Origen envisaged the existence of a physical, terrestrial Paradise – akin, perhaps, to Zihuatanejo – which would comprise a place for spiritual instruction and training. In his words:

> This will be a place of instruction and, so to speak, a lecture room or school for souls, in which they may be taught about all that they had seen on earth and may also receive some indications of what is to follow in the future.[11]
>
> *(Origen 1973: 152)*

Important though future eschatology is, Origen did not thereby reject the value of the present. For Origen, only God is totally incorporeal (see McGinn 1999: 374), with the terrestrial realm, and its inhabitants, a tangible and fertile spiritual training ground for eschatological encounter where we are afforded the opportunity to reflect upon past sins and be restored to our original primeval and prelapsarian state of perfection. The idea that Shawshank-Zihuatanejo might function as a school for souls in need of reform or purification is not wide of the mark on this reading. This idea of the material as a site of spiritual education is an important component of the film. Just as Origen sees this world as a school for improvement – and, indeed, as Danielou attests, everything since the Fall was, for Origen, a means of education (Danielou 1955: 276) – Andy sees education as a necessary tool for the edification of his fellow inmates within an otherwise constraining and impoverished environment. This is demonstrated in the film by the tuition he offers the other inmates, most notably Tommy Williams (Gil Bellows) who is afforded the opportunity to read and write and who, thanks to Andy's patience and diligence, manages to pass his high school equivalency examinations.

This emphasis on the importance of the material ties in also with Chilton's attestation that '"Heaven" as cosmographic place now occupies the central position once occupied by the eschatological kingdom of God in Jesus' teaching' (Chilton 2000: 93). It also accords with Origen's own assertion that when the saints depart from this life they will 'remain in some place situated on the earth, which the divine Scripture calls "paradise"' (Origen 1973: 152).[12] There is the obvious, and important, difference in that the inhabitants of this film, in contradistinction to the inhabitants of Origen's graduate school, have not yet died – not in a material or physical sense at any rate, though the film is keen to play up the idea that Andy's escape from Shawshank is a rebirth of sorts. We see this, for instance, in Kermode's analysis that from an environment 'in which anal rape was once the order of the day, Andy now commits the most extraordinary act of escapology, literally bursting out of Shawshank's rectum to be reborn again in the cleansing waters of a new world' (Kermode 2003: 74–75). This is a realised escapology (!), no less, and the fact that we see Andy holding his arms out in cruciform pose underscores the none-too-subtle Christological provenance and symbolism afforded by this scene.

Elucidating though it is, however, to find points of convergence between Origen's and *Shawshank*'s teachings on eschatology, or to attempt to equate Andy's rebirth from the underworld, or hell, of Shawshank prison with Origen's teaching on hell–salvation, it is worth stressing that this is not an entirely representative case study. Indeed, conducive though Origen's approach to the topic of hell may be to *The Shawshank Redemption*, it is quite atypical of the way hell has been portrayed both cinematically and theologically over the centuries. In the case of Origen, the decision was made in 553 CE at the meeting of the Ecumenical Council in Constantinople to ban Origen's works, as a result of which only fragments of his writings survive in the Greek today. No fourth- or fifth-century mainstream Christian theologian went as far as Origen had done in the third century in reinterpreting the themes of resurrection, judgement, heaven and hell. Rather, they objected to 'his radically spiritual and internalized reinterpretation of the eschatological tradition' (Hebblethwaite 1984: 52). In Chester's words, 'A few voices, from Origen onward, suggested ways for the wicked to be purified and repent, but the mainstream view was much more uncompromising' (Chester 2004: 247). Indeed, as regards the doctrine of hell, hardly any fourth- or fifth-century thinker agreed with Origen on its temporary or remedial nature, as reflected by Augustine's position that the only teaching consistent with Scripture is that there will be an everlasting anguish of the damned. A case in point is Matthew 13:40–42 where we learn that:

> Just as the weeds are gathered and burned with fire, so will it be at the close of the age. The Son of man will send his angels, and they will gather out of his kingdom all causes of sin and all evildoers, and throw them into the furnace of fire; there men will weep and gnash their teeth.

In Matthew 25:46, also, we learn that whereas the righteous will enter into eternal life the wicked 'will go away into eternal punishment'. Revelation 14:10 speaks, similarly, of the wicked being 'tormented with fire and sulphur ... [a]nd the smoke of their torment goes up for ever and ever; and they have no rest, day or night'. The scope allowed by Origen for the wicked to be cleansed of their wrongdoing and to be redeemed accordingly was lost on Augustine who preferred to see hell as a much more static and permanent place of destruction and punishment from which no-one would be exempt (even unbaptised infants) except by God's grace. Writing in his *City of God*, Augustine identified hell as a bottomless pit containing a lake of fire – a real, material fire – and brimstone where the bodies of sinners would be tormented, without being consumed, forever (see Augustine 1998: 1068).[13] Hick likewise cites Augustine as insisting 'at great length and with many pre-scientific analogies that the damned are embodied and are able to burn everlastingly in literal flames' (Hick 1976: 198–99).

That said, Augustine is not the most consistent of writers, as he did accept the tenability of spiritual readings of Scripture, as in his discussion of Mark 9:47–48 which speaks of how it is better 'to enter the kingdom of God with one eye than with two eyes to be thrown into hell, where their worm does not die, and the fire is not quenched'. As Walls puts it: 'What is at issue for Augustine is how the worm and the fire are to be understood' (Walls 1992: 141). For Augustine, some understand both the worm and the fire in a spiritual sense (such that the fire signifies the spiritual agony of someone who repents too late while the worm stands for the sorrow which consumes their heart) while, for others, the fire is a literal description of what will happen to the body and the worm is a metaphor for spiritual punishment (see Walls 1992: 141). Ultimately, though, Augustine did come down on the side of a literal reading. As he wrote in *The City of God*, 'I find it easier to say that "fire" and "worm" both pertain to the body than to suppose that neither does', and that the reason scripture is silent regarding the spiritual pain of the damned is because it is 'necessarily understood that, in a body thus suffering, the soul will also be tormented by fruitless repentance' (Augustine 1998: 1065).[14] Spiritual pain, though very real, is thus auxiliary in Augustine's eyes to corporal punishment.

Augustine and Dante's legacy in popular culture

Significantly, then, Augustine's teachings leave rather less room for interpretation than Origen's more supple and spiritualised interpretation, and have also found a more favourable and familiar domicile in art, literature and film. This is especially evinced in the horror genre which is characteristically (even fanatically) obsessed with delineating the literal and material suffering and torment of the damned. A case in point are medieval morality, miracle and mystery plays, whose titles include *The Wakefield Pageant of the Harrowing of Hell*, also known as *Extraction of Souls from Hell* (see Anonymous 2006: <www.gutenberg.org/files/19481/19481-h/19481-h.htm#wakefield_hell>), which is one of the oldest English miracle plays, dating from around the thirteenth century, and which concerns Christ's descent into hell between the period of his crucifixion and resurrection. It was common in such literature for Death to be allegorised as Satan and for the Seven Deadly Sins, which emanated from hell, to be personified (see Turner 1995: 123). Pulpit manuals from the period, such as Honorius of Autun's twelfth-century *Elucidarium*, also presented extremely explicit images of the punishments that the damned could be expected to undergo, such as, in Turner's words, 'unquenchable fire, unbearable cold, worms and snakes, disgusting stench, demons with whips, horror-filled darkness' (Turner 1995: 113), and so on. This was, in short, an uncompromisingly literalistic, combative and horror-oriented period in which, in Lorimer's words, 'The Last Judgment is featured in most medieval cathedrals, hell's mouth … wide open', where 'the damned are cast headlong into the flames' (Lorimer 1984: 78).

Dante's *Inferno* is arguably the most sophisticated and detailed depiction of the topography of hell that we have in literature – so influential, in fact, that it has completely changed the way hell has henceforth been conceived. Prior to its creation in the thirteenth century, it was not uncommon for hell to have been imaged as existing above, rather than below, the earth (see Bailey & Yates 1996 [b]: 330), a picture quite unrecognisable to us today. In the *Inferno*, hell is described so lucidly and precisely that it amounts almost to a travel guide or manual of the underworld, which lies at the centre of the earth, the point farthest removed from heaven (see Russell 1986: 108). It contains an imaginatively rich evocation of nine circles of hell, starting with the circle of limbo which houses the souls of virtuous pagans, to the last three circles where we find those who are violent (circle seven), fraudsters, thieves and false prophets (circle eight) and, in tier nine, the circle of traitors. At the centre of this last circle lies the arch-traitor Satan – 'trapped, a grotesque parody of a king, the emperor of the miserable kingdom, ruling the wretched in his anti-city' (Russell 1997: 160), and 'frozen fast and mindlessly weeping as he devours the shades of Judas Iscariot, Brutus, and Cassius'[15] (Turner 1995: 141). Accordingly, this is no arbitrary or merely allegorical representation of hell. The damned exist here as very real, and, with the exception of limbo where no-one is punished, very tormented physical and bodily selves. Between the fifth and sixth circles, for example, lies the distinction between the Lower and Upper circles of hell, separated by the River Styx in whose swamp 'the angry tear at one another, while under the mud the slothful and sullen gurgle incoherently' (Turner 1995: 137). When Jerry Walls thus writes sympathetically of the view that hell is a very real place where the damned will be resurrected in their bodies, and that, in his words, 'I am inclined to think it would be *closer* to the truth to say hell is on some faraway planet than to deny that it is a place' (Walls 1992: 153), it would not be wide of the mark to see how Dante's legacy (and Augustine's before him) has contributed to the framing of such a position.

Dante is never less than graphic in what has proven to be a highly influential forerunner to modern cinematic portrayals of hell. This is quite explicitly borne out by the third-person action-adventure video game titled *Dante's Inferno*, the tagline of which is 'Go to Hell', which was released in 2010. The game's official web site (<www.dantesinferno.com>) displays at the top of the screen the warning 'Abandon all hope, ye who enter here' and invites those who surf the US version of the site to 'Select a circle of Hell' from the nine choices available, along with the somewhat enigmatic invitation to 'Check back on the 9th of every month for a new circle of hell'. It also promises to 'take gamers to the western world's most definitive view of the afterlife as created in the 13th century by the Italian poet Dante Alighieri'

(<www.ea.com/uk/game/dantes-inferno>). Dante, reconceived here as a Temple Knight, undertakes an epic journey through the nine gates of Hell to rescue the soul of his wife, Beatrice. According to the game's product details, 'Just like the poem, players will descend through Dante's unique nine circles of Hell', namely limbo, lust, gluttony, greed, anger, heresy, violence, fraud and treachery, with each circle featuring 'distinct environments, enemies and story elements befitting the sins committed by their inhabitants' (<www.ea.com/uk/game/dantes-inferno>). It helps, of course, that

> Dante fights through the nine circles armed with Death's Scythe and Beatrice's Holy Cross, with magic powers and a deep, customizable upgrade system helping the player take full advantage of a fast and fluid gameplay experience that will never run at lower than 60 frames per second.
>
> *(<www.ea.com/uk/game/dantes-inferno>)*

We have certainly come a long way in just a decade and a half from when Turner wrote that 'The architectural ingenuity Dante put into his landscape of Hell has always fascinated readers', with modern editions of the *Divine Comedy*, of which *Inferno* is the first of three canticles, carrying 'maps and diagrams, while illustrators have presented not only the characters and monsters of the story but also the wonderful underground embankments, moats, castles, paved trenches, and the city of Dis [the so-called fiery capital of Hell, guarded by fallen angels, that encompasses all of Lower Hell] with walls of red-hot iron' (Turner 1995: 133). For, in the present day and age we can go one stage better, with hell conceived as a full High Definition, widescreen, interactive experience in which, due to the technological acumen of Visceral Games, 'Each circle has its own distinct look, with demons, monsters, damned and geography that are crafted straight from the poem's vivid descriptions' (<www.ea.com/uk/game/dantes-inferno>).

The Dantean connection can also be seen to pervade much of contemporary cinema, albeit in more subtle ways. Indeed, in *Literature and Film as Modern Theology*, published in 2000, William Ferrell draws an explicit correlation between the protagonist of *Shawshank* and Dante. The grounds for Ferrell's argument are that, like Dante, Andy Dufresne 'is required to descend into hell and live to tell about it' (Ferrell 2000: 61), and that the 'motivation for [Andy's] journey into the underworld becomes one man's search for paradise' (Ferrell 2000: 71). That said, Ferrell is more interested in the metaphorical, and mythological, aspects of Dufresne's underworld encounter than in seeing the maximum security prison which houses him as a literal hell. We can see this from where he expresses an interest in the extent to which *Shawshank* and the other films and novels he looks at, which include *Shane, Field of Dreams* and *One Flew Over The Cuckoo's Nest*, draw on 'a recurrent theme or archetype that in its telling connects to ancient myth' (Ferrell 2000: 22). Ferrell's specific interest is in the myths of messianic redeemer-figures who, even when in hell, can enable viewers and readers to 'find a meaning or purpose for life' (Ferrell 2000: 63). An example of this is when Dufresne's journey from hell to paradise functions mythologically as a way of defining 'the importance of hope for all of us' (Ferrell

2000: 71). In Ferrell's words, 'In the final analysis, everyone receives what he ought to get, implying that right will eventually triumph when or if one does not lose hope; at the very least it has a chance' (Ferrell 2000: 72).

Ferrell's Dantean interpretation is, however, quite an atypical one. Instead of focusing on the very real material dimension to the hell that Shawshank represents, Ferrell suggests, in quite reductionistic terms, that the hell that Andy experiences is no more than a means to a redemptive, and paradisiacal, end, where the attainment of the beach in Mexico functions metaphorically as the overcoming of adversity by hope. While Ferrell is perfectly entitled to focus on the hero-myth and archetypal dimensions of *Shawshank*, in order to fully comply with the Dantean and Augustinian, rather than the Origenistic, formula hell has to be seen as a very real *place*. In this regard, Ferrell's reading is actually closer to John Milton's understanding of hell in *Paradise Lost* than to that of Dante's *Inferno*. This is because whereas for Dante hell has a very real geographical location at the centre of the earth, Milton's hell was 'for all its geographical features' more properly to be understood as 'a cavernous interior underworld' (Turner 1995: 188). Indeed, for Milton hell is not actually in the earth (though, as Russell points out, the physical imagery used to describe it comes from the imagined interior of the earth [see Russell 1986: 108]). Rather, for Milton (and, I would argue, Ferrell), hell is nowhere – 'a perfect metaphor for the absolute non-being of evil' (Russell 1986: 109). Turner similarly writes that Milton's hell 'seems to be located on, or rather inside another planet altogether' (Turner 1995: 184), and that to 'map Milton's cosmos logically is impossible' (Turner 1995: 186). Applied to *Shawshank*, a Dantean reading would have to acknowledge that, whatever the metaphorical or psychological significance or ramifications of Andy's underworld journey, the maximum security prison in which Andy resides *is* hell and that the prison bars are material and real. For Ferrell, in contrast, Andy's attainment of paradise is only able to take place 'because of a graphic *yet metaphoric* rebirth' (Ferrell 2000: 72; my its.) which has been created as a result of his 'ingenuity and will' (Ferrell 2000: 73).

While this seeming reluctance to allow for a fully spiritual or allegorical reading might seem unduly restrictive, cinematic representations of hell have tended more towards the Augustinian (and Dantean) than towards the Origenistic (and Miltonian). This comes to the fore in a *High Plains Drifter* (1973), a supernatural western, directed by Clint Eastwood, and a homage to his mentors Don Siegel and Sergio Leone, whose tagline is, portentously, 'Welcome to Hell'. Eastwood's Stranger is the reincarnation, the film implies, of a former town marshal, Jim Duncan, who was whipped to death while the townsfolk stood idly by and who we are to believe has returned from the dead in order to dispense retribution to his three murderers. He is asked to save the small mining town of Lago in the American southwest from the same trio of vengeful, escaped convicts. In return for protecting them, the Stranger instructs the citizens to paint the town red and to rename it 'Hell'. When the desperadoes subsequently wreak revenge against the town for the year they have just spent in jail, they literally set Hell aflame, prompting Patrick McGee to write, in his 2007 publication *From Shane to Kill Bill: Rethinking the Western*, that 'Eastwood's vision is more Augustinian than Marxist' (McGee 2007: 194). In other words, there is a metaphysical and supernatural dimension to the corruption to which the film bears witness – to the point that Eastwood's impassive and invulnerable character is, as McGee sees it, 'the spirit of divine authority and the instrument of transcendent morality' (McGee 2007: 194) – which presupposes, in Augustinian terms, the inherent evil of a fallen and depraved humanity 'rather than the humanly constructed social injustice' (McGee 2007: 194) of the world. To this end, Eastwood's western is very much in the mould of the nineteenth-century Gothic novel where, as Turner points out, hell tended to be recreated on earth, and horror and terror were employed for titillation rather than moralising purposes (see Turner 1995: 216).

That said, of course, it is hard to discern much in the way of moral instruction in this film other than the suggestion that Lago, a modern day Sodom, deserves to be raised to the ground after a human life was sacrificed in the name of greed and ostensible progress. If anything, Eastwood's film goes even further than such literature where, in Turner's words, 'Punishment was almost always the lot of the innocent; the guilty did the punishing' (Turner 1995: 216). For, in *High Plains Drifter*, we observe an entire town, with few exceptions, enmeshed in guilt – 'hiding behind words like faith, peace and trust', to cite the words of the hotelier's wife, Sarah Belding (Verna Bloom) – in order to cover up the murder of their principled marshal. It is only fitting, then, that the Stranger should pit all of the inhabitants of Lago, where there are no innocents left, against one another. Despite the film's at times surreal and mystical symbolism (and what the *Time Out* reviewer Paul Taylor refers to as a 'genuine weirdness to the movie that totally escaped other post-spaghetti American Westerns, with a real sense of exorcism running both through and beyond it' [Taylor 2001: 506]), the film could not be more emphatic that Hell is a very real, terrestrial, geographical place – specifically, the fictional town of Lago, filmed on the shores of California's Mono Lake (see <www.imdb.com/title/tt0068699/locations>). Indeed, writing in the August 1973 edition of the *Monthly Film Bulletin*, at the time of the film's release, Nigel Andrews attested that Eastwood's Stranger might be seen as 'the Angel of Death who ushers the town into Hell', and that 'the transformation of Lago into a flaming, red-painted hell provides the story with an impressively eerie climax' (Andrews 1973: 170).

Much the same could be said about Harold Ramis' comedy *Groundhog Day* (1993). Though ostensibly a tale of redemption in the Ebenezer Scrooge mould (see Deacy 2005: 65) in the respect that its protagonist, an egocentric TV weatherman, Phil Connors (Bill Murray), is similarly presented as 'a decayed soul getting the chance to pick himself up, dust himself off and start all over again' (Gilbey 2004: 9), the picture is also remarkable for its delineation of a small, rural Pennsylvanian town (population 6,072) called Punxsutawney[16] as a hellish location of endless repetition. Indeed, as Gilbey puts it, 'Punxsutawney is for Phil a kind of expanded Room 101, no less claustrophobic and terrifying than Winston Smith's ordeal by rats' (Gilbey 2004: 8–9) in Orwell's seminal *1984*. After all, whereas Scrooge is at least accompanied by ghosts, who provide a commentary (albeit without words in the case of the Ghost of Christmas Yet to Come) on his plight, 'Phil is abandoned without instruction or insight in his icy, isolated hell' (Gilbey 2004: 11). Although, by the end of the film,

Punxsutawney is transformed into somewhere where Phil *chooses* to live ('It's so beautiful. Let's live here'), this film, about a self-centred man doomed to live out one single day for an eternity, never deviates from the idea that hell is a geographical entity rather than a product of its protagonist's warped mind. No matter how hard he tries, even after successfully committing suicide a multitude of different ways – and even after, as in the original version of Danny Rubin's screenplay, managing to escape by plane in order to visit his mother in Ohio (Gilbey 2004: 65) – Phil always returns, without exception, to Hell-Punxsutawney at six o'clock the following morning.

Another conspicuous delineation on celluloid of Hell as a tangible, material place is Martin Scorsese's *Taxi Driver* (1976), a film that has also been the subject of considerable theological scrutiny over the years (see e.g. Deacy 2001: 113–20). *Taxi Driver* is a bleak, intensive and almost hallucinatory study of the alienation of a former Vietnam veteran, Travis Bickle (Robert De Niro), who plies his trade as a taxi driver on the 'mean streets' of New York City, and whose voice-over narration underscores the disgust he feels at working in a city 'where all the animals come out at night – whores, skunks, pussies, buggers, queens, fairies, dopers, junkies'. My own focus to date has been on the extent to which Scorsese's vision of the diseased human condition sheds light on the Christian concept of redemption. A case in point is Travis' subsequent decision to stand up against, in his own words, 'the scum, the cunts, the dogs, the filth, the shit' which might be construed as having a messianic quality, amounting even to what Lawrence Friedman designates 'a holy calling' (in Deacy 2001: 116). Indeed, Scorsese himself has even spoken in interviews about how the course of action that Travis takes, whereby he murders a pimp and his associates in order to rescue a 12-year-old prostitute, Iris (Jodie Foster), from the streets in order that she may return home, is not altogether dissimilar from what St Paul set out to do in the respect that Travis 'believes he's doing right' as he seeks to 'clean up life, clean up the mind, clean up the soul' (in Deacy 2001: 116). Like the saints in the Christian tradition, further, Scorsese has spoken of how Travis possesses an 'energy' and sense of moral righteousness whereby 'he sees something ugly or dirty and he has to clean it up', such that he believes that what he is doing constitutes 'good work' (in Deacy 2001: 116).

Yet, pertinent though it may be to see Travis' cleansing and purification of the morally diseased city streets in redemptive terms, to the point, even, that he is seen to be taking on the self-appointed role of 'God's agent' (Deacy 2001: 115), the point remains that the filth and sordidness of the streets of New York in this film amount to the realisation of a very concrete and tangible hell. Back in 2001, I wrote that, from a theological perspective, Travis' predicament may be seen to accord with the Christian understanding of hell (Deacy 2001: 114). Yet, my focus then was on the way in which *Taxi Driver* epitomises the idea of hell not as an actual material site used by God to punish the wicked but as a metaphor for spiritual misery (Deacy 2001: 114). Referring to book four of Milton's *Paradise Lost*, in which Satan says 'Which way I fly is Hell; myself am Hell' (in Deacy 2001: 114), I was seeking to build upon the point made by Jerry Walls that, rather than a remote, inconceivable mystery, 'hell stands in clear continuity with our experience in this world', and that, in this world, we may experience 'a foretaste of hell' (Walls 1992: 142). Accordingly, when Walls writes that 'hell is sometimes conceived as an experience of complete isolation', in which 'the damned are like prisoners in solitary confinement, whose misery is compounded by the fact that they must bear it utterly alone' (Walls 1992: 145), this could be said to correspond to the world of Travis Bickle in which Rosalie Savage writes of his being banished 'to the hell of his isolation' (in Deacy 2001: 115) in an existence that is devoid of proper human interaction.

Feasible though such a reading is, however, it would be wrong to overlook the extent to which hell is more than merely a state of Travis' alienated, dysfunctional and aberrant mind or imagination. Walls himself thinks that hell must possess a physical dimension of some kind to be fully intelligible, on the grounds that, in Christianity, it is traditionally supposed that the damned will be resurrected in their bodies and thus that 'there will be a bodily dimension to their suffering' (Walls 1992: 151). We are, ultimately, according to Walls, embodied persons, and thus, in contrast, say, to the mind-dependent predilection of H.H. Price, there has to be 'a bodily aspect to who we are, what we become, and what we experience' (Walls 1992: 152). Although Walls writes that Dante saw the fire of hell as an image for spiritual misery and as an internal fire which burns violently in the hearts of the wicked (Walls 1992: 142), such an overtly allegorical reading overlooks the physical and geographical aspect to hell that Dante has so painstakingly mapped out. Similarly, in *Taxi Driver*, while a symbolical or psychological reading is obviously important, New York as a terrestrial hell is not simply a metaphor. From the film's initial shot, in which, in Stern's words, 'From centre screen steam gushes, swirling like light out of a manhole, polluted light, glitteringly opaque … [t]he bumper of a yellow checker cab moves in slow motion through the steam' (in Deacy 2001: 115), the idea of hell is physically evoked. Marie Connelly even goes so far as to comment that 'the smoke, red filters, and greenish distortions of light make the city look like Dante's *Inferno*' (in Deacy 2001: 115). Indeed, just as Dante descends into Hell to save Beatrice, so Travis enters the very real, tawdry underworld of New York City, with guns and knives as his weapons, in order to rescue Iris from a life of prostitution. Travis may well be what Jake Horsley, in a chapter entitled 'Citizens of Hell', calls 'a man whose inner hell has seeped out in the world around him' (Horsley 2005: 82), thus lending the film a fully fledged expressionistic quality. But this does not disguise the fact that the city as portrayed in the film is degenerate, diseased and literally needs cleaning up.[17]

Hell as entertainment

With such considerations in mind, Alice Turner is wrong when she writes that the cinematic and televisual treatment of hell is 'mostly gothic and trivial, a chance for set designers and special-effects people to strut their stuff' (Turner 1995: 242–43). Whether we are Augustinian or Origenistic in our sensibilities, hell continues to play a pivotal role in contemporary film, and possesses more than a 'mere' entertainment function. *Groundhog Day* is ostensibly a comedy, but the light, frivolous ending belies what was, especially in Rubin's first draft, 'a very existential script', to the point that Rubin even attests that he 'saw it as an epic – like *Siddhartha* – a young man's journey through life' (in Gilbey 2004: 15). Gilbey also writes that, in terms of the multiple forms of suicide that, in vain, Phil Connors commits – by electrocution, walking in front of a speeding truck, jumping from the roof of a tall building, as well as the encounters with death we have not seen but which Phil confesses to, namely, that he has been 'stabbed, shot, poisoned, frozen, hung', to the point that 'I've killed myself so many times I don't even exist any more' – rarely in a movie 'are we forced to confront so starkly the extinction of a main character' (Gilbey 2004: 68). Indeed, as Gilbey puts it, 'The suicide montage in *Groundhog Day* lasts less than two minutes, but its effect on the film is momentous' (Gilbey 2003: 68–69). The film has already proven to be a rich resource of theological, biblical and religious commentary, as the work produced on this film by Robert Jewett and in my own *Faith in Film* testifies.[18] Hindu and Buddhist scholars have also found *Groundhog Day* to be worthy of intellectual analysis, as evinced by Michele Marie Desmarais' recent examination of how the film comprises an 'accurate' (Desmarais 2009: 286) study of *samsara*, *karma* and *moksa*. Whereas at the start of the film, in her words, 'Connors displays the consequences of negative acts and their fruition', he later 'acquires knowledge, performs good acts and eventually transcends his own self-interest through love' (Desmarais 2009: 286). This liberation from the cycle of life parallels, according to Desmarais, the three paths to *moksa*, or liberation, that can be found in the *Bhagavad Gita*, namely the paths of knowledge, action and devotion (Desmarais 2009: 286). Further, in a 2001 article for the non-academic publication *Philosophy Now*, Matthew Coniam even called the film 'one of the most cogent and intelligent extended metaphors for the central tenets of humanist existentialism ever presented on a cinema screen' (Coniam 2001: 10). Gilbey further writes that *Groundhog Day* 'is stimulating enough to be worthy of moral debate' (Gilbey 2004: 87) while nevertheless successfully functioning as a work of entertainment.

Such a close interrelation between 'hell' and 'entertainment' is not simply restricted to contemporary film. As Turner puts it, 'Even the most supposedly pious and church-ridden periods of Christian history, the Middle Ages and the Puritan Reformation, offer examples of Merry Hell' (Turner 1995: 4). Medieval mystery plays are a case in point, in which hell is the site not of sombre or morbid reflection but of 'devilish pratfalls, firecrackers, and crude toilet doggerel' (Turner 1995: 90), in which the Devil himself, with his tail, horns and cloven feet, is a kind of grandiose trickster. The 1616 Jacobean play *The Devil is an Ass*, written by Ben Jonson, epitomises such a representation. In the Elizabethan play *Doctor Faustus*, further, the protagonist, a sixteenth-century scholar at the University of Wittenberg who sells his soul to the devil in return for 24 years of fame, power and hedonism, converses with Lucifer's servant, the demon Mephistopheles, who facilitates the contract with Lucifer, quite facetiously about hell:

> Learn thou of Faustus manly fortitude
> And scorn those joys thou never shalt possess.

Go bear those tidings to great Lucifer:
Seeing Faustus hath incurred eternal death
By desperate thoughts against Jove's deity,
Say, he surrenders up to him his soul,
So he will spare him four-and-twenty years,
Letting him live in all voluptuousness,
Having thee ever to attend on me,
To give me whatsoever I shall ask,
To tell me whatsoever I demand,
To slay mine enemies and aid my friends,
And always be obedient to my will.[19]

(Marlowe 2005: 17)

In Act I, scene 4, we witness two devils chasing a clown (Marlowe 2005: 19), and a key, if diversionary, component of Act II, scene 1 consists of Mephistopheles laying on the spectacle of devils dancing, and even at one point supplying Faustus, who has just asked to be given a wife, with a devil brandishing fireworks (Marlowe 2005: 25). When, in Act II, scene 3 a pageant of the Seven Deadly Sins is laid on for Faustus, after which Lucifer leaves a book for Faustus which will enable him to transform his appearance into any shape he desires, it is quite fitting that Faustus should be advised that 'in hell is all manner of delight' (Marlowe 2005: 33).[20] Faustus expends a great deal of his time in ostentatious and flippant displays of magical powers, as when in an alternative version of the play, from 1616, he wields a false head and calls on Mephistopheles to torture three would-be assassins who have just been boasting about decapitating what they thought was Faustus' real head (Marlowe 2005: 100–102).[21] This suggests that, though doomed to damnation, Faustus is quick to exploit the comic potential afforded by his fate. He also has time to play a trick on a horse-dealer in Act IV, scene 1, who is not amused that the horse Faustus has sold him has disappeared (Marlowe 2005: 43). After pulling at Faustus' leg to wake him, the Horse-courser is horrified when Faustus' leg comes away in his hands (Marlowe 2005: 44).

We do, of course, see a similar use of hell for comedic purposes in contemporary film, with *Deconstructing Harry* (Woody Allen, 1997), *Bedazzled* (Harold Ramis, 2000), *Little Nicky* (Steven Brill, 2000) and *Drag Me to Hell* (Sam Raimi, 2009) among some of the more recent manifestations. Indeed, *Deconstructing Harry* has Satan (Billy Crystal) residing on the bottom, ninth level of an air-conditioned hell that resembles a Playboy Club adorned by topless women, a jazz band and a percolating jacuzzi. After descending in an elevator through the various floors populated by members of the National Rifle Association, the media, right-wing extremists, escaped war criminals, television lawyers and televangelists, the protagonist, Harry Block (Woody Allen), threatens to kidnap his true love after herself being abducted by the Devil (quite a variation on Dante). Block thinks he might even have the upper hand over Satan – 'I'm more powerful than you because I'm a bigger sinner. Because you're a fallen angel and I never believed in God or heaven or any of that stuff'.

One of the more ribald celluloid representations of hell is in the Adam Sandler comedy *Little Nicky*. Here, Nicky (Adam Sandler), the youngest son of the Devil (Harvey Keitel), 'ascends' to New York in order to bring back his errant siblings, accompanied by a foul-mouthed talking bulldog, who are intent on disturbing the balance between good and evil on which the order of the cosmos is contingent. First, the brothers, Adrian (Rhys Ifans) and Cassius (Tom Lister Jr.), freeze, and thereby lock the gates of hell, and then they quite literally create their own hell on New York's 'mean streets' – where a preacher urges his congregation to sin and the city's mayor lowers the drinking age to ten. Although the film presents hell in traditional terms as a red and fiery kingdom, populated by demons and decorated with gargoyles, the emphasis is on bawdy humour. For example, the gatekeeper to hell wears breasts on his head, tarantulas transform into humans, jellyfish fly and Satan rapidly disintegrates each time we see him (as, with the gates of hell closed, there are no new souls for the Devil to feed on). He begins by losing an ear and is later reduced to just two arms supporting his mouth. As Bob Graham wrote in the *San Francisco Chronicle* upon the film's release, 'Hell looks like a Halloween party or, better yet, a theme restaurant' (Graham 2000: <www.sfgate.com/cgi-bin/article.cgi?f=/c/a/2000/11/10/DD21779.DTL>) with the Devil taking the part of the maitre d'. This is, of course, rather far removed from *Doctor Faustus* which, at root, is an eminently serious, indeed tragic, play, in which Faustus presses Mephistopheles relentlessly about the nature of hell and he is plagued by guilt and doubt at the end of his 24 years, conceding that he has 'damned both body and soul' (Marlowe 2005: 50)[22] and is beyond redemption. Hell, as well as being a rich opportunity for playfulness and a lack of decorum, is also a very real location[23] to which Faustus is doomed to spend all eternity, as when Faustus' Bad Angel urges him in Act V, scene 2 of the 1616 version of the play to stare into 'that vast perpetual torture-house', wherein 'There are the furies tossing damnèd souls / On burning forks ... There are live quarters broiling on the coals, / That ne'er can die. This ever-burning chair / Is for o'er-tortured souls to rest' (Marlowe 2005: 119).[24] *Little Nicky*, in marked contrast, is, according to one reviewer, full of 'physical pratfalls, moments of gross-out exuberance, and extreme expressions of political incorrectness' (Berardinelli 2000: <www.reelviews.net/movies/l/little_nicky.html>). Similarly, in the words of *Christian Spotlight on Entertainment* reviewer Curtis D. Smith, the inclusion of 'two headbanging dorks, an ambiguously gay roommate, a cross-dressing wacko, a talking dog and a crazy, blind street preacher' have little to offer to the film 'beyond pointless, quasi-comic gobbledygook and general boorishness' (Smith 2000: <www.christiananswers.net/spotlight/movies/2000/littlenicky.html>).

In this respect, *Little Nicky*'s closest historical counterpart may be the thirteenth-century parody *Saint Pierre et le Jongleur* – a comic and irreverent treatment of Christ's Harrowing of Hell in which a penniless minstrel is left by Lucifer in charge of the souls of the damned. While Lucifer is out gathering souls, the *jongleur* enters into a gambling match with St Peter, using the souls in his care as the stake. St Peter wins and all of the souls are subsequently able to enter heaven, including, after the Devil in turn throws him out of hell, the *jongleur* himself (see Owen 1955: 60–61). *Little Nicky* similarly ends on a note of triumph as Nicky's mother turns out to be a celestial angel, Holly

(Reese Witherspoon), and at the end, he manages to 'save' his father and is dispatched from the kingdom of hell forever. Such a predilection for 'good' to prevail over 'evil' is also, of course, a staple of the other films addressed in this chapter. In *The Shawshank Redemption*, an earthly hell is superseded by the attainment of redemption on a Mexican beach, while in *Groundhog Day* Punxsutawnsey is transformed from a hellish site of endless repetition into a town that Phil Connors wants to call home. *Taxi Driver* arguably ends with Travis no longer a pathologically lonely and alienated individual but, as I have argued elsewhere, someone who is capable of social interaction, as his banter with his taxi driver colleagues at the end of the film testifies (see Deacy 2001: 117). The anonymous and outcast Travis is also accorded an heroic status (by the press and by the parents of Iris whom he rescues from the streets), and, according to one school of thought, 'Travis the Savior has been resurrected' (in Deacy 2001: 118). Finally, in *High Plains Drifter*, it is no coincidence that, after the Stranger has raised Hell to the ground, he literally ascends, on horseback, from Hell into the unspoilt, natural – even primordial – Edenic paradise represented by the mountains at the film's denouement.

Of course, there are many films in which evil *does* have the last word. The horror genre, with such staples as *Rosemary's Baby* (Roman Polanski, 1968), *The Omen* (Richard Donner, 1976) and *Carrie* (Brian De Palma, 1976) as well as recent fare as *The Unborn* (David S. Goyer, 2009), together with the category of *film noir* with its unflinching depiction of unhealthy and untrustworthy human relationships and a cruel, unheroic, claustrophobic and fatalistic universe, highlight the extent to which evil is not always so transparently redeemed by good. Polanski's *Chinatown*, for example, epitomises the *film noir* world where no-one is immune from corruption, not even the detective Jake Gittes (Jack Nicholson) who, in taking on what he thinks is a simple case of marital infidelity, finds himself confronting what John G. Cawelti calls 'a depth of evil and chaos so great that he is unable to control it' (in Deacy 2001: 48). John May further writes that it is 'cohesively malignant … catastrophic … in its evil … sudden and inexplicable in its outbreaks of violent chance' (in Deacy 2001: 48). The ending of Polanski's *Rosemary's Baby*, in which a young mother, played by Mia Farrow, discovers that she has given birth to the Devil's son, is another instance of unmitigated horror realised on celluloid. But, these tend to be the exceptions rather than the rule, and it is instructive that Polanski himself has indicated that the hope-less denouement of *Chinatown* (1974) does not necessarily imply that good has been surmounted by evil. In his words:

> If it all ended with happy endings, we wouldn't be sitting here talking about this film today. If you … feel … there's a lot of injustice in our world, and you want to have people leaving [the] cinema with a feeling that they should do something about it in their lives, [then] if it's all dealt for them by the filmmakers they just forget about it over dinner, and that's it.
>
> *(in Deacy 2005: 37)*

It is, on this reckoning, up to the viewer to decide whether to passively allow evil to win out, or to attempt to work towards a better world and to be active participants in the goal of personal and societal transformation and redemption.

Quite simply, where hell is itself specifically invoked or documented in film, it tends to be a means towards a celestial end. This is epitomised by the ending of *What Dreams May Come*, where the anguish of hell is merely provisional in form, making way as it does for what is presented as the infinitely more pleasurable experience of being reunited in heaven with one's hitherto estranged family members.[25] At first sight, such a reductionist approach might be seen to undermine, or at the very least dilute, the effectiveness of picturing hell on celluloid. But, it does suggest, albeit paradoxically, that filmmakers are, on the whole, involved in the same type of enterprise as many theologians today for whom hell is deemed to be a vital *but ultimately deficient* doctrine. Indeed, central though Augustine's corporeal and graphic depiction of hell as a literal place of torture, where bodies would burn forever without being consumed, happens to be, it is not the way either filmmakers – with their penchant for seeing evil being supplanted by good, as the endings of *The Shawshank Redemption*, *Groundhog Day*, *Taxi Driver* and *High Plains Drifter* typify – or most mainstream theologians understand the issue. Hick is concerned, for instance, that, on Augustine's schema, 'the sheer monotony of the continuous pain would produce diminishing returns of agony' (Hick 1976: 199), and that 'for a conscious creature to undergo physical and mental torture through unending time ... is horrible and disturbing beyond words' (Hick 1976: 200–201). This objection to the teaching of hell on moral grounds stretches back at least as far as the Victorian period, where John Stuart Mill was one of many contemporaries outraged by the spectacle of everlasting torment. His own father, James Mill, was similarly concerned that at the heart of Christianity lay the notion that God had created the human race in full knowledge that the vast majority of its members would eventually be consigned to an eternal hell (see Walls 1992: 5). For Charles Darwin, likewise:

> I can indeed hardly see how anyone ought to wish Christianity to be true; for if so the plain language of the text seems to show that the men who do not believe, and this would include my Father, Brother and almost all my best friends, will be everlastingly punished. And this is a damnable doctrine.
>
> *(Darwin 1958: 87)*

These sentiments were echoed in the twentieth century by Bertrand Russell, for whom belief in hell amounted to one serious defect in Christ's moral character, such that 'I do not myself feel that any person who is profoundly humane can believe in everlasting punishment' (in Walls 1992: 5). Badham refers, further, to the abhorrent notion 'that the spectacle of the sufferings of the damned will provide one of the greatest joys of the saints in heaven' (Badham & Badham 1984: 62). This idea derived from the aforementioned Revelation 14:10, with its talk of the damned being 'tormented with fire and sulphur' in the presence of the holy angels and the Lamb, and was in turn taken up in the twelfth century by scholastic theologian and bishop Peter Lombard. According to Lombard, 'the elect shall go forth ... to see the torments of the impious, and seeing this they will not be affected with grief, but will be satiated with joy at the sight of the unutterable calamity of the impious' (in Badham &

Badham 1984: 62). Aquinas similarly subscribed to the view in *Summa Theologica* that, as MacGregor puts it, 'the blessed in heaven will be granted a perfect view of the punishment of the damned and will have no pity on them' (MacGregor 1992: 179–80).[26] Badham quite properly points out that this 'notion is appalling, not least from the supposition that God would arrange such a display in order to enhance the gratitude of the redeemed' (Badham & Badham 1984: 62). As Badham puts it:

> I believe that the notion of raising a man from the dead simply that he might be punished for the evil he committed during his life seems an obnoxious doctrine to most people today; especially since eternal punishment must of necessity be infinitely out of proportion to any conceivable crime.
>
> *(Badham 1976: 49)*

Accordingly, for both many filmmakers and theologians, in the words of early-twentieth-century biblical scholar Canon B.H. Streeter, 'Traditional pictures of hell are morally revolting' (in Aldwinckle 1972: 97). This is in spite of the fact that traditional images of hell, with their extravagant, flamboyant and excessive delineation of bodies roasting and of devils adorned with horns, lend themselves to such striking visual expression. It is all the more ironic, therefore, that where filmmakers have striven to document hell on celluloid it has been for comedic purposes, as in the case of *Deconstructing Harry*, or, as in the case of *Drag Me to Hell* with its skilful blend of humour and the macabre – what *Sight and Sound* reviewer Jasper Sharp calls the 'laugh-out loud outrageousness' of its special effects which nevertheless stops short of tipping 'proceedings into the realms of pure silliness' (Sharp 2009: 62) – as a means of titillation and shock-value. It is also noteworthy that, for all the rich (not to mention lurid) opportunities afforded to filmmakers, very few films are set entirely within hell (*Little Nicky* perhaps comes closest). In *Deconstructing Harry*, for example, despite the expensive and imposing vision of a red-hot and fiery underground hell, less than five minutes of screen time is set there, and the scene concerned, for all its visual and literal splendour, is explicitly presented as a work of fiction. For, the protagonist is an author suffering from writer's block, and the episode set in hell amounts to his way of creatively trying to overcome his affliction by rendering in supernatural form all of the demons that are preventing him from producing his next novel. The Devil, for example, represents the character, played by Billy Crystal, of his former best friend, Larry, who has taken advantage of Harry's lacuna by running off with his girlfriend, Fay (Elisabeth Shue). Even Ernst Lubitsch's dazzling technicolor construction of hell in the 1943 classic *Heaven Can Wait*, in which Don Ameche plays Henry Van Cleve, a 70-year-old playboy who thinks that his earthly transgressions more than warrant everlasting damnation, only flaunts its spectacular set pieces at the beginning and end. The main body of the film comprises a retrospective journey through the kind-hearted and ingenuous Casanova's past life which, as we increasingly come to see, makes him an unsuitable candidate for hell after all (to the point that the Devil sends him 'Upstairs'). Such representations are far removed from those traditional theological pictures of hell in which, as MacGregor points out, both Protestant and Roman

Catholic thinkers have dwelt on the graphic details of the damned being roasted first on the left side and then baked on the right side for twenty million years each. MacGregor continues that while the burning process was taking place, 'serpents would be perpetually stinging the victim and each sting would produce an agony greater than that of all the stings that all the vipers in the world would produce if they all were able to sting at the same place at the same time' (MacGregor 1992: 179).

Although the technological means are thus available in abundance to filmmakers to luridly document the eternal suffering of the damned, films that attempt to visualise hell are ultimately involved in a far more sensitive and nuanced enterprise. As the trajectory of Henry Van Cleve perhaps typifies, it is too much of a caricature to suppose that we are eternally bound for either heaven or hell as if we are all, at the point of death, in such a spiritual state as to warrant *either* eternal salvation *or* eternal damnation, with no point in between. Even Satan's son in *Little Nicky* turns out to be 'too good' for hell to be his natural domicile, and although the protagonists of *Heaven Can Wait* and *Deconstructing Harry* both argue their case that they deserve to be in hell their residence there is no more than transitory and fleeting. In theological terms, moreover, Origen even took the line, as we have already discussed, that the Devil himself could one day be saved. To this end, it is not entirely surprising that film-makers are disinclined to revisit Augustine or Aquinas but to take the line, rather, that most of us float between the polarities of good and evil. As Aldwinckle succinctly attests, 'Few men and women, if any, are in such a spiritual condition at death as to merit either heaven or hell in the traditional sense', in the respect that, in actuality, some people 'have a long life in which to come to repentance and faith' whilst others 'are cut off in their prime, not to mention those who die in infancy' (Aldwinckle 1972: 136). According to Hick, likewise, 'the absolute contrast of heaven and hell, entered immediately after death, does not correspond to the innumerable gradations of human good and evil', and that 'justice could never demand for finite human sins the infinite penalty of eternal pain' (Hick 1976: 201).

Without denying that horrifying images of hell do abound, Badham could just as easily be writing about filmmakers when he argues that among theologians and religious practitioners today there is an increasing tendency 'to move away from such images and to emphasise instead the need for moral reflection and progress in the life beyond' (Badham 1995: 124). Filmmakers themselves may not be explicitly asking the questions posed by Aldwinckle as to how a loving God could 'assign some of His children to eternal bliss and others to eternal separation from Himself on the basis of what seems to be an arbitrary moment of time, namely physical death' (Aldwinckle 1972: 136), as well as how any person

> of sensitive conscience and compassion would really want to receive eternal life from a God who is content to assign the vast majority of the human race to eternal punishment in a hell where suffering is purely retributive, and by definition can have no value either as purifying or in the sense of rehabilitation.
>
> *(Aldwinckle 1972: 103)*

But, it is clear that hell is increasingly being seen by both filmmakers and theologians as no more than 'a temporary state leading to purification' (Badham 1995: 125). Indeed, to apply Badham's words to the trajectories of Andy Dufresne, Phil Connors, Travis Bickle and Henry Van Cleve, among others, all of whom are finite beings undergoing a process of evolution and growth of sorts and who experience hell as a very real but also, most importantly, a very temporary stage in their respective psychological and emotional journeys, 'many writers have insisted that the horrifying imagery should be interpreted symbolically rather than factually' (Badham 1995: 125).

7

CONCLUSION

Using film to revisit eschatology

Having established that both filmmakers and theologians often share many of the same values and insights when it comes to undertaking their respective eschatological forays, what our discussion to date has also, paradoxically, shown is that films ostensibly about the afterlife are very rarely interested in the afterlife *per se*. To an extent this is inevitable, as, in keeping with Kant's distinction between the *noumenal* realm – the world as it is in itself – and the *phenomenal* realm – the much more limited world we can apprehend through our finite senses (see Kant 2007: 258–62) – no filmmaker is ever able to undertake anything other than an albeit imaginative and creative *interpretation* of how the afterlife might look or feel. Even those people who, as our discussion in Chapter 3 has demonstrated, have had a close brush with death in the form of a Near-Death Experience have not actually *survived* death. Their NDE may have had a transformative impact on them, and may even have convinced them that physical death does not have the last word. But, the fact that they have returned to tell the tale militates against the idea that NDEs provide definitive answers as to what, if anything, will happen to 'me' (howsoever conceived) once 'I' have irrevocably crossed the threshold of death. While it is sensible, therefore, to treat afterlife-themed films with a certain degree of caution, this is not to say that they have only limited theological provenance or potential. On the contrary, many of the films discussed, *Flatliners* (Joel Schumacher, 1990) perhaps being the most flagrant example, go beyond the one-dimensional and static model of the afterlife as typified by Augustine, for whom heaven and hell are places of reward and punishment, respectively, where one can expect to receive everlasting salvation or everlasting damnation depending on our pre-mortem character and behaviour (as if this is ever singularly consistent) on earth. In lieu of such a limited and stationary model, many filmmakers are much more interested in conceiving of the afterlife in a manner more consonant with that of Origen as a spiritual, moral and rehabilitative training ground where we have the capacity to evolve and change. The medical students in *Flatliners*, for example, experience death not simply as a place of punishment (though they *are* punished for their past misdemeanours). Crucially, they are afforded the opportunity to atone and to mature. To this end, there is something far more efficacious about the way many filmmakers have treated the theme of the afterlife than can be said about some of their theological counterparts. It would be a misnomer, therefore, to suggest that, due to the reductionistic and terrestrial nature of most afterlife-themed films, film is an impoverished, patchy or defective site of eschatological meaning. Quite simply, theologians have much to learn from their celluloid counterparts and there is more to what filmmakers can do than merely bear witness to or somehow replicate on film the teachings and images of religious traditions.

At the same time, however, there is no room for complacency. For all the obvious moral advantages, as outlined at the end of the previous chapter, that attend those celluloid endeavours which depart from the traditional depiction, so repulsive to the liberal mindset of John Stuart Mill, Bertrand Russell and Paul Badham, which portray hell as a place of torture, the downside is that many cinematic portrayals of the afterlife are rather vacant and lack specific contours. *Vanilla Sky* (Cameron Crowe, 2001) is a case in point, in which the afterlife – if that is even what it is, the film being rather hard to pin down on almost any level – is a rather nebulous and indeterminate realm. As the video brochure of Life Extension Corporation explains at one point to the protagonist, David Aames (Tom Cruise), 'Your life will continue as a realistic work of art painted by you minute to minute, and you'll live it with the romantic abandon of a summer day with the feeling of a great movie, or a pop song you've always loved', and with 'no memory of how it occurred, save for the knowledge that everything simply improved'. The emotional odyssey undertaken in this film by Aames, while hardly consonant with the teachings of any particular tradition – indeed, the film seems to be an amalgamation of aspects of Christianity, Buddhism and Scientology – does rather reinforce Peter Stanford's contention, written in the same year that *Vanilla Sky* was released, that 'for novelists, film-makers, artists, song-writers and even advertising executives, heaven remains an attractive, instantly recognisable, elastic metaphor, the symbol of the ultimate happy ending or wish-fulfilment' (Stanford 2002: 325).

Of course, the film does not quite lend itself to that straightforward an interpretation. This is evinced by the murkier undercurrents running through the narrative, in which Aames is forced to confront and relive his own disfiguration and the tragic death of one (or even both) of his girlfriends, which seems to precipitate his 'death' from the cycle of consciousness at the film's denouement. But, there is only so much eschatological insight one can extract from a film which may well invite, even necessitate, on the part of the audience what Danny Graydon, in his BBC review of the film, calls 'some serious yet ultimately highly rewarding mental weightlifting' (Graydon 2002: <www.bbc.co.uk/films/2002/01/17/vanilla_sky_2002_review.shtml>), yet which is disappointingly let down by its presentation of a protagonist with a limited character trajectory. He is the same rich, pampered, unable to commit emotionally, appearance-obsessed, millionaire playboy at the end of the film as he was at the beginning. In place of rich spiritual or theological insight, Todd McCarthy's *Variety* review gets to the hub of where the film is lacking in profundity. According to McCarthy, *Vanilla Sky* 'ultimately heads into an elaborate mumbo-jumbo zone that strenuously plays head trips over familiar issues of reality vs. fantasy, who's who and what characters are alive or dead' (McCarthy 2001: <www.variety.com/review/ VE1117916556.html?categoryid=31&cs=1&p=0#ixzz13OFJLQZI>). Peter Bradshaw, writing in the *Guardian*, is even less impressed, calling the film an 'extraordinarily narcissistic high-concept vanity project', both 'cumbersome and bombastic' and 'lumbered' with nothing more sophisticated than 'pseudo-futuristic ideas' (Bradshaw 2002: <www.guardian.co.uk/film/2002/jan/25/culture.reviews>).

Representations of the devil and ghosts

Such a perceived lack of depth applies also to films specifically about eschatological figures and agencies, most notably the character of the devil. This is quite ironic considering that, as the previous chapter has outlined, hell, howsoever it is depicted, plays such a pivotal role in films from a variety of different genres, ranging from slapstick comedy (*Little Nicky*) and horror (*Drag Me to Hell*) to westerns (*High Plains Drifter*) and psychological dramas (*Taxi Driver*). Yet, as Kelly J. Wyman pertinently suggests, it is hard to find any other creature throughout the history of artistic expression who has been so devoid of intrinsic meaning as Satan. In her words, 'For many Christians, both Protestant and Catholic, the Devil is certainly not meaningless. However, the variety of images and conceptions of him does make the character of Satan rather vacant' (Wyman 2004: <www.unomaha.edu/jrf/Vol8No2/wymandevil. htm>). Wyman's argument is that, despite being so influential a figure, as exemplified by our earlier discussion of *Doctor Faustus* and Dante's *Inferno*, there has been no advancement or development in his personality or physical appearance at least since the Middle Ages (see Wyman 2009: 309).

This is a legitimate point, which stretches back even further to the entirely ambivalent picture of the devil that we can glean from scripture. In the Book of Job Satan is one of the attendants in God's heavenly court – effectively a quasi-legal accuser or tempter who administers affliction on the righteous, God-fearing Job in order to test the durability and limitlessness of his faith – who acts under God's jurisdiction. However, in Revelation the character of the devil has mutated into the much more autonomous 'prince of this world' and the personification of evil where he is engaged in a cosmic battle with God for the souls of humankind (see e.g. Revelation 20:1–10). What we do not know is whether the devil is human, fallen angel, comedic foil, beast of the apocalypse, or – along the lines of what happens to the 12-year-old Regan (Linda Blair) in *The Exorcist* (William Friedkin, 1973), whose experiments with a Ouija board have (literally) diabolical ramifications – a mysterious spiritual power whose mission is to possess the spirit of the weak. In films, likewise, it is just as questionable that the devil is really made known to us. Satan is Arnold Schwarzenneger's foe and nemesis in *End of Days* (Peter Hyams, 1999), a sexual predator and arch-exploiter of women – yet who is easily outmatched when the women join forces and plot revenge, thus suggesting he is little more than a comic fool – in *The Witches of*

Eastwick (George Miller, 1987), and a slick-talking executive lawyer in *The Devil's Advocate* (Taylor Hackford, 1997) who seeks to continue his reign by the creation, through incestuous procreation, of the antichrist. In Wyman's words, although films may be 'a way to investigate his character and to fill a void of knowledge about the Devil', and even though one may find patterns in the way that the devil is presented on film, 'the only real constant in films with diabolical subject matter is that there is no consistency' (Wyman 2009: 300).

We should thus exercise caution before looking to films for exhaustive, authoritative or definitive answers about eschatological subject matter. The fact that, to date, there has not really been much academic discussion about the subject of Satan in film only serves to highlight the need for further research to be conducted in this area. Indeed, Jeffrey Burton Russell's 1986 monograph *Mephistopheles: The Devil in the Modern World* accords only a brief and sporadic treatment to the representation of Satan in cinema in the penultimate chapter. In like manner, Alice K. Turner's otherwise far-reaching and comprehensive *The History of Hell*, published in 1995, has only an even more cursory (less than two pages) and somewhat dismissive reference to the treatment of hell in film in which, as we have already noted, she writes that 'Treatment of Hell in the movies or on television is mostly gothic and trivial, a chance for set designers and special-effects people to strut their stuff' (Turner 1995: 242–43). One possible exception is Nikolas Schreck's 2001 publication *The Satanic Screen*, though this is more of an illustrative guide to films about the devil than a sustained theological treatment of the topic. To this end, the result is not dissimilar to James Robert Parish's *Ghosts and Angels in Hollywood Films* which provides a potentially useful encyclopedic synopsis of 264 movies that depict ghosts and angels ranging from 1914's *The Ghost Breaker* (Oscar Apfel & Cecil B. DeMille) to the 1991 TV movie *Hi Honey – I'm Dead* (Alan Myerson), but which is far more descriptive than analytical, with its focus on each film's production details and cast list, plot summary, box office takings, press reviews and (if applicable) awards details. It is also difficult to ascertain exactly what Parish's rationale for selecting relevant films happens to be. He includes films involving haunted houses (see Parish 1994: x) and finds room for *The Return of the Jedi* (Richard Marquand, 1983) – even though there is not a single reference to ghosts or angels in his entry for this second *Star Wars* (George Lucas, 1977) sequel – yet he rules out *The Shining* (Stanley Kubrick, 1980) and *Poltergeist* (Tobe Hooper, 1982) on the rather arbitrary premise that, while they deal with 'extra-dimensional "creatures" who are not merely living beings who have passed on to another state', they 'stress the horrific' and 'focus on the gruesome to a highly graphic, gratuitous degree' (Parish 1994: xi). In other words, Parish seems to be saying, they are simply too frightening to be included in a book about ghosts.

In terms of filling a void in the character of Satan, ghosts or angels in film, much of the extant literature, in tandem with the depth of many of the films themselves, is thus disappointingly thin. There is, simply, no uniform picture that emerges. This point is typified by Tom Ruffles in his astute observation that cinematic ghosts can be both threatening *and* friendly, helpful *and* obstructive, and comic *and* pathetic, to the extent that the cinematic ghost 'straddles too wide a spectrum and is ultimately pressed into service in too many causes to be confined by a single shape and style' (Ruffles 2004: 202). This lacuna is not simply restricted, however, to *cinematic* litera- ture on ghosts. Rather, it is very much in keeping with the representation of ghosts in the Bible, where references are few and far between. The most familiar exceptions to this are the account in 1 Samuel 28:14 where Saul, the first King of Israel, consults the witch of Endor and asks for the prophet Samuel to be raised from the earth and the story in Mark 6:49 where the disciples mistake Jesus walking on the sea for a ghost (whereupon we learn that 'they all saw him, and were terrified'). No systematic doctrine or teaching exists, however, to undergird such depictions, even though, as Geoffrey Parrinder attests in his examination of the way ghosts have been understood across a range of African, Indian, Burmese, Thai, Chinese and Japanese belief systems, 'Notions of ghosts and spirits as restless, perhaps unburied or una- venged, beings with a message to convey or a task to fulfill abound in popular belief in many countries' (Parrinder 1989: 245). Combined with the fact that, in Cowan's words, 'ghost movies have generated box office receipts around the world for dec- ades' (Cowan 2009: 411) – in films such as *Dead of Night* (Alberto Cavalcanti, Charles Crichton, Basil Dearden & Robert Hamer, 1945), *Portrait of Jennie* (William Dieterle, 1948), *Beetlejuice* (Tim Burton, 1988), *Truly, Madly, Deeply* (Anthony Minghella, 1990), *Ghost Dad* (Sidney Poitier, 1990), *Casper* (Brad Silberling, 1995), *The Others* (Alejandro Amenábar, 2001), *Ghost Town* (David Koepp, 2008) and *Hereafter* (Clint Eastwood, 2010) – it is not surprising that such an eclectic, yet eschatologically sparse, assortment of diffuse representations abound. Such texts and films may exercise our imaginations and may even challenge and provoke us, but it would be folly to look to them for clear or highly developed intimations of immortality.

Angels in scripture and film

We have also only to look to the rather miscellaneous 'genre' of angel films to see how and why the present conversation is a rather limited one. Garrett is no doubt correct that 'angel-mania has bombarded American culture in recent years with images, stories, and TV shows' (Garrett 2007: 5). This is evinced by Emma Heathcote- James' study, published in 2002, in which the claim is made that since the 1990s 'Angels have invaded the media, through fashion, films, TV talk shows, music, advertising, magazines, newspapers … and, of course, the internet', to the extent that 'increasing numbers of British people are claiming to have had angel encounters' (Heathcote-James 2002: 12). Heathcote-James refers, for example, to the presence in Britain of what she terms 'angel group therapy sessions in which one can communicate with angels for help with problems as well as meditation workshops to enable visualisation of personal guar- dians' (Heathcote-James 2002: 14). Gustav Niebuhr, Professor of Religion and the Media at Syracuse University, wrote in an article for the *New York Times* in 1997 to this end that 'Fascination with angels has run at high tide in recent years, and there's little sign that it's letting up. One can read angel books, mail angel postcards, mark the days on angel calendars, attend workshops on guardian angels' (Niebuhr 1997: <www. nytimes.com/1997/04/06/arts/in-the-bible-they-don-t-talk-so-much.html>), and so on. But, it is hard to sustain a serious theological conversation with a body of films which, on Garrett's own admission, 'are so barely worth watching', as when in *Michael* (Nora Ephron, 1996) the suggestion is that angels 'have nothing better to do than hang around honkytonks and resurrect dead pets' (Garrett 2007: 5). This is not to say that such films are completely devoid of theological value. After all, as a number of writers have suggested, it is not such a leap from affirming belief in God or Heaven to holding that angels also exist. David Brown, for instance, argues that if one believes in God then there can be no serious difficulty in believing in other disembodied beings (Brown 1995: 49), and Ruffles similarly attests that 'Angels in a film demonstrate that Heaven exists, placing them in an Afterlife framework' (Ruffles 2004: 136). For Garrett, too, 'Angelology is a way of talking about God without having to talk about God', on the grounds that if 'you believe in angels, then you have to acknowledge the One who sent them' (Garrett 2007: 5).

But, the differences between what little scriptural information we can glean about angels and what their celluloid counterparts are able to tell us are stark. In the Bible, angels are depicted as an ontologically different species to that of humans. In the extracanonical Book of Enoch, there is an attempt to link the Nephilim of Genesis 6:4 – where we learn of the race of giants born to mortal women who had had sexual relations with 'the sons of God' – with a rebel angelic sect. In 1 Enoch 6, for instance, we learn that

> ... it came to pass when the children of men had multiplied that in those days were born unto them beautiful and comely daughters. And the angels, the children of the heaven, saw and lusted after them, and said to one another: 'Come, let us choose us wives from among the children of men and beget us children'.
>
> *(1 Enoch 6:1–3)*

This is, admittedly, a disputed interpretation. St Augustine, for instance, was inclined to interpret the reference in Genesis 6 to 'the sons of God' to refer not to an angelic host but to a community of mortal and depraved *humans* who, because of their having formerly been in a covenantal relationship with God, were identified as 'the sons of the Lord your God' (see e.g. Deuteronomy 14:1).[1] But, throughout the Bible there is a very clear trend towards seeing angels as being of supernatural origin. In Revelation 8, for instance, we hear of the seven angels standing before God, following the opening by the Lamb of the seventh seal, in which we learn that the 'first angel blew his trumpet, and there followed hail and fire, mixed with blood, which fell on the earth; and a third of the earth was burnt up ... and all green grass was burnt up' (Revelation 8:7). In Revelation 10:5, reference is made to an angel standing on the sea, and in Revelation 14:6, meanwhile, we read of 'another angel flying in midheaven, with an eternal gospel to proclaim to those who dwell on earth'. In Revelation 18:21, moreover, we learn of 'a mighty angel' who 'took up a stone like a great millstone and threw it into the sea'. We read also in Mark 1:13 of Jesus being ministered to by angels while he was dwelling, without food or sustenance, in the wilderness for 40 days.

In many films, in contrast, angels often tend to be no more than guardian angels whose job is to dispense advice and to give succour to humans in distress. We see this to be the case, for example, with Clarence (Henry Travers) in *It's a Wonderful Life* (Frank Capra, 1946) whose function is little more than that of a glorified social worker or psychotherapist whose mission is to help George Bailey (James Stewart) recover a sense of self-worth at a time of suicidal despair (cf. Ruffles 2004: 138). Cinematic angels even look like humans, as with Dudley (Denzel Washington) in *The Preacher's Wife* (Penny Marshall, 1996) and Seth (Nicolas Cage) in *City of Angels* (Brad Silberling, 1998). In these two instances, the angels even fall in love with humans (in the shape of the Whitney Houston and Meg Ryan characters, respectively), a situation rendered even more complicated in the case of *The Preacher's Wife* where we are led to believe that Dudley is actually a human being who died some three decades earlier and has been sent from heaven (though by whom it is not entirely clear) to give aid to a dispirited inner city pastor. There is no biblical foundation to the notion that angels are human beings who have died, or for that matter that they can even possess a specific gender. Even in *Switch* (Blake Edwards, 1991), a film that, as was discussed in Chapter 1, creatively explores the possibility that a misogynistic male may stand a better chance of entering heaven when reincarnated as a female, and even presents God as a sexless entity who speaks in both male and female voices, it is significant that, at the end, Steve/Amanda nevertheless has to choose – even though s/he has all eternity to make his/her decision – as to whether to become a male or a female angel. This is a far cry from the biblical portrait where angels are integral elements in an indissolubly cosmic framework, in which they are either a body of celestial beings who act as emissaries for humankind on God's behalf or else they are fallen angels. In the latter case, they are so named after, as in Milton's reimagining of the Creation story, they have been persuaded by the archangel Lucifer to rebel against God, as a result of which they are expelled from the heavenly kingdom and, as indicated in the Book of Enoch, condemned to a life of wickedness on earth.

Towards a more syncretic perspective

A further difficulty that arises when one attempts to conflate cinematic and scriptural depictions of the afterlife concerns the tendency in many films to borrow from the teachings and philosophies of more than one religious tradition at one and the same time. A key example is when filmmakers juxtapose, whether consciously or otherwise, the Hindu or Buddhist understanding of transmigration and reincarnation, in which it is believed that the particular karma an individual has built up in his or her past will have a corresponding bearing on the conditions they will face in the afterlife, with belief in the Christian conception of heaven. Such syncretism may at first glance appear congenial, inasmuch as it looks as though attempts are being made to transcend the particularities and limitations of any one specific tradition or culture by appealing to a common core of religious experience that can be inclusive rather than exclusive. But, the end result characteristically seems to fit neither eastern nor western formulations and ends up being difficult to reconcile with either. This is an important issue for theology and religious studies discussion, highlighting as it does that inter-disciplinary perspectives, including the comparative study of different religious tradi-tions, need to be taken seriously within Christian theology. Viable though it is for the Christian theologian to engage with the rudiments of Christian doctrines and other teachings when entering into dialogue with film, the conversation should not merely be a two-sided one, between 'Christianity' on the one hand and 'film' on the other, as if either two are discrete, monolithic and homogeneous entities in the first place. If anything, it is at least a three- or even four-sided exchange.

To give an example, although in the case of Christianity there are obvious differ-ences in how belief in an afterlife can be understood – as our previous examination of debates concerning resurrection, immortality and mind-dependent worlds has evinced – there is a staple, and non-negotiable, assumption in Christian conceptions of the afterlife that the individual persists. There is a possible exception to this picture in some of the cruder interpretations of the Beatific Vision that have been composed over the centuries. Aquinas, for example, saw the Beatific Vision as a final timeless and bodiless state where we would be at one with God and would share in God's eternal changelessness (see Vardy 1995: 18–20), yet which would, by definition, be ontologically different from anything we experience now in our far from static, body-oriented, social world. But, even this aspect of Christian teaching is far removed from what amounts to the very kernel of Buddhist teaching that we do not possess a soul and that there is no permanent or objective essence to any person. Indeed, in Neumaier-Dargyay's words, 'In general, Buddhism perceives the entire universe as a web of interdependent fleeting moments that constantly transform and reproduce themselves', such that there are no essences or substances 'that provide islands of permanence in a sea of impermanence' (Neumaier-Dargyay 2000: 89). On this basis, there can be no afterlife as such. It may be possible to talk about rebirth or reincar-nation. But, this is not technically an afterlife as, in terms of the laws of karma, it is not so much 'me' that is reincarnated as 'the result of what I have done in and with my life and lives' (Neumaier-Dargyay 2000: 89). The fact that we do not usually have any cognisance, in the form of a memory, of any past lives only reinforces the point that there need be no physico-mental continuation from one life to another for the process of karma to be intelligible. This is in marked contrast to, say, H.H. Price's conception of the afterlife which assumes, as a prerequisite, that it is our memories, wishes and desires from our present lives on earth that sustain our post-mortem journey.

In many afterlife-themed films, however, it is taken as a given that the complete memory of a previous life will be known to us in our subsequent incarnation(s). We see a prime example of this in *Heaven Can Wait* (Warren Beatty & Buck Henry, 1978) in that the protagonist who is reborn, Joe Pendleton (Warren Beatty), initially retains all of the memories of his previous life as a footballer even though he is inhabiting a completely new body. Technically, his is not a reincarnation as such as, due to a celestial mishap (hardly a Buddhist notion), Pendleton is allowed to 'own' somebody else's body on a temporary basis until a more permanent one is found.

But, even though, when that eventually comes, Pendleton loses all memory of his previous 'rebirth', his former girlfriend, Betty Logan (Julie Christie), still recognises him as the same person and they are able to fall in love (all over again). The same motif is used at the end of *What Dreams May Come* (Vincent Ward, 1998), in which Chris (Robin Williams) and Annie (Annabella Sciorra) elect to be reborn in order that, as they are soul mates, they will invariably 'find' one another all over again. This happens even though they have been reborn into two different cultures – he in Philadelphia, she in India – and have different ethnic and racial backgrounds. In an even less subtle way, in *Chances Are* (Emile Ardolino, 1989), Alex Finch (Robert Downey, Jr.) slowly comes to the realisation that he is actually the reincarnation of the late husband of his girlfriend's mother. Hick may be correct when he observes that it is sometimes thought in Hinduism that 'the full memory of each successive life, as experienced "from within", accumulates in the reincarnating being and is lodged at a deep unconscious level within each of the new empirical selves which it produces' (Hick 1976: 329). But, such an interpretation actually seems closer to Hollywood's model of reincarnation than Hinduism's. Indeed, in the Upanishads there is no reference to memory for proof of reincarnation (see Parrinder 1995: 83), and in Buddhism, also, the ability to remember past lives is very much an alien concept. In Eckel's words, from a Buddhist point of view, 'What I was yesterday is gone. What I am now is just a flickering moment in the process of becoming something new. Life itself is a process of death and rebirth' (Eckel 2001: 75).

Of course, this is not to say that Hollywood's forays into the territory of reincarnation have nothing to contribute to eschatology. On the contrary, such films often imaginatively re-work core elements of Hindu and Buddhist belief-systems. We see this in *Dead Again* (Kenneth Branagh, 1991) where the theme of reincarnation is addressed from the perspective not of a dead person discovering that he or she has been reborn into the body of a new person, but of a living person, played by Emma Thompson, coming to the realisation that a dead person is living out their afterlife through her nightmarish dreams. Rather than a place we go to after we die, the film's premise would seem to be that another person's afterlife is being vicariously lived out through our nightmares – it is not surprising to this end that Thompson's character is an amnesiac – and, conversely, our own lives are being lived out through the visions and dreams of the dead. Cinematically provocative though such a rendering is, however, it tells us rather more about how filmmakers are picking and choosing from a range of Buddhist- or Hindu-related teachings than about those teachings *per se*. A similar treatment can be evinced in *Field of Dreams* (Phil Alden Robinson, 1989) where, in addition to the conflation of Christian and secular eschatological ideas that different theologians and commentators have identified in this film (see Chapter 1), Caroline M. Cooper, writing in the *Literature/Film Quarterly*, refers to the 'ghosts' of the now deceased baseball legends who enigmatically return to play a few games on the family's Iowa cornfield as having been reincarnated (in Ruffles 2004: 73). Yet, it would be misleading to see in this film a straightforward outworking of reincarnation motifs. This is not least because, in stark contrast to Buddhist or Hindu teachings on the subject where one's souls – if we can even call them that, at least from a Buddhist standpoint – are thought to have been transferred into new bodies, in the schema delineated in Robinson's whimsical picture the likes of Shoeless Joe Jackson (Ray Liotta) and Archibald 'Moonlight' Graham (Frank Whaley/Burt Lancaster) are shown playing *in their own bodies* and so are instantly recognisable to Kinsella and the few other characters fortunate enough to be able to so bear witness. Quite how their bodies are in optimum physical condition – it is as though they have never grown old – is also a moot point.

It is thus the differences, rather than the correlations, between religious and cinematic depictions of reincarnation that come to the fore. Indeed, it is by far the exception rather than the rule for a Hollywood film about reincarnation to show any signs that the filmmakers are familiar with what religious traditions have to say on the topic. A case in point is *Defending Your Life* (Albert Brooks, 1991), in which the afterlife resembles a Disneyland theme park (with its fantasy hotels and shuttle buses) in which the occupants are required to demonstrate not whether their actions and behaviour on earth were sufficiently virtuous or righteous so as to merit a higher or lower level of rebirth. Rather, the criterion for advancement (or regression) is whether or not the dead can prove in a courtroom scenario that they had sufficiently demonstrated courage and bravery over against fear or terror. As Haunton puts it, the film's premise seems to be that humans 'are among the lower forms of consciousness in the universe, and only by overcoming their fear and anxiety can they merit forward progression towards higher states of being' (Haunton 2009: 256). The judgement that they face seems to draw on a variety of theological and philosophical teachings, including the Christian understanding of the Last Judgement, the Hindu or Buddhist idea of reincarnation, as well as the mystical sense of personal enlightenment. As with *Made in Heaven* (Alan Rudolph, 1987) where the afterlife is specifically identified as 'Heaven', the suggestion is that the afterlife is a kind of Origenistic training ground in which individuals can either ascend or descend to different levels of spiritual development, yet in both pictures the ultimate *telos* is a return to earth. In Buddhist teachings the ultimate goal is the attainment of *Nirvana* in which one transcends the cycle of life–death–rebirth to achieve union with what Parrinder calls 'the supreme Being-Consciousness-Bliss' (Parrinder 1973: 106). In Hinduism, also, the ultimate goal is an alternative to the endless cycle of *samsara*, namely, the attainment of *moksa* – what Brian K. Smith calls 'an eternal and changeless state of salvation that not only overcomes death but also frees one from continual rebirth' (Smith 2000: 98). Such a state is the antithesis of rebirth. Indeed, as Smith puts it, 'Such an afterlife entails a kind of mystical union with the Cosmic One, the unifying principle of the cosmos' (Smith 2000: 115). This is all fundamentally different to the philosophy undergirding *Defending Your Life* and *Made in Heaven* in which rebirth (and the reuniting of soul mates in the latter) is the supreme goal, and which could not be more distinct from the Hindu belief in the eternal immortality of the liberated soul and where the goal is to escape from the cycle of life and rebirth altogether.

To be fair, it is not the case that all Hindu teachings on this matter are uniform. As Smith points out, indeed, in many Hindu texts there is a sense in which the deceased individual undergoes 'a kind of double retribution, first in another world of reward or punishment and then again in the type of rebirth one receives in this world' (Smith 2000: 109). In other words, rather than be straightforwardly reborn as a result of our previous actions and behaviour in our past life or lives, there is a sense in which one is also likely to face reward or punishment at a stage in another world *before* rebirth takes effect. Badham notes, moreover, that in many Hindu texts, as well as in Pure Land Buddhism, reincarnation itself is said to take place *in other worlds* (Badham 1995: 124). Similarly, although the Tibetan Book of the Dead counsels that the states of conscious experience that are encountered after death are projections of one's mind (see e.g. Levine 1990: 228), there is an implicit assumption that the soul will undergo experiences following physical death and the next phase of existence (illusory though these experiences may ultimately prove to be). Badham speaks, for instance, of how the Tibetan Book 'speaks of the dying person seeing the radiant, pure and immutable light of Amida Buddha before passing into what is explicitly described as a world of mental-images' (Badham 2005: 40). When, in *Defending Your Life*, therefore, we see characters undergoing conscious experiences between rebirths, this is not completely at odds with Hindu or Buddhist teachings, especially when we take into consideration the fact that in the Vedic texts references are made to the many different varieties of heavens and hells within Hinduism. This is illustrated by Smith's contention that, in the Vedas, 'Heaven is a place where the pleasant things of this life are found in unlimited quantities and are enjoyed forever' (Smith 2000: 106), while, conversely, the Vedas also describe various hells to which individuals will be consigned.[2] The fact that Smith is even able to entertain the notion that one may be able to 'die again' (Smith 2000: 108) after experiencing heaven in Hinduism does, then, suggest that the rather fluid boundaries that seem to apply in the likes of *Made in Heaven* and *Defending Your Life* are not completely wide of the mark.

Concluding thoughts

What is apparent from the above discussion is that it is the eclecticism of the ideas that we can find in so many films about the afterlife that render all attempts to impose a simple and uncomplicated correlation between what religious traditions and their cinematic counterparts have to say on this topic so problematical. The fact that Tom Ruffles contends that *Jacob's Ladder* (Adrian Lyne, 1990) can be construed as both a New Age version of Christianity and a Buddhist outworking of how 'the material is an illusion, and spiritual progression depends upon the sloughing off of the sense of self' (Ruffles 2004: 192), in which the protagonist appears to be progressing to some form or another of the unravelling of ego or even *Nirvana*, is an obvious case in point. Yet, any renunciation that Jacob Singer (Tim Robbins) undergoes must be qualified by the fact that what seems to be spurring him on in the last scene towards some form of enlightenment is the strength of his attachment towards his (deceased) son (see Ruffles 2004: 237). Is Jacob letting go of the self, in accordance with Buddhist teachings? Or is he re-attaching himself to familial ties, thereby allowing for a more Christian-compatible corporate and familial type of afterlife in which (in accordance with the later Augustine) the individual persists in community? If so, however, how do we square this with the fact that Jacob does not seem to know that his life appears to be over? Is he thus in *denial* of death? Added to this is the further problem that in Christianity any eschatological hope has an unapologetically theocentric dimension. It is, in other words, God who is the source and foundation of all afterlife activity. Since the film makes no reference to a creating and sustaining divine being, does this thereby mean that *Jacob's Ladder* – or for that matter any of the other films we have been addressing – has no contribution to make to (in this particular context) a Christian theological conversation?

The answer is that this is emphatically not the case. In terms of the revised correlational model as proposed by Lynch (2005), it is more profitable to look at how the differences between theological and cinematic texts can enable us to find a third way that moves beyond the rather static and linear model which supposes that theological traditions or cinematic works are monolithic and homogeneous entities that can only be meaningfully or constructively brought together when the values of one are in tandem with those of the other. Since it is difficult to find an afterlife-themed film which merely correlates with or 'bears witness' to a specific religious or theological tradition then any such resulting conversations are necessarily going to be rather unsophisticated and undemanding, and hardly worthy of serious scholarly attention. If, on the other hand, films can have the effect of enabling theologians to reassess theological principles and paradigms that they had not previously accorded much attention, then the resulting exchange is likely to be far more profitable. In my own case, for example, prior to undertaking this research I had not given any serious thought to the question of *animal* immortality. I was familiar with the teachings in the Upanishads that, while most individuals are reborn as human beings rebirth in non-human forms such as that of an animal or plant is also possible (see Long 1989: 171; Rambachan 2000: 80; Smith 2000: 112–13), as well as with the problem from within a Christian perspective of how, as encapsualted by Moltmann, our personal identity can be preserved if one is to subscribe to the possibility of animal rebirth. In Moltmann's words, 'If I am reborn as a human being, I must be able to preserve my soul's human identity. If I am reborn as an animal … this identity cannot be preserved' (Moltmann 2000: 250). In a number of films, however – including *What Dreams May Come* and *Dean Spanley* (Toa Fraser, 2008) – it is implicitly supposed that animals will partake in the afterlife. Indeed, in the former Chris Nielson's dog is the first thing he sees when he arrives in heaven (prompting him to joke: 'Boy, I screwed up. I'm in dog Heaven'), while in the latter we discover that an Anglican clergyman in Edwardian England is the reincarnation of a spaniel. So integral is the role of the domestic dog to the characters in this film, moreover, that *Dean Spanley* would seem to echo C.S. Lewis' teaching that (as Walls puts it) 'domestic pets may enjoy a degree of personality in relationship with their masters and that this personality has promise of being restored in heaven', and that 'pets may be a part of a web of affection and love that will be a fit object of redemption and preservation' (Walls 2002: 90–91).

In traditional terms, to accord any due weight to such films would manifestly be absurd, even a debasement of the 'serious' business of theology. For Aquinas, indeed, the existence of the soul does not apply to animals in the same way that it applies to humans. The reason for this is that whereas the human soul is indestructible, the souls of animals perish along with their bodies at the point of death (see Lorimer 1984: 79). Quite simply, for Aquinas, there cannot be any sort of transmigration or reincarnation of human souls into animal bodies (or, for that matter, vis-à-vis the premise of *Dean Spanley*, animal souls into human bodies). But, this is not the only picture available. For example, Paul Badham makes the instructive point that 'If God created man for fellowship with him, one would expect this also to apply to other life forms of comparable intellectual and moral development' (Badham & Badham 1984: 54). Badham's premise is that, rather than diminished, one's understanding of God may actually be expanded if it is held that God's 'purposes extend far more widely than simply concern for the spiritual wellbeing of our own species' (Badham & Badham 1984: 54). In evolutionary terms, for instance, Badham argues that the line of demarcation between humans and other animals is more permeable than fixed, and 'can best be represented by a rising curve rather than definitive steps' (Badham & Badham 1984: 47). Curiously, however, one of the most accessible and provocative endorsements of this contentious position can be found in a late 1980s children's cartoon, *All Dogs Go to Heaven* (Don Bluth, 1989). The premise of this film is that not all humans go to heaven because they are not all intrinsically good, whereas canine afterlives *can* be countenanced. The film itself is hardly theologically profound – to this end, the *Halliwell's Film Guide* review is not alone in its assessment that this is a technically skilful animated fantasy which 'goes to waste in a confused and confusing narrative' (Walker 1995: 26). But, what it does have the capacity to do is something that should no longer be alien to theology, namely, to inspire us to ask pressing questions not just about the values of the films that we watch, important though these may be. Rather, films – no matter how 'secular', no matter how shallow or banal – function no less importantly when they enable us to ask whether the values that underpin our theological positions are really any more cogent, any more consistent, any more defensible just because they may happen to be more established and have been around for longer than their cinematic counterparts. Can *All Dogs Go to Heaven* challenge Aquinas? Can *The Shawshank Redemption* (Frank Darabont, 1994) enable us to revisit the way we categorise and understand 'heaven'? Can *Working Girl* (Mike Nichols, 1988) shed new light on the way we conceptualise the 'New Jerusalem'? Surely they can, they must, and they already do.

NOTES

Introduction

1 That said, though, in his 1994 biography of Jack Nicholson, Patrick McGilligan wrote that in preparing to play the role of the Devil Incarnate the actor 'pored over Gustave Doré's illustrations for Dante's Inferno, and delved into St. Thomas Aquinas' (McGilligan 1994: 350–51), so there may not be quite such a discordance between the academic and the populist.

2 A good example of this can be seen with respect to the question of violence. On the one hand, we live in a world – and this has particularly been the case in modern America in recent years – in which conservative forms of Christianity have increasingly been back on the agenda and there has been an innate suspicion of secularity, to the effect that only films which are deemed suitable for family viewing and which promote family values can thus be countenanced (the writings of Michael Medved are a case in point [see Medved 1993: 10]). However, in order to properly understand the world today, we can do nothing other than bring culture and theology into serious dialogue – otherwise, debate becomes stunted. Conservatives like Medved deplore the way violence seeps into films, but they overlook the very real sense in which religion and violence are historically inter-connected. Whether we are talking about the Day of Atonement in Judaism or the Cross in Christianity, violence is not some external 'other' which is at odds with the 'non-violent' nature of religious traditions. Rather, as René Girard has shown us, the history of religion *per se* is based on violence – in that, in religious traditions, violence is characteristically directed against a sacrificial scapegoat, who takes on the role of 'a sub-stitute for all the members of the community, offered up by the members themselves' (Girard 1988: 8). For Girard, 'The sacrifice serves to protect the entire community from *its own* violence; it prompts the entire community to choose victims outside itself' (Girard 1988: 8). Even though, as primitive society evolved, humankind gradually drew 'away from violence' and eventually lost sight of it, it is not possible for 'an actual break with violence' ever to take place – indeed, no sooner has it appeared to go away than it will 'always stage a stunning, catastrophic comeback' (Girard 1988: 307). It would thus be more profitable for those more conservative voices who denounce films to pay attention first to just how rudimentary a part violence played in the origins of Christianity. The way in which conservative critics applauded Mel Gibson's *The Passion of the Christ* (2004) as passionately as they vilified Quentin Tarantino's *Kill Bill: Volume 2*

(2004), which was on release in the same period in spring 2004, only serves to illustrate the point that, for some, violence will be condemned in one context, only to be condoned in another, for no other reason than that the said violence is believed in the former case to have a Christian *telos* or goal. My own view here is that one cannot have it both ways, and theologians must therefore interact with popular culture in late modernity to help fine-tune and contextualise a debate which has, perhaps, become too one-sided of late.

3 This material will be covered in detail in the penultimate chapter of this book.

1 Mapping the afterlife in theology, eschatology and film

1 Among film theorists in particular, the religious nature and orientation of film is substantially overlooked, if not altogether dismissed, as a viable or authoritative interpretation. As Gaye Ortiz indicated in 1998, whenever a new book on theology and film is published 'the academics in film studies titter and scornfully dismiss churchy types who dare to bring God into the rarefied presence of cinematic discourse' (Ortiz 1998: 173). For Bryan Wilson, if religious questions are dealt with in film studies at all it tends to be as a purely 'peripheral phenomenon in contemporary social organization' (cited in Martin 1995: 2) where the forces of secularisation are taken for granted, and Paul Giles wrote in 1992 that 'it is still not easy to discuss religion within a contemporary cultural context' since the prevailing ethos is that the academic study of culture 'is, *per se*, a rationalistic enterprise' which has no room for 'the mumbo jumbo of spiritual belief' (Giles 1992: 6). This is not helped by the recent success of Richard Dawkins' *The God Delusion* (2006), Christopher Hitchens' *God Is Not Great: How Religion Poisons Everything* (2007) and other writings on the New Atheism which serve to demonstrate that there is still a widespread suspicion, certainly at a popular level, that discourse involving religion has anything positive to offer in the contemporary world.

2 Categorising someone as a film, rather than a theology, specialist is always going to be a fraught endeavour, however. Ruffles teaches communication skills and film studies, but he has also been a member of the Council of the Society for Psychical Research since 1990 and was for some years coordinator of the Anglia Paranormal Research Group.

3 In cinema, there have been several notable treatments of the phenomenon of imaginary playmates, including *Harvey* (Henry Koster, 1950), in which James Stewart's character has a six-foot invisible rabbit as a friend, and *A Beautiful Mind* (Ron Howard, 2001), a biopic of the Nobel Prize winning mathematician John Nash (Russell Crowe), whose hard-drinking university roommate turns out to be imaginary, and one of many symptoms of Nash's lifelong battle with paranoid schizophrenia.

4 See the introduction to this book where Chester's point is developed.

5 As the discussion in Chapter 5 will demonstrate, it is commonplace in many churches today to sidestep this very topic, with many theologians taking the view that belief in a physical or literal heaven, at any rate, is a superstition that can and must be discarded in the modern world.

6 Stoeger has a PhD in astrophysics from Cambridge University, but he is also staff scientist for the Vatican Observatory Research Group and has been involved in interdisciplinary dialogue between science and theology.

7 See e.g. Flew and Varghese (2008).

8 To this end, we can add also Al Gore's documentary on global warming, *An Inconvenient Truth* (Davis Guggenheim, 2006), in which the message is clear: if we change our attitude towards the environment, we can save our planet. The *telos* is unmistakably terrestrial in form.

9 We will explore this paradox in Chapter 4, in the context of debates surrounding realised eschatology.

10 This raises all sorts of questions, of course, as to whether a secular philosophy such as Marxism can be construed as a religion. Though Marx himself was an anti-religious

thinker, he envisaged the heralding of a new age, namely, the coming to fruition of a utopian commonwealth, where there would be no conflict, and which would last forever – this is hardly devoid of eschatological value.

11 Notwithstanding Sam Raimi's humorous homage to the genre, *The Quick and the Dead* (1995), in which Sharon Stone is cast as a female gunslinger who outshoots all of her male adversaries, the western hero is characteristically male.

12 See e.g. Badham's point that the 'traditional doctrine teaches that there will be one definitive last judgement in which the whole of humankind is separated into two groups' (Badham & Badham 1984: 59) – the saved and the damned, respectively. It is plainly the case that this event will not happen at the point of our individual deaths. Rather, to cite from Matthew 25: 31, it will take place 'When the Son of man comes in his glory' and proceeds to 'sit on his glorified throne'. Verse 32 continues that 'Before him will be gathered all the nations, and he will separate them one from another as a shepherd separates the sheep from the goats'.

13 Even in his *City of God*, Book XIII, Ch. 22, Augustine refers to the bodies of the saints in heaven as being able to eat and drink, even though they will not need to do so in view of the fact that 'they will be endued with the reward of an immortality so certain, and so inviolable in every way, that they will not eat except when they wish' (Augustine 1998: 569). See also McDannell and Lang: 'The human community was now seen to continue in the other world, with the body taking on more material qualities than his earlier philosophy had allowed' (McDannell & Lang 1990: 66).

14 This quotation is from Book XXII, Ch. 24.

15 We find a similar instance of inconsistency in the work of British philosopher and parapsychologist Henry H. Price, whose work on mind-dependent worlds will be discussed in detail in Chapter 3. Although the notion of telepathic communication was crucial to his thinking, his earlier writings tended to construe telepathy as involving ideas which persist independently of the conscious minds which create them (see Dilley 1995: xix). There is also an inconsistency in Price concerning whether we have our own mind-dependent worlds or whether such a world is a shared environment. Whereas in many passages Price took the line that two people's minds do not possess the *same* image, he elsewhere saw telepathy as 'activities of a *single* image moving from one mind into another or materialising itself in the effort to get the conscious attention of some other mind' (Dilley 1995: xvi).

16 We find a similar confusion in Zoroastrianism where it is hard to discern whether one is judged immediately after death or on the fourth day afterwards (see MacGregor 1992: 102).

17 This is a frustrating claim, as Greene and Krippner do not supply the reference in *The City of God*. At best, this would appear to be an *interpretation* of what Augustine says, rather than something that can specifically be found in the text.

18 The significance of the claim is, however, undermined by the lack of a specific reference in *The City of God*.

19 This quotation is from Book XXII, Ch. 21.

20 Indeed, it does help matters that the quotation continues: ' ... just as the spirit, even when carnal and subject to the flesh, is still spirit and not flesh' (Augustine 1998: 1152).

2 Resurrection or immortality?

1 Paul Fiddes would also add to the list the novels of Doris Lessing (see Fiddes 2000: 7).

2 There is also the consideration that in Mark 16:12 we learn that after appearing first to Mary Magdalene 'he appeared in another form to two of [the disciples]'.

3 This citation is from *The City of God*, Book XXII, Ch. 19.

4 This citation is also from Book XXII, Ch. 19.

5 See e.g. Matthew 10:30: 'But even the hairs of your head are all numbered'.

6 *The City of God*, Book XXII, Ch. 20.

7 *The City of God*, Book XXII, Ch. 21.
8 In Scotland in July 1996 scientists created the first successfully cloned mammal, Dolly the Sheep. When the news was announced in February 1997 it was met with controversy. The following is taken from the British Science Museum web site: 'Dolly the sheep became a scientific sensation when her birth was announced in 1997. Her relatively early death in February 2003 fuels the debate about the ethics of cloning research and the long-term health of clones' (<www.sciencemuseum.org.uk/antenna/dolly>).
9 It is important to stress, here, that for Aquinas the soul itself is not the person, for we are a composite of soul and body. The soul is simply the form of the material body (see e.g. Lorimer 1984: 79), and Aquinas still believed that there must be a bodily resurrection (the resurrection body being qualitatively, rather than numerically, identical to the earthly body). Aquinas took the line that after death the soul goes either to purgatory or hell, and that those in purgatory, though enduring great pain, would at least eventually attain the Beatific Vision (see Vardy 1995: 15).
10 Note, though, the emphasis in Matthew's Gospel on the fact that the two Marys 'came up and took hold of his feet and worshipped him' (Matthew 28:9), thus laying emphasis on the *physical* nature of Jesus' body. We do, though, learn from Matthew 28:17 that, when the 11 disciples saw Jesus post-resurrection, 'some doubted'.
11 Fiddes' more measured understanding of the relationship between body and soul is of course quite distinct from Descartes' thorough-going dualist position, whereby 'it is certain that I am really distinct from my body, and could exist without it' (in Lorimer 1984: 93). Being immaterial, Descartes saw the soul as not being subject to bodily decomposition and as surviving the body's death.
12 This citation is from *On First Principles*, Book II, Ch. X.3.
13 *On First Principles*, II.X.3.
14 *On First Principles*, II.X.3.

3 Near-death experiences and mind-dependent worlds in theology and film

1 It is, though, worth bearing in mind the Fenwicks' qualification that 28 per cent of respondents in one of his surveys did not feel that the experience changed them in any significant or permanent way (Fenwick & Fenwick 1996: 149).
2 Water has provided the visual cue for life reviews in a number of films, including *Made in Heaven* (Alan Rudolph, 1987), *Beetlejuice* (Tim Burton, 1988), *Ghost Dad* (Sidney Poitier, 1990), *Switch* (Blake Edwards, 1991), *Intersection* (Mark Rydell, 1994) (where the protagonist's life flashes before his eyes during a car accident and we see him swimming through water) and *Dragonfly* (Tom Shadyac, 2002) (where the protagonist, played by Kevin Costner, nearly drowns at the scene of a bus accident which claimed the life of his wife, precipitating a life review and NDE on his part, which includes the appearance of his late wife before him – she appears in resplendent glory, emanating white light). In these films, the overriding theme is that 'the drowning, by entering a domain inimical to the living, are on a voyage of self-discovery as well as across the threshold of death' (Ruffles 2004: 126).
3 Of course, not everyone will be persuaded as to the merits of taking any sort of discourse about parapsychology and the supernatural seriously. It does not help, for example, that one of the more popular movies about the paranormal is *Ghostbusters* (Ivan Reitman, 1984), in which a trio of parapsychologist investigators, who are fired from their university posts after their research is exposed as fraudulent, set up a freelance ghost-extermination business. For, as Ruffles points out, 'Confronted with the most momentous opportunity to study life after death ever afforded to science, the [principal characters] are in effect glorified vermin catchers' (Ruffles 2004: 116), and the film itself is derided in *Halliwell's Film Guide* as a '[c]rude farce with expensive special effects' (in Walker 1995: 451).

4 The data here is ambiguous, however. According to Fenwick and Fenwick, e.g., 42 per cent of people actually become more spiritual as a result of having an NDE (Fenwick & Fenwick 1995: 149).

5 We witness just such an argument in *Dragonfly*, in which an eye surgeon explains away NDEs in these very terms: 'The tunnel is literal tunnel vision, and the white light is the gradual bleaching out of the optic screen. As it grows bigger, it would seem like you're moving toward it'. The protagonist's father, a retired doctor, also construes NDEs in similarly reductionistic terms: 'Obviously, the brain is still functioning on some subliminal level, soaking up all the last bits of what's left to hear and see'.

6 *Confessions*, Book XI.39.

4 Towards a cinematic realised eschatology

1 In such a scenario, the words and imagery employed will characteristically amount to no more than an imperfect approximation of that which will be revealed or encountered post-death, in a manner analogous to Plato's talk in the *Republic* of the analogy between the world of Ideal Forms and the forms we perceive through our senses in present experience.

2 Cf. Matthew 12:28: 'the Kingdom of God has come upon you'.

3 We can see this in Altizer and Hamilton's *Radical Theology and the Death of God*, in the preface of which they write that 'radical theology must finally understand the Incarnation itself as effecting the death of God' (Altizer & Hamilton 1966: xii).

4 Badham made this point in a paper (entitled 'Eschatology, Death and the Afterlife in Modern Christian Thought') he gave at a conference that I co-organised at the Katholische Akademie, Schwerte, Germany, in June 2009. I am currently in the process of editing, with Ulrike Vollmer, the papers given at this conference for publication in 2011, the title of which is *Seeing Beyond Death: Images of the Afterlife in Theology and Film* (Marburg: Schueren Verlag).

5 Heaven and the New Jerusalem as a place on earth

1 In his commentary on article four, Gibson, writing in 1902, effectively marginalises the importance of this reference to heaven (which he stresses is a psychological state rather than a place): 'The fact of the Ascension, though clearly stated, has comparatively little stress laid upon it in Holy Scripture' (Gibson 1902: 189).

2 The fact that heaven is so easily able to combine agricultural and metropolitan elements is unsurprising in view of the nomadic, desert-based nature of the Israelites in the Hebrew Bible, for whom even the city of Jerusalem lies atop Mount Zion. The Book of Revelation also concludes with the vision of the New Jerusalem where 'the street of the city was pure gold' (Revelation 21:21) and that 'through the middle of the street of the city' flows 'the river of the water of life' (Revelation 22:1). Added to this, 'on either side of the river' lies 'the tree of life with its twelve kinds of fruit', the leaves of which 'were for the healing of the nations' (Revelation 22:2). It is not a very steady picture – how does the (singular) tree of life lie on *both* sides of the river? – but it does demonstrate just how interconnected the pastoral and the urban were in the ancient world.

3 We learn that Antiochus IV Epiphanes robbed the Temple, banned circumcision, Sabbath observance and the reading of the Torah before rededicating the Temple to Zeus and permitting Gentiles also to worship there.

4 *Purgatorio*, canto XXVIII, lines 31–58.

5 For Christopher Columbus, indeed, the New Indies were believed to be located close to the earthly paradise – in Delumeau's words, 'Deeply impressed by the beauty of Haiti, he declared this island to be unmatched in all the world because it was covered with all sorts of trees that seemed to touch the sky and never lost their leaves' (Delumeau 2000: 109).

6 Andy's wife is the only character with whom he has had any sort of tangible relationship, but it could be argued (and I am grateful to Sara Barnes for pointing this out) that Andy *does* have a relationship of sorts with Rita Hayworth and the other 'poster girls' whose images are imaginatively employed to conceal the evidence of his prison escape scheme.

7 See also Dan Heaton's online review, posted May 2001, which points out that 'Through the opening credits, the camera pans over the skyscrapers of New York City while a rousing tune about the *"new Jerusalem,"* [sic] plays. For countless people struggling like Tess, this metropolis does represent the holy place they're all striving to reach' (Heaton 2001: <www.digitallyobsessed.com/displaylegacy.php?ID=1188>).

8 It is worth pointing out to this end that the New Jerusalem was originally understood, as in the writings of Ezra and Nehemiah, to refer to a future earthly city which would in fact rise from the ashes of the old city which had been destroyed following the Exile (see McGrath 2003: 9). But, McGrath points out, 'with the passing of time, Jewish hopes began to crystallize around the idea of a heavenly Jerusalem – a future city, beyond this world, filled with the "glory of the Lord," in which God is seated on a throne' (McGrath 2003: 9). There is, however, no unanimity on this matter, as evinced by Russell's point that for later Jewish rabbis the most prevalent view was that Zion would be reconstructed on earth: 'The resurrection of the body and the judgment will take place in the geographical Jerusalem at the end of time, and there the Kingdom of the Lord will be established' (Russell 1997: 39).

9 Note, though, that according to Russell the 'glorified earthly Jerusalem was the model for, and gradually merged with, the heavenly city of Jerusalem' (Russell 1997: 32), thus suggesting that the geographical Jerusalem preceded its celestial counterpart.

10 When King Solomon brought the Ark of the Covenant into the Jerusalem Temple, in the Holy of Holies, the term Zion – which had once referred to a small Jebusite fortress – was used to refer to the Temple Mount (see Russell 1997: 31). In Russell's words, 'From the time of Solomon, Zion by metonymy represented Jerusalem and even all Israel' (Russell 1997: 31–32).

11 The figure 12 is designed to evoke the 12 tribes of Israel and the 12 apostles of Jesus. As well as 12 gates guarded by 12 angels, we learn from Revelation 21:12 that 'on the gates the names of the twelve tribes of the sons of Israel were inscribed' and from Revelation 21:14 that 'the wall of the city had twelve foundations, and on them the twelve names of the twelve apostles of the Lamb'. The clear suggestion is that both Jews and Christians are (re)united within the sanctuary of the New Jerusalem.

12 According to Revelation 21:25, 'its gates shall never be shut by day – and there shall be no night there'.

13 As well as being the quintessence of all that is urban and all that is agricultural, it is notable that the New Jerusalem is also identified here with Christ, in the form of the Lamb, and, in Revelation 21:2, with a person, in that the author writes that the city came down from heaven 'prepared as a bride adorned for her husband'.

14 The Pygmalion link is established in the following claim by Janet Maslin in her *New York Times* review of the film: 'Tess decides to masquerade as an executive in order to sell the idea she thinks Katharine [Parker] was stealing, and she arranges a head-to-toe overnight transformation without needing help from a fairy godmother' (Maslin 1988: <http://movies.nytimes.com/movie/review?res=940DE5DD153AF932A15751-C1A96E948260>).

15 That said, though, according to film reviewer Simon Rose, 'Before being given the Disney treatment, the script [of *Pretty Woman*] was darker (she was a cocaine addict, among other things) and it ended with her walking out on him' (Rose 1995: 297).

16 The 'schoolgirl' link is made by this reviewer in relation to the fact that 'Jack, her affectionate insider, her loving "trainer," bestows upon Tess a metal school lunchbox (complete with an apple for the teacher and an admonition to "play nice with the other kids") on her way to her first day at her new job' (Goldsmith 2006: <www.notcoming.com/reviews/workinggirl>).

17 The ostensible fairy-tale link is reinforced by another of Sigourney Weaver's screen perso-nae as when in 1997 she played the Wicked Stepmother in a made-for-TV adaptation of the Brothers Grimm fairy-tale *Snow White: A Tale of Terror* (Michael Cohn, 1997). The tag line for this film was, perhaps fittingly in light of the present discussion, 'The fairy tale is over'.

18 *Shawshank* was released in American cinemas in September 1994 and in Britain the following February.

19 See the Box Office Mojo website (<www.boxofficemojo.com/movies/?id=shaws hankredemption.htm>) for information concerning the film's theatrical performance.

20 *The River Wild* (Curtis Hanson, 1994), starring Meryl Streep as a Montana white water rafting guide in a family-in-peril suspense thriller, was at number 2 with takings that same weekend of $7,109,765.

21 Statistics for these three films are from the above website at <www.boxofficemojo.com/weekend/chart/?yr=1994&wknd=40&p=.htm>.

22 The regularly updated poll can be accessed at <www.imdb.com/chart/top>.

23 The possibility that *Shawshank* bears witness to a Christian understanding of hell will be considered in the next chapter.

24 In Marsh's words, this is the kind of film 'which a major network can put out on eve-ning prime-time TV without causing great offense, guaranteeing good TV ratings' (Marsh 1997 [a]: 194).

25 One DVD reviewer, writing in 2007, writes specifically, albeit critically, about Shirley's 'path towards personal redemption' (see Mavis 2007: <www.dvdtalk.com/reviews/27986/shirley-valentine>).

26 When, in the course of my undergraduate teaching in December 2010, I cited this passage from Jewett, the response from my students was far from enthusiastic. The perception was that if the film were really to bear witness to American ethnocentrism then Red would not have been a black man.

27 An obvious case in point would be the Burning Bush episode in Exodus 3 where 'the angel of the Lord appeared to [Moses] in a flame of fire out of the midst of a bush' (v. 2) and attests: 'I have seen the affliction of my people … I have come down to deliver them out of the hand of the Egyptians, and to bring them up out of that land' (vv. 7–8).

28 For more on this, see Deacy 2008 [b]: 129–40.

6 Punishment or rehabilitation?

1 It is, perhaps, fitting to this end that the location used for filming the prison scenes, the Ohio State Reformatory, is now a haunted house attraction, one of whose events, which ran in the autumn of 2009, was called the 'Hell on Earth Haunted Prison Experience' (<www.hauntedx.com>).

2 *On First Principles*, Book II, Ch. X.4.

3 *On First Principles*, II.X.4.

4 *On First Principles*, II.X.3.

5 *On First Principles*, II.X.5.

6 *On First Principles*, III.VI.6.

7 *On First Principles*, III.VI.9.

8 *On First Principles*, III.VI.6.

9 The most obvious instance is the depiction of the film's hypocritical Warden, who, on the one hand, has a penchant for encouraging the inmates to read and, by definition, live by the Bible's teachings and precepts, while, on the other, falling short by the personal example he sets. Indeed, Norton presides over money laundering, torture and murder, and Kermode is, perhaps, not entirely wide of the mark when he describes him as 'demonic' (Kermode 2003: 14). Reinhartz similarly designates Norton a 'diabolical figure who has the power to cast Andy down to the nether realms of the jail (both literally and morally)' (Reinhartz 2003: 135).

10 This concept will be examined in more detail in the concluding chapter.

11 *On First Principles*, II.XI.6.

12 *On First Principles*, II.XI.6.

13 *The City of God*, Book XXI, Ch. 10.

14 *The City of God*, Book XXI, Ch. 9.

15 According to Dante, Satan has three faces – red in the middle (denoting Judas), black on the left-hand side (denoting Brutus) and yellow on the right-hand side (denoting Cassius). See *Inferno*, XXXIV.61–67: 'That wretch up there whom keenest pangs divide / Is Judas called Iscariot ... His head within, his jerking legs outside; / As for the pair whose heads hang hitherward: From the black mouth the limbs of Brutus sprawl – / See how he writhes and utters never a word; / And strong-thewed Cassius is his fellow thrall' (Dante 1949: 286–87).

16 Though set in Punxsutawney, the film was actually filmed in Woodstock, Illinois, as revealed when, in scenes set on the town's square, the inscription on one of the stores can be identified as 'Woodstock Jewellers'.

17 We can contrast this to Scorsese's experience of filming *Bringing Out the Dead* (1999) more than two decades later, when the city *had* been cleaned up under its mayor, Rudy Giuliani, as a result of which the film needed to be set in the early 1990s in order for the portrayal of the city to look authentic.

18 See e.g. Jewett 1999: 88–103 and Deacy 2005: 61–68.

19 Act I, Scene 3, lines 85–97.

20 Line 162.

21 Act IV, Scene 2 of the so-called B-text, which is 12 years older than the text cited above; see Marlowe 2005: xiii–xiv, xvi.

22 Act V, Scene 2, line 11.

23 To this end, it must be noted that this is but one interpretation of hell on offer in Marlowe's play. Elsewhere, in Act II, Scene 1, lines 117–22, Mephistopheles informs Faustus: 'Hell hath no limits, nor is circumscrib'd / In one self place, for where we are is Hell, / And where Hell is there must we ever be ... All places shall be Hell that is not Heaven' (Marlowe 2005: 24). As Turner puts it, Mephistopheles thus 'suffers the searing pain of deprivation rather than physical torment' (Turner 1995: 167). She acknowledges, though, that at the end Faustus is doomed to an actual physical hell and that, at the end, a 'curtain is whisked away to uncover the dreadful Hellmouth' (Turner 1995: 168).

24 Act V, scene 2, lines 117–22.

25 Though, of course, in this instance heaven is itself superseded, as was discussed in Chapter 2.

26 See *Summa Theologica*, Pt. III, supplement question 94, article 1, cited in Badham & Badham 1984: 62.

7 Conclusion

1 In *The City of God*, Book XV, Ch. 23, Augustine wrote: ' ... it is not true, as some suppose, that these sons of God were angels of God in such a way that they were not also men' (Augustine 1998: 683), and that 'According to the canonical Scriptures, then, both Hebrew and Christian, there is no doubt that there were many giants before the Flood, and that these were citizens of the earth-born society of men' (Augustine 1998: 684).

2 The example Smith cites is that 'Those who consume food in this world without first sacrificing some of it to the gods will enter one of a variety of hells where revenge is exacted' (Smith 2000: 106).

BIBLIOGRAPHY

Aldwinckle, R. (1972) *Death in the Secular City: A Study of the Notion of Life after Death in Contemporary Theology and Philosophy*, London: George Allen & Unwin.

Allison, D.C. (1999) 'The Eschatology of Jesus', in J.J. Collins (ed.) *The Encyclopedia of Apocalypticism, Volume I: The Origins of Apocalypticism in Judaism and Christianity*, New York: Continuum: 267–302.

Altizer, T.J.J. and Hamilton, William (1966) *Radical Theology and the Death of God*, New York: Bobbs-Merrill.

Anderson, R.S. (1986) *Theology, Death and Dying*, Oxford: Blackwell.

Andrew, G. (1991) *The Films of Nicholas Ray: The Poet of Nightfall*, London: Letts.

——(2001) Review of *Fearless*, in J. Pym (ed.) *Time Out Film Guide*, 10th edition, London: Penguin: 377.

——(2001) Review of *Prelude to a Kiss*, in J. Pym (ed.) *Time Out Film Guide*, 10th edition, London: Penguin: 919–20.

——(2001) Review of *Vice Versa*, in J. Pym (ed.) *Time Out Film Guide*, 10th edition, London: Penguin: 1247.

Andrews, N. (1973) Review of *High Plains Drifter*, *Monthly Film Bulletin*, 40/475: 169–70.

Anonymous (2006) 'The Wakefield Pageant of the Harrowing of Hell', a.k.a. 'Extraction of Souls from Hell', in E. Rhys (ed.) *Everyman and Other Old Religious Plays*. Online. Available HTTP: <www.gutenberg.org/files/19481/19481-h/19481-h.htm#wakefield_hell> (accessed 31 December 2010).

Augustine, St (1969) *The Confessions of St. Augustine*, ed. R.W. Dyson, New York: Airmont.

——(1998) *The City of God against the Pagans*, ed. & trans. R.W. Dyson, Cambridge: CUP.

Auster, A. and Quart, L. (1988) *How the War was Remembered: Hollywood and Vietnam*, New York: Praeger.

Babington, B. and Evans, P.W. (1993) *Biblical Epics: Sacred Narrative in the Hollywood Cinema*, Manchester: Manchester University Press.

Badham, P. (1976) *Christian Beliefs about Life after Death*, London & Basingstoke: Macmillan.

——(1995) 'Death and Immortality: Towards a Global Synthesis', in D. Cohn-Sherbok and C. Lewis (eds) *Beyond Death: Theological and Philosophical Reflections on Life after Death*, Basingstoke & London: Macmillan: 119–26.

——(2005) 'The Experiential Grounds for Believing in God and a Future Life', *Modern Believing*, 46/1: 28–43.

——and Badham, L. (1984) *Immortality or Extinction?*, 2nd edn, London: SPCK.

——and Ballard, P. (1996) 'Facing Death: An Introduction', in P. Badham and P. Ballard (eds) *Facing Death: An Interdisciplinary Approach*, Cardiff: University of Wales Press: 1–4.

Bailey, L.W. and Yates, J. (1996) [a] 'Introduction', in L.W. Bailey and J. Yates (eds) *The Near-Death Experience: A Reader*, New York & London: Routledge: 1–23.

——(1996) [b] Introduction to C. Zaleski, 'Evaluating Near-Death Testimony', in L.W. Bailey and J. Yates (eds) *The Near-Death Experience: A Reader*, New York & London: Routledge: 330.

Barr, J. (1973) *The Bible in the Modern World*, London: SCM.

Barth, K. (1961) *Church Dogmatics, III.3: The Doctrine of Creation*, ed. G.W. Bromiley and T. F. Torrance, trans. G.W. Bromiley and R.J. Ehrlich, Edinburgh: T & T Clark.

Baugh, L. (1997) *Imaging the Divine: Jesus and Christ-Figures in Film*, Kansas City: Sheed & Ward.

BBC News (2006) 'Anna Ford talks tough on ageism', 9 April. Online. Available HTTP: <news.bbc.co.uk/1/hi/programmes/panorama/4892178.stm> (accessed 10 October 2009).

——(2008) (a) 'Nurse writes book on near-death', 19 June. Online. Available HTTP: <news.bbc.co.uk/1/hi/wales/7463606.stm> (accessed 31 December 2010).

——(2008) (b) 'Scott settles Five legal action', 5 December. Online. Available HTTP: <news.bbc.co.uk/1/hi/entertainment/7764644.stm> (accessed 10 October 2009).

Beavis, M.A. (2003) 'Angels Carrying Savage Weapons: Uses of the Bible in Contemporary Horror Films', *Journal of Religion and Film*, 7/2. Online. Available HTTP: <www.unomaha.edu/jrf/Vol7No2/angels.htm> (accessed 28 December 2010).

Berardinelli, J. (2000) Review of *Little Nicky*, in *Reelviews*. Online. Available HTTP: <www.reelviews.net/movies/l/little_nicky.html> (accessed 24 November 2010).

Berger, A.S. (1987) *Aristocracy of the Dead: New Findings in Postmortem Survival*, Jefferson NC & London: McFarland.

Berger, J. (1991) 'Every Time We Say Goodbye', *Sight and Sound*, 1/2: 14–17.

Blackmore, S.J. (1992) *Beyond the Body: An Investigation of Out-of-the-Body Experiences*, Chicago: Academy Chicago Publishers.

——(1993) *Dying to Live: Near-Death Experiences*, Buffalo NY: Prometheus Books.

——(1996) 'Near-Death Experiences: In or Out of the Body?', in L.W. Bailey and J. Yates (eds) *The Near-Death Experience: A Reader*, New York & London: Routledge: 285–97.

Blenkinsopp, J. (1983) *Wisdom and Law in the Old Testament*, New York: OUP.

Bonhoeffer, D. (1959) *The Cost of Discipleship*, London: SCM.

——(1963) *Letters and Papers from Prison*, 5th impression, London: Fontana.

Botting, H.D.H. (1991) 'Intimations of Immortality: An Analysis of the Basis of Belief in an Afterlife', MA thesis, University of Calgary.

Bradshaw, P. (2001) Review of *The Others*, in *The Guardian*, 2 November. Online. Available HTTP: <www.guardian.co.uk/film/2001/nov/02/nicolekidman> (accessed 31 December 2010).

——(2002) Review of *Vanilla Sky*, in *The Guardian*, 25 January. Online. Available HTTP: <www.guardian.co.uk/film/2002/jan/25/culture.reviews> (accessed 31 December 2010).

Braude, S. (2006) 'John Beloff: Scientist who put parapsychology on the academic map', *The Guardian*, 4 July. Online. Available HTTP: <www.guardian.co.uk/science/2006/jul/04/obituaries.guardianobituaries> (accessed 19 November 2010).

Brinkley, D. (1996) 'Saved by the Light', in L.W. Bailey and J. Yates (eds) *The Near-Death Experience: A Reader*, New York & London: Routledge: 61–70.

Brooks, X. (2002) Review of *Vanilla Sky*, in *Sight and Sound*, 12/2: 63–64.

Brown, D. (1995) 'The Christian Heaven', in D. Cohn-Sherbok and C. Lewis (eds) *Beyond Death: Theological and Philosophical Reflections on Life after Death*, Basingstoke & London: Macmillan: 42–53.

Brown, S. (1997) 'Optimism, Hope, and Feelgood Movies: The Capra Connection', in C. Marsh and G. Ortiz (eds) *Explorations in Theology and Film: Movies and Meaning*, Oxford: Blackwell: 219–32.

Brussat, F. and M.A. (date unknown) Review of *Working Girl*, in *Spirituality and Practice*. Online. Available HTTP: <www.spiritualityandpractice.com/films/films.php?id=2750> (accessed 23 November 2010).

Bultmann, R. (1958) *Jesus Christ and Mythology*, New York: Charles Scribner's Sons.
——(1972) [a] 'New Testament and Mythology', in H.W. Bartsch (ed.) *Kerygma and Myth: A Theological Debate*, Vol. 1, trans. R.H. Fuller, London: SPCK: 1–44.
——(1972) [b] 'The Case for Demythologising: A Reply', in H.W. Bartsch (ed.) *Kerygma and Myth*, Vol. 2, trans. R.H. Fuller, London: SPCK: 181–94.
——(1976) *Theology of the New Testament*, Vol. 2, trans. K. Grobel, London: SCM.
Canby, V. (1991) Review of *Switch*, in *The New York Times*, 10 May. Online. Available HTTP: <movies.nytimes.com/movie/review?res=9D0CE7D8113CF933A25756C0A967958260> (accessed 31 December 2010).
Chester, A. (2004) 'Eschatology', in G. Jones (ed.) *The Blackwell Companion to Modern Theology*, Oxford: Blackwell: 243–57.
Chilton, B. (2000) 'Christianity', in J. Neusner (ed.) *Death and the Afterlife*, Cleveland: The Pilgrim Press: 79–96.
Chitty, S. (1974) *The Beast and the Monk: A Life of Charles Kingsley*, London: Hodder & Stoughton.
Cho, F. (2009) 'Buddhism', in J. Lyden (ed.) *The Routledge Companion to Religion and Film*, London & New York: Routledge: 162–77.
Clarke, P. (1995) 'Beyond Death: The Case of New Religions', in D. Cohn-Sherbok and C. Lewis (eds) *Beyond Death: Theological and Philosophical Reflections on Life after Death*, Basingstoke & London: Macmillan: 127–36.
——and Byrne, P. (1993) *Religion Defined and Explained*, Basingstoke: Macmillan.
Coates, P. (2003) *Cinema, Religion and the Romantic Legacy*, Aldershot: Ashgate.
Cohn-Sherbok, D. (1996) *God and the Holocaust*, Leominster: Gracewing.
Collins, A.Y. (1999) 'The Book of Revelation', in J.J. Collins (ed.) *The Encyclopedia of Apocalypticism, Volume I: The Origins of Apocalypticism in Judaism and Christianity*, New York: Continuum: 384–414.
Collins, J. (1993) 'Genericity in the 90s: eclectic irony and the new sincerity', in J. Collins, H. Radner and A.P. Collins (eds) *Film Theory Goes to the Movies*, London: Routledge: 242–63.
Collins, J.J. and Fishbane, M. (1995) 'Introduction', in J.J. Collins and M. Fishbane (eds) *Death, Ecstasy, and Other Worldly Journeys*, New York: State University of New York: ix–xvi.
Combs, R. (1978) Review of *Heaven Can Wait*, in *Monthly Film Bulletin*, 45/537: 201–2.
——(1989) [a] Review of *Working Girl*, in *Monthly Film Bulletin*, 56/663: 99–100.
——(1989) [b] 'Slaves of Manhattan', *Sight and Sound*, 58/2: 78.
Coniam, M. (2001) 'Rodents to Freedom!', *Philosophy Now*, 32, June/July: 10–11.
Cowan, D. (2009) 'Horror and the Demonic', in J. Lyden (ed.) *The Routledge Companion to Religion and Film*, London & New York: Routledge: 403–19.
Cox, H. (1966) *The Secular City*, New York: Macmillan.
——(1975) '"The Secular City" – Ten Years Later', *The Christian Century*, 28 May, XCII/20: 544–47.
Daley, B.E. (1991) *The Hope of the Early Church: A Handbook of Patristic Eschatology*, Cambridge: CUP.
Danielou, J. (1955) *Origen*, New York: Sheed & Ward.
Dante (1949) *The Divine Comedy 1: Hell*, trans. D. L. Sayers, London: Penguin.
——(1977) *The Divine Comedy 2: Purgatory*, trans. D. L. Sayers, Harmondsworth: Penguin.
Darwin, C. (1958) *The Autobiography of Charles Darwin 1809–1882*, ed. N. Barlow, London: Collins.
Davies, D. (2008) *The Theology of Death*, London: T & T Clark.
Davies, S. (2009) Review of *Dean Spanley*, in *Sight and Sound*, 19/1: 60.
Dawkins, R. (2006) *The God Delusion*, London: Transworld.
Deacy, C. (2001) *Screen Christologies: Redemption and the Medium of Film*, Cardiff: University of Wales Press.
——(2005) *Faith in Film: Religious Themes in Contemporary Cinema*, Aldershot: Ashgate.
——(2008) [a] '"Escaping" from the world through film: Theological perspectives on the "real" and the "reel"', in G. Hallbäck and A. Hvithamar (eds) *Recent Releases: The Bible in Contemporary Cinema*, Sheffield: Sheffield Phoenix Press: 12–29.

——(2008) [b] 'The Pedagogical Challenges of Finding Christ Figures in Film', in G.J. Watkins (ed.) *Teaching Religion and Film*, Oxford: OUP: 129–40.

——and Ortiz, G. (2008) *Theology and Film: Challenging the Sacred/Secular Divide*, Oxford: Blackwell.

Delumeau, J. (2000) *History of Paradise: The Garden of Eden in Myth and Tradition*, trans. M. O'Connell, Urbana & Chicago: University of Illinois Press.

Desmarais, M.M. (2009) 'Karma and Film', in W.L. Blizek (ed.) *The Continuum Companion to Religion and Film*, London & New York: Continuum: 281–89.

Dilley, F.B. (1995) 'Editor's introduction', in F.B. Dilley (ed.) *Philosophical Interactions with Parapsychology: The Major Writings of H. H. Price on Parapsychology and Survival*, Basingstoke: Macmillan: ix–xix.

Dodd, C.H. (1944) *The Apostolic Preaching and its Developments*, London: Hodder & Stoughton.

Doore, G. (1990) 'Introduction', in G. Doore (ed.) *What Survives? Contemporary Explorations of Life After Death*, Los Angeles: Jeremy P. Tarcher, Inc.: 1–4.

Ebert, R. (1989) Review of *Field of Dreams*, in *Chicago Sun-Times*, 21 April. Online. Available HTTP: <rogerebert.suntimes.com/apps/pbcs.dll/article?AID=/19890421/REVIEWS/904210302/1023> (accessed 31 December 2010).

——(1990) Review of *Pretty Woman*, in *Chicago Sun-Times*, 23 March. Online. Available HTTP: <rogerebert.suntimes.com/apps/pbcs.dll/article?AID=/19900323/REVIEWS/3230305/1023> (accessed 23 November 2010).

——(1999) Review of *Stigmata*, 1 January. Online. Available HTTP: <rogerebert.suntimes.com/apps/pbcs.dll/article?AID=/19990101/REVIEWS/901010302/1023> (accessed 31 December 2010).

Eckel, M.D. (2001) 'If I Should Die before I Am Awakened: Buddhist Reflections on Death', in L.S. Rouner (ed.) *If I Should Die*, Notre Dame IN: University of Notre Dame Press: 71–93.

Edgar, A. (1996) 'The Importance of Death in Shaping our Understanding of Life', in P. Badham and P. Ballard (eds) *Facing Death: An Interdisciplinary Approach*, Cardiff: University of Wales Press: 154–67.

Elley, D. (ed.) (1994) *Variety Movie Guide*, London: Hamlyn.

Ellison, A. (1995) 'Human Survival of Death: Evidence and Prospects', in D. Cohn-Sherbok and C. Lewis (eds) *Beyond Death: Theological and Philosophical Reflections on Life after Death*, Basingstoke & London: Macmillan: 173–82.

Falsani, C. (2009) *The Dude Abides: The Gospel According to the Coen Brothers*, Grand Rapids, MI: Zondervan.

Feinstein, D. (1990) 'Personal Mythologies of Death and their Evolution', in G. Doore (ed.) *What Survives? Contemporary Explorations of Life After Death*, Los Angeles: Jeremy P. Tarcher, Inc.: 255–64.

Fenwick, P. and Fenwick E. (1996) 'The Near-death Experience', in P. Badham and P. Ballard (eds) *Facing Death: An Interdisciplinary Approach*, Cardiff: University of Wales Press: 133–53.

Ferrell, W.K. (2000) *Literature and Film as Modern Theology*, Westport CT: Praeger.

Fiddes, P.S. (2000) *The Promised End: Eschatology in Theology and Literature*, Oxford: Blackwell.

Flew, A. with Varghese, R.A. (2008) *There is a God: How the World's Most Notorious Atheist Changed His Mind*, New York: HarperCollins.

Floyd, N. (1991) Review of *Almost an Angel*, in *Monthly Film Bulletin*, 58/685: 38–39.

Foucault, M. (1967) *Madness and Civilization: A History of Insanity in the Age of Reason*, trans. R. Howard, London: Tavistock.

Fox, K. and McDonagh, M. (2003) *The Eleventh Virgin Film Guide*, London: Virgin Books.

Fox, M. (2003) *Religion, Spirituality and the Near-Death Experience*, London: Routledge.

French, P.A. (1997) *Cowboy Metaphysics: Ethics and Death in Westerns*, Oxford: Rowman & Littlefield.

Garrett, G. (2007) *The Gospel According to Hollywood*, Louisville & London: Westminster John Knox.

Gauld, A. (1982) *Mediumship and Survival: A Century of Investigations*, London: Heinemann.

Gibson, E.C.S. (1902) *The Thirty-Nine Articles of the Church of England*, London: Methuen.

Gilbey, R. (2004) *Groundhog Day*, London: British Film Institute.

Giles, P. (1992) *American Catholic Arts and Fictions: Culture, Ideology, Aesthetics*, Cambridge: CUP.

Gill, R. (2006) *A Textbook of Christian Ethics*, 3rd edn, London: T & T Clark.

Girard, R. (1988) *Violence and the Sacred*, trans. P. Gregory, London: Athlone.

Goldsmith, L. (2006) Review of *Working Girl*, in *Not coming to a theater near you*. Online. Available HTTP: <www.notcoming.com/reviews/workinggirl> (accessed 23 November 2010).

Graham, B. (2000) 'Heaven Help Us: Adam Sandler is Satan's spawn in the effects-laden comedy *Little Nicky*', *San Francisco Chronicle*, 10 November. Online. Available HTTP: <www.sfgate.com/cgi-bin/article.cgi?f=/c/a/2000/11/10/DD21779.DTL> (accessed 24 November 2010).

Graydon, D. (2002) Review of *Vanilla Sky*, in BBC Movies, 24 January. Online. Available HTTP: <www.bbc.co.uk/films/2002/01/17/vanilla_sky_2002_review.shtml> (accessed 31 December 2010).

Greene, F.G. and Krippner, S. (1990) 'Panoramic Vision: Hallucination or Bridge into the Beyond?', in G. Doore (ed.) *What Survives? Contemporary Explorations of Life After Death*, Los Angeles: Jeremy P. Tarcher, Inc.: 61–75.

Greyson, B. and Evans Bush, N. (1996) 'Distressing Near-Death Experiences', in L.W. Bailey and J. Yates (eds) *The Near-Death Experience: A Reader*, New York & London: Routledge: 209–30.

Grosso, M. (1990) 'Fear of Life after Death', in G. Doore (ed.) *What Survives? Contemporary Explorations of Life After Death*, Los Angeles: Jeremy P. Tarcher, Inc.: 241–54.

Haas, A.M. (1999) 'Otherworldly Journeys in the Middle Ages', in B. McGinn (ed.) *The Encyclopedia of Apocalypticism, Volume II: Apocalypticism in Western History and Culture*, New York: Continuum: 442–66.

Hall, L. (2003) *Swinburne's Hell and Hick's Universalism: Are We Free to Reject God?*, Aldershot: Ashgate.

Hallisey, C. (2000) 'Buddhism', in J. Neusner (ed.) *Death and the Afterlife*, Cleveland: The Pilgrim Press: 1–29.

Haunton, C. (2009) 'Filming the Afterlife', in W.L. Blizek (ed.) *The Continuum Companion to Religion and Film*, London & New York: Continuum: 251–59.

Heathcote-James, E. (2002) *Seeing Angels*, London: John Blake.

Heaton, D. (2001) Review of *Working Girl*, in *digitallyOBSESSED!* Online. Available HTTP: <www.digitallyobsessed.com/displaylegacy.php?ID=1188> (accessed 23 November 2010).

Hebblethwaite, B. (1984) *The Christian Hope*, Basingstoke: Marshall, Morgan & Scott.

Heidegger, M. (1962) *Being and Time*, Oxford: Blackwell.

Henderson, I. (1963) *Myth in the New Testament*, 6th impression, London: SCM.

Hick, J. (1973) 'Towards a Christian Theology of Death', in T. Penelhum (ed.) *Immortality*, Belmont, CA: Wadsworth: 141–57.

——(1976) *Death and Eternal Life*, London: Collins.

Hitchens, C. (2007) *God is Not Great: How Religion Poisons Everything*, London: Atlantic.

Holmwood, L. (2009) 'Strictly ageism? Row as Arlene Phillips, 66, is axed for a 30-year-old', *The Guardian*, 17 July. Online. Available HTTP: <www.guardian.co.uk/media/2009/jul/17/arlene-phillips-strictly-come-dancing> (accessed 10 October 2009).

Hoover, S.M. (2006) *Religion in the Media Age*, Abingdon: Routledge.

Horsley, J. (2005) 'Citizens of Hell', in P.A. Woods (ed.), *Scorsese: A Journey through the American Psyche*, London: Plexus.

Jasper, D. (1997) 'On Systematizing the Unsystematic: A Response', in C. Marsh and G. Ortiz (eds) *Explorations in Theology and Film: Movies and Meaning*, Oxford: Blackwell: 235–44.

Jewett, R. (1999) *Saint Paul Returns to the Movies: Triumph over Shame*, Cambridge: Eerdmans.

Kant, I. (2007) *Critique of Pure Reason*, ed. & trans. M. Weigelt, London: Penguin.

Kastenbaum, R. (1996) 'Near-Death Reports: Evidence for Survival of Death?', in L.W. Bailey and J. Yates (eds) *The Near-Death Experience: A Reader*, New York & London: Routledge: 247–64.

Kempley, R. (1988) Review of *Working Girl*, in *The Washington Post*, 21 December. Online. Available HTTP: <www.washingtonpost.com/wp-srv/style/longterm/movies/videos/workinggirlrkempley_a0c9d9.htm> (accessed 23 November 2010).

——(1989) (a) Review of *Field of Dreams*, in *The Washington Post*, 21 April. Online. Available HTTP: <www.washingtonpost.com/wp-srv/style/longterm/movies/videos/fieldofdreamspgkempley_a09fb9.htm> (accessed 31 December 2010).

——(1989) (b) Review of *Shirley Valentine*, in *The Washington Post*, 15 September. Online. Available HTTP: <www.washingtonpost.com/wp-srv/style/longterm/movies/videos/shirleyvalentinerkempley_a0c997.htm> (accessed 31 December 2010).

Kermode, M. (2003) *The Shawshank Redemption*, London: British Film Institute.

Kolker, R.P. (1988) *A Cinema of Loneliness*, Oxford: OUP.

Kovacs, L. (1999) *The Haunted Screen: Ghosts in Literature and Film*, London: McFarland.

Kozlovic. A.K. (2004) 'The Structural Characteristics of the Cinematic Christ-Figure', *Journal of Religion and Popular Culture*, Vol. 8. Online. Available HTTP: <www.usask.ca/relst/jrpc/art8-cinematicchrist.html> (accessed 31 December 2010).

Küng, H. (1984) *Eternal Life?*, trans. E. Quinn, London: Collins.

Lachs, J. (2001) 'The Vague Hope of Immortality', in L.S. Rouner (ed.) *If I Should Die*, Notre Dame IN: University of Notre Dame Press: 127–39.

Lerner, R.E. (1999) 'Millennialism', in B. McGinn (ed.) *The Encyclopedia of Apocalypticism, Volume II: Apocalypticism in Western History and Culture*, New York: Continuum: 326–60.

Lester, D. (2005) *Is There Life After Death?: An Examination of the Empirical Evidence*, Jefferson NC & London: McFarland.

Levenson, A.T. (2000) *Modern Jewish Thinkers: An Introduction*, Northvale NJ: Jason Aronson Inc.

Levine, S. (1990) 'What Survives?', in G. Doore (ed.) *What Survives? Contemporary Explorations of Life After Death*, Los Angeles: Jeremy P. Tarcher, Inc.: 223–32.

Lewis, C. (1995) 'Beyond the Crematorium – Popular Belief', in D. Cohn-Sherbok and C. Lewis (eds) *Beyond Death: Theological and Philosophical Reflections on Life after Death*, Basingstoke & London: Macmillan: 199–206.

Lewis, H.D. (1973) *The Self and Immortality*, Basingstoke: Macmillan.

Livingston, J.C. (1971) *Modern Christian Thought: From the Enlightenment to Vatican II*, London: Collier Macmillan.

Long, J.B. (1989) 'The Underworld', in L.E. Sullivan (ed.) *Death, Afterlife, and the Soul*, London: Collier Macmillan: 161–73.

Lorimer, D. (1984) *Survival? Body, Mind and Death in the Light of Psychic Experience*, London: Routledge & Kegan Paul.

——(1990) 'Science, Death, and Purpose', in G. Doore (ed.) *What Survives? Contemporary Explorations of Life After Death*, Los Angeles: Jeremy P. Tarcher, Inc.: 99–110.

——(1995) 'The Near-Death Experience: A Glimpse of Heaven and Hell?', in D. Cohn-Sherbok and C. Lewis (eds) *Beyond Death: Theological and Philosophical Reflections on Life after Death*, Basingstoke & London: Macmillan: 164–72.

Lynch, G. (2005) *Understanding Theology and Popular Culture*, Oxford: Blackwell.

McCarthy, T. (2001) Review of *Vanilla Sky*, in *Variety*, 9 December. Online. Available HTTP: <www.variety.com/review/VE1117916556.html?categoryid=31&cs=1&p=0#ixzz13OFJLQZI> (accessed 31 December 2010).

McDannell, C. and Lang, B. (1990) *Heaven: A History*, 2nd edn, New Haven & London: Yale University Press.

McGee, P. (2007) *From Shane to Kill Bill: Rethinking the Western*, Oxford: Blackwell.

McGilligan, P. (1994) *Jack's Life: A Biography of Jack Nicholson*, London: Hutchinson.

McGinn, B. (1999) 'The Last Judgment in Christian Tradition', in B. McGinn (ed.) *The Encyclopedia of Apocalypticism, Volume II: Apocalypticism in Western History and Culture*, New York: Continuum: 361–401.

McGrath, A.E. (2001) *Christian Theology: An Introduction*, 3rd edn, Oxford: Blackwell.

——(2003) *A Brief History of Heaven*, Oxford: Blackwell.

MacGregor, G. (1982) *Reincarnation as a Christian Hope*, London & Basingstoke: Macmillan.

——(1992) *Images of Afterlife: Beliefs from Antiquity to Modern Times*, New York: Paragon.

Mahan, J.H. (2002) 'Celluloid Savior: Jesus in the Movies', *Journal of Religion and Film*, 6/1. Online. Available HTTP: <www.unomaha.edu/jrf/celluloid.htm> (accessed 31 December 2010).

Marlowe, C. (2005) *Doctor Faustus*, ed. D.S. Kastan, New York and London: W.W. Norton.

Marsh, C. (1997) [a] 'The Spirituality of *Shirley Valentine*', in C. Marsh and G. Ortiz (eds) *Explorations in Theology and Film: Movies and Meaning*, Oxford: Blackwell: 193–205.

——(1997) [b] 'Did You Say "Grace"?: Eating in Community in *Babette's Feast*', in C. Marsh and G. Ortiz (eds) *Explorations in Theology and Film: Movies and Meaning*, Oxford: Blackwell: 207–18.

——(1998) 'Religion, Theology and Film in a Postmodern Age: A Response to John Lyden', *Journal of Religion and Film*, 2/1. Online. Available HTTP: <www.unomaha.edu/jrf/marshrel.htm> (accessed 23 November 2010).

——(2004) *Cinema and Sentiment: Film's Challenge to Theology*, Carlisle: Paternoster Press.

——(2007) [a] *Theology Goes to the Movies: An Introduction to Critical Christian Thinking*, London & New York: Routledge.

——(2007) [b] 'On Dealing with What Films Actually Do to People: The Practice and Theory of Film Watching in Theology/Religion and Film Discussion', in R.K. Johnston (ed.) *Reframing Theology and Film: New Focus for an Emerging Discipline*, Grand Rapids: Baker Academic: 145–61.

Martin, J.W. (1995) 'Introduction: Seeing the Sacred on the Screen', in J.W. Martin and C.E. Ostwalt Jr. (eds) *Screening the Sacred: Religion, Myth, and Ideology in Popular American Film*, Boulder: Westview Press: 1–12.

——and Ostwalt, C.E. (1995) 'Mythological Criticism', in J.W. Martin and C.E. Ostwalt Jr. (eds) *Screening the Sacred: Religion, Myth, and Ideology in Popular American Film*, Boulder: Westview Press: 65–71.

Maslin, J. (1988) 'The Dress-for-Success Story Of a Secretary from Staten Island', *New York Times*, 21 December. Online. Available HTTP: <http://movies.nytimes.com/movie/review?res=940DE5DD153AF932A15751C1A96E948260> (accessed 23 November 2010).

Matheson, R. (2008) *What Dreams May Come*, 2nd edn, New York: Tor.

Matthews, P. (1999) Review of *What Dreams May Come*, in *Sight and Sound*, 9/1: 59–61.

Maude, C. (2001) Review of *Flatliners*, in J. Pym (ed.) *Time Out Film Guide*, 10th edition, London: Penguin: 394.

Mavis, P. (2007) Review of *Shirley Valentine*, in *DVD Talk*, Online. Available HTTP: <www.dvdtalk.com/reviews/27986/shirley-valentine> (accessed 23 November 2010).

Medved, M. (1993) *Hollywood vs. America: Popular Culture and the War on Tradition*, New York: HarperCollins.

Miller, L. and Grenz, S.J. (1998) *Fortress Introduction to Contemporary Theologies*, Minneapolis: Fortress.

Miller, P.D. (2000) 'Judgment and Joy', in J. Polkinghorne and M. Welker (eds) *The End of the World and the Ends of God: Science and Theology on Eschatology*, Harrisburg PA: Trinity Press International: 155–70.

Milne, T. (1987) Review of *Made in Heaven*, in *Monthly Film Bulletin*, 54/646: 335–37.

——(2001) Review of *Here Comes Mr Jordan*, in J. Pym (ed.) *Time Out Film Guide*, 10th edition, London: Penguin: 501.

Moltmann, J. (1967) *Theology of Hope*, trans. J.L. Leitch, New York: Harper & Row.

——(1981) *The Trinity and the Kingdom of God*, trans. M. Kohl, London: SCM.

——(1993) *The Way of Jesus Christ: Christology in Messianic Dimensions*, trans. M. Kohl, Minneapolis: Fortress Press.

——(1996) *The Coming of God: Christian Eschatology*, trans. M. Kohl, Minneapolis: Fortress Press.

——(2000) 'Is There Life After Death?', in J. Polkinghorne and M. Welker (eds) *The End of the World and the Ends of God: Science and Theology on Eschatology*, Harrisburg PA: Trinity Press International: 238–55.

Moody, R. (1975) *Life After Life*, Atlanta: Mockingbird.

Moorhead, J.H. (1999) 'Apocalypticism in Mainstream Protestantism, 1800 to the Present', in S.J. Stein (ed.) *The Encyclopedia of Apocalypticism, Volume III: Apocalypticism in the Modern Period and the Contemporary Age*, New York: Continuum: 72–107.

More, St T. (1965) 'Utopia', in E. Surtz and J.H. Hexter (eds) *The Complete Works of St. Thomas More*, Vol. 4, New Haven and London: Yale University Press.

Morgan, R. (1998) 'Rudolf Bultmann', in D. F. Ford (ed.) *The Modern Theologians: An introduction to Christian theology in the twentieth century*, 2nd edn, Oxford: Blackwell: 68–86.

Neumaier-Dargyay, E.K. (2000) 'Buddhism', in H. Coward (ed.) *Life after Death in World Religions*, 4th edn, Maryknoll, New York: Orbis: 87–104.

Niebuhr, G. (1997) 'In the Bible, They Don't Talk So Much', *New York Times*, 6 April. Online. Available HTTP: <www.nytimes.com/1997/04/06/arts/in-the-bible-they-don-t-talk-so-much.html> (accessed 25 November 2010).

Nuckols, B. (2008) Review of *Working Girl*, in *Ill-Informed Gadfly*. Online. Available HTTP: <http://illinformedgadfly.com/?p=354> (accessed 23 November 2010).

Origen (1973) *On First Principles*, trans. G.W. Butterworth, Gloucester MA: Peter Smith.

Ortiz, G. (1998) 'Theology and the Silver Screen', *The Month: A Review of Christian Thought and World Affairs*, 31/5: 171–74.

Ostwalt, C. (2003) *Secular Steeples: Popular Culture and the Religious Imagination*, Harrisburg PA: Trinity International.

——(2008) 'Teaching Religion and Film: A Fourth Approach', in G. J. Watkins (ed.) *Teaching Religion and Film*, Oxford: OUP: 35–54.

Owen, D.D.R. (1955) 'The Element of Parody in *Saint Pierre et Le Jongleur*', *French Studies*, 9/1: 60–63.

Parish, J.R. (1994) *Ghosts and Angels in Hollywood Films: Plots, Critiques, Casts and Credits for 264 Theatrical and Made-for-Television Releases*, Jefferson NC & London: McFarland.

Parrinder, G. (1973) *The Indestructible Soul: The Nature of Man and Life after Death in Indian Thought*, London: George Allen & Unwin.

——(1989) 'Ghosts', in L.E. Sullivan (ed.) *Death, Afterlife, and the Soul*, London: Collier Macmillan: 240–45.

——(1995) 'The Indestructible Soul – Indian and Asian Beliefs', in D. Cohn-Sherbok and C. Lewis (eds) *Beyond Death: Theological and Philosophical Reflections on Life after Death*, Basingstoke & London: Macmillan: 80–94.

Penelhum, T. (1970) *Survival and Disembodied Existence*, London: Routledge & Kegan Paul.

——(2000) 'Christianity', in H. Coward (ed.) *Life after Death in World Religions*, 4th edn, Maryknoll, New York: Orbis: 31–47.

Phelps, E.S. (1869) *The Gates Ajar*, Boston: Fields, Osgood & Co.

——(1883) *Beyond the Gates*, Boston: Houghton, Mifflin & Co.

Phillips, D.Z. (1970) *Death and Immortality*, London: Macmillan.

Plato (1974) *The Republic*, 2nd edition, trans. D. Lee, Harmondsworth: Penguin.

Polkinghorne, J. (1995) *Serious Talk: Science and Religion in Dialogue*, Harrisburg PA: Trinity Press International.

——(2000) 'Eschatology: Some Questions and Some Insights from Science', in J. Polkinghorne and M. Welker (eds) *The End of the World and the Ends of God: Science and Theology on Eschatology*, Harrisburg PA: Trinity Press International: 29–41.

——and Welker, M. (2000), 'Introduction: Science and Theology on the End of the World and the Ends of God', in J. Polkinghorne and M. Welker (eds) *The End of the World and the Ends of God: Science and Theology on Eschatology*, Harrisburg PA: Trinity Press International: 1–13.

Pope, R. (2007) *Salvation in Celluloid: Theology, Imagination and Film*, London: T & T Clark.

Price, H.H. (1973) 'Survival and the Idea of "Another World"', in T. Penelhum (ed.) *Immortality*, Belmont CA: Wadsworth: 21–47.

——(1995) [a] 'Some Philosophical Questions about Telepathy and Clairvoyance', in F.B. Dilley (ed.) *Philosophical Interactions with Parapsychology: The Major Writings of H. H. Price on Parapsychology and Survival*, Basingstoke: Macmillan: 35–39.

——(1995) [b] 'Mind Over Matter and Mind Over Matter', in F.B. Dilley (ed.) *Philosophical Interactions with Parapsychology: The Major Writings of H. H. Price on Parapsychology and Survival*, Basingstoke: Macmillan: 61–76.

——(1995) [c] 'Some Aspects of the Conflict between Science and Religion', in F.B. Dilley (ed.) *Philosophical Interactions with Parapsychology: The Major Writings of H. H. Price on Parapsychology and Survival*, Basingstoke: Macmillan: 3–16.

——(1995) [d] 'What Kind of a "Next World"?', in F.B. Dilley (ed.) *Philosophical Interactions with Parapsychology: The Major Writings of H. H. Price on Parapsychology and Survival*, Basingstoke: Macmillan: 263–69.

Rambachan, A. (2000) 'Hinduism', in H. Coward (ed.) *Life after Death in World Religions*, 4th edn, Maryknoll, New York: Orbis: 66–86.

Rauschenbusch, W. (1920) *Christianity and the Social Crisis*, London: Macmillan.

Reinhartz, A. (2003) *Scripture on the Silver Screen*, Louisville KY: Westminster John Knox.

Richardson, J. (1991) *Existential Epistemology: A Heideggerean Critique of the Cartesian Project*, Oxford: Clarendon.

Ring, K. (1990) 'Shamanic Initiation: Imaginal Worlds, and Light after Death', in G. Doore (ed.) *What Survives? Contemporary Explorations of Life After Death*, Los Angeles: Jeremy P. Tarcher, Inc.: 204–15.

——(1996) 'Near-Death Experiences: Implications for Human Evolution and Planetary Transformation', in L.W. Bailey and J. Yates (eds) *The Near-Death Experience: A Reader*, New York & London: Routledge: 181–97.

Robinson, J.A.T. (1963) *Honest to God*, London: SCM.

——(1968) *In the End, God: A Study of the Christian Doctrine of the Last Things*, 2nd edn, London: Collins.

Rose, S. (1995) *Classic Film Guide*, Glasgow: HarperCollins.

Ruffles, T. (2004) *Ghost Images: Cinema of the Afterlife*, Jefferson NC & London: McFarland.

Russell, J.B. (1981) *Satan: The Early Christian Tradition*, Ithaca & London: Cornell University Press.

——(1986) *Mephistopheles: The Devil in the Modern World*, Ithaca & London: Cornell University Press.

——(1997) *A History of Heaven: The Singing Silence*, Princeton NJ: Princeton University Press.

——(2006) *Paradise Mislaid: How We Lost Heaven – And How We Can Regain It*, Oxford: OUP.

Sartori, P. (2008) *Near-Death Experiences of Hospitalized Intensive Care Patients: A Five Year Clinical Study*, New York: Edwin Mellen Press.

Schwartz, D. (2008) Review of *Working Girl*, in *Ozus' World Movie Reviews*. Online. Available HTTP: <http://homepages.sover.net/~ozus/workinggirl.htm> (accessed 23 November 2010).

The Scotsman (2009) 'X-Factor judges accused of ageism', 22 September. Online. Available HTTP: <news.scotsman.com/entertainment/XFactor-judges-accused-of-ageism.5667957.jp> (accessed 10 October 2009).

Scott, B.B. (1994) *Hollywood Dreams and Biblical Stories*, Minneapolis: Fortress.

Segal, E. (2000) 'Judaism', in H. Coward (ed.) *Life after Death in World Religions*, 4th edn, Maryknoll, New York: Orbis: 11–30.

Sharp, J. (2009) Review of *Drag Me to Hell*, in *Sight and Sound*, 19/7: 62.

Skrade, C. (1970) 'Theology and Films', in J.C. Cooper and C. Skrade (eds) *Celluloid and Symbols*, Philadelphia: Fortress: 1–24.

Smith, B.K. (2000) 'Hinduism', in J. Neusner (ed.) *Death and the Afterlife*, Cleveland: The Pilgrim Press: 97–115.

Smith, C.D. (2000) Review of *Little Nicky*, in *Christian Spotlight on Entertainment*. Online. Available HTTP: <www.christiananswers.net/spotlight/movies/2000/littlenicky.html> (accessed 24 November 2010).

Smith, J.I. (1989) 'The Afterlife', in L.E. Sullivan (ed.) *Death, Afterlife, and the Soul*, London: Collier Macmillan: 81–95.

Smith, N. (2001) Review of *Lost Souls*, in BBC Movies, 10 January. Online. Available HTTP: <www.bbc.co.uk/films/2001/01/10/lost_souls_2001_review.shtml> (accessed 31 December 2010).

Soskice, J.M. (2000) 'The Ends of Man and the Future of God', in J. Polkinghorne and M. Welker (eds) *The End of the World and the Ends of God: Science and Theology on Eschatology*, Harrisburg PA: Trinity Press International: 78–87.

Stanford, P. (2002) *Heaven: A Traveller's Guide to the Undiscovered Country*, London: HarperCollins.

Stern, R.C., Jefford, C.N. and DeBona, G. (1999) *Savior on the Silver Screen*, New York: Paulist Press.

Stevenson, I. and Greyson, B. (1996) 'Near-Death Experiences: Relevance to the Question of Survival after Death', in L.W. Bailey and J. Yates (eds) *The Near-Death Experience: A Reader*, New York & London: Routledge: pp. 201–6.

Stevenson, J. [revised W.H.C. Frend] (ed.) (1992) *A New Eusebius: Documents illustrating the history of the Church to AD 337*, 4th impression, London: SPCK.

Stoeger, W.R. (2000) [a] 'Scientific Accounts of Ultimate Catastrophes in our Life-Bearing Universe', in J. Polkinghorne and M. Welker (eds) *The End of the World and the Ends of God: Science and Theology on Eschatology*, Harrisburg PA: Trinity Press International: 19–28.

——(2000) [b] 'Cultural Cosmology and the Impact of the Natural Sciences on Philosophy and Culture', in J. Polkinghorne and M. Welker (eds) *The End of the World and the Ends of God: Science and Theology on Eschatology*, Harrisburg PA: Trinity Press International: 65–77.

Stone, B.P. (1998) 'Religious Faith and Science in *Contact*', *Journal of Religion and Film*, 2/2. Online. Available HTTP: <www.unomaha.edu/jrf/stonear2.htm> (accessed 31 December 2010).

Strachan, R.H. (1920) *The Fourth Gospel*, London: SCM.

Strick, P. (1990) Review of *Flatliners*, in *Monthly Film Bulletin*, 57/682: 320–21.

——(1992) Review of *Switch*, in *Sight and Sound*, 1/9: 53–54.

Tanner, K. (2000) 'Eschatology Without a Future?', in J. Polkinghorne and M. Welker (eds) *The End of the World and the Ends of God: Science and Theology on Eschatology*, Harrisburg PA: Trinity Press International: 222–37.

Tart, C. (1990) 'Who Survives? Implications of Modern Consciousness Research', in G. Doore (ed.) *What Survives? Contemporary Explorations of Life After Death*, Los Angeles: Jeremy P. Tarcher, Inc.: 138–51.

——(1996) 'Who Might Survive the Death of the Body?', in L.W. Bailey and J. Yates (eds) *The Near-Death Experience: A Reader*, New York & London: Routledge: 321–27.

Taylor, E. (1996) *William James on Consciousness Beyond the Margin*, Princeton: Princeton University Press.

Taylor, P. (2001) Review of *High Plains Drifter*, in J. Pym (ed.) *Time Out Film Guide*, 10th edition, London: Penguin: 506.

Tillich, P. (1963) *Systematic Theology, Volume III: Life and the Spirit: History and the Kingdom of God*, Chicago: University of Chicago.

——(1964) *Theology of Culture*, New York: Oxford University Press.

——(1979) *The Courage to Be*, 11th impression, Glasgow: Collins.

——(2004) 'Art and Ultimate Reality', in G.E. Thiessen (ed.) *Theological Aesthetics: A Reader*, London: SCM: 209–17.

Tober, L.M. and Lusby, S. (1989) 'Heaven and Hell', in L.E. Sullivan (ed.) *Death, Afterlife, and the Soul*, London: Collier Macmillan: 151–60.

Turner, A.K. (1995) *The History of Hell*, London: Robert Hale Ltd.

Vardy, P. (1995) 'A Christian Approach to Eternal Life', in D. Cohn-Sherbok and C. Lewis (eds) *Beyond Death: Theological and Philosophical Reflections on Life after Death*, Basingstoke & London: Macmillan: 13–26.

Volf, M. (2000) 'Enter into Joy! Sin, Death, and the Life of the World to Come', in J. Polkinghorne and M. Welker (eds) *The End of the World and the Ends of God: Science and Theology on Eschatology*, Harrisburg PA: Trinity Press International: 256–78.

Walker, J. (ed.) (1995) *Halliwell's Film Guide*, 11th edn, London: HarperCollins.

Wall, J.M. (1970) 'Biblical Spectaculars and Secular Man', in J.C. Cooper and C. Skrade (eds) *Celluloid and Symbols*, Philadelphia: Fortress: 51–60.

Walls, J.L. (1992) *Hell: The Logic of Damnation*, Notre Dame & London: University of Notre Dame Press.

——(2002) *Heaven: The Logic of Eternal Joy*, Oxford: OUP.

Walsh, R. (2005) *Finding St. Paul in Film*, New York & London: T & T Clark.

Ware, K. (1995) '"Go Joyfully": The Mystery of Death and Resurrection', in D. Cohn-Sherbok and C. Lewis (eds) *Beyond Death: Theological and Philosophical Reflections on Life after Death*, Basingstoke & London: Macmillan: 27–41.

Watts, F. (2000) 'Subjective and Objective Hope: Propositional and Attitudinal Aspects of Eschatology', in J. Polkinghorne and M. Welker (eds) *The End of the World and the Ends of God: Science and Theology on Eschatology*, Harrisburg PA: Trinity Press International: 47–60.

Wilkinson, K. (2001) Review of *The 6th Day*, in J. Pym (ed.) *Time Out Film Guide*, 10th edition, London: Penguin: 1065.

Wilson, A.N. (1995) 'Life after Death: A Fate Worse than Death', in D. Cohn-Sherbok and C. Lewis (eds) *Beyond Death: Theological and Philosophical Reflections on Life after Death*, Basingstoke & London: Macmillan: 183–98.

Wyman, K. J. (2004) 'The Devil We Already Know: Medieval Representations of a Powerless Satan in Modern American Cinema', *Journal of Religion and Film*, 8/2. Online. Available HTTP: <www.unomaha.edu/jrf/Vol8No2/wymandevil.htm> (accessed 25 November 2010).

——(2009) 'Satan in the Movies', in W.L. Blizek (ed.) *The Continuum Companion to Religion and Film*, London & New York: Continuum: 300–309.

Zaleski, C. (1987) *Otherworld Journeys: Accounts of Near-Death Experiences in Medieval and Modern Times*, Oxford: OUP.

——(1995) 'Death and Near-Death Today', in J.J. Collins and M. Fishbane (eds) *Death, Ecstasy, and Other Worldly Journeys*, New York: State University of New York: 383–407.

INDEX